COMPARATIVE MANAGEMENT

Ballinger Series in
BUSINESS IN A GLOBAL ENVIRONMENT

S. Prakash Sethi, Series Editor

Center for Management
Baruch College
The City University of New York

COMPARATIVE MANAGEMENT
A Regional View

Edited by

RAGHU NATH

Joseph M. Katz Graduate School of Business
University of Pittsburgh

BALLINGER PUBLISHING COMPANY
Cambridge, Massachusetts
A Subsidiary of Harper & Row, Publishers, Inc.

International Standard Book Number: 0-88730-136-3

Library of Congress Catalog Card Number: 87-17459

Printed in the United States of America

Library of Congress Cataloging-in-Publication Data

Comparative management.

    (Ballinger series in business in a global environment)
    Includes index.
    1. Comparative management. I. Nath, Raghu.
II. Series.
HD30.55.C656 1987   658   87-17459

    ISBN 0-88730-136-3

For my wife, Lily, and our daughters, Ritika and Nitika

Contents

List of Figures

List of Tables

Preface

Two distinctive features of this book are its framework and the process by which it was assembled.

The book's development was guided by an open systems framework (Chapter 1), involving the interaction between the business and management system and its environment. In the comparative management field, there have been two major areas of work: one has concentrated on the environment whereas the other has focused on comparing business and management systems. Our framework integrates these two perspectives, resulting in the incorporation of both macrolevel (environmental) and microlevel (organization) factors. Further, the framework is compatible with current thought in the international strategy field, where the emphasis is on assessing both the environment- and organization-level factors and achieving a strategic fit between them.

Seven aspects of the environment included in the framework are the cultural milieu, the socio-political context, the economic system, the legal system, technology, transportation and communications, and the industry structure. Prior models in comparative management have focused primarily on discussion of economic, political, and legal factors. However, in recent years there has been an increasing emphasis on the role of culture. For example, a special symposium at the Academy of Management Annual Meeting held in August 1985 discussed the role of culture in comparative management. Also, many recent popular books have focused on the role of corporate culture. Comparative and policy studies have emphasized the importance of sociopolitical context. Though the literature in the management and comparative management fields has not usually dealt with infrastructure issues (such as technology, communications, and transportation), international executives and economic development specialists have emphasized the importance of infrastructure. Issues related to infrastructure were the focal point of discussion at the "Partnerships Dialogue Conference" held in May 1985 in Pittsburgh. This conference was attended by leaders of government, business, labor, academic institutions, and media from over twenty-five countries.

At the microlevel, most of the comparative studies have focused on management philosophy, attitudes, and practices. In addition to these, we have included in the framework such areas as organization structure, processes, and policies, which have occupied an important place in organizational, policy, and strategy research.

In conclusion, we have drawn on a variety of sources to develop the framework, including scholars as well as leading international executives. Scholarly inputs have come from multidisciplinary sources such as international and comparative management, organization studies, policy research, system theory, economics, sociology, anthropology, area and economic development studies.

The second distinctive feature of the book is the process by which it was developed. The guiding perspective was geocentric rather than ethnocentric. A multistage process comprising the following action steps was implemented:

- First, as outlined above, a broad and comprehensive framework was developed, which integrated inputs from both scholarly studies and practicing international executives.
- Second, six regions or nations were selected to represent the worldwide diversity along economic, political, and cultural dimensions. These six regions or nations are the United States, Japan, Europe, China, Africa, and Latin America. We would have liked to include other regions and nations such as Australasia, South Asia, Middle East, and the four newly industrialized Pacific Rim countries (Hong Kong, Korea, Singapore, and Taiwan), but this would have made the book too long and unmanageable. In fact, limiting the volume to six regions or nations was the most difficult decision we had to make.
- Third, scholars were selected to write chapters on particular regions or countries based on the dual criteria of their knowledge-based expertise and cultural sensitivity. Therefore, the various authors of this book constitute a truly cross-cultural team of scholars.
- Fourth, an ideographic approach was used to develop each chapter. Using the framework as a broad guideline, each scholar developed

those themes that were appropriate to his or her region or country. Reading Chapters 2 through 7 will give the reader a good sense of the diversity that characterizes our world today.

• Fifth, after individual chapters were completed, a comparative analysis was conducted to identify similarities and differences between the regions and countries studied. Results of this analysis are reported in Chapter 8. In addition to suggesting fruitful areas for future research, results of the comparative analysis provide useful guidelines for the development of international business strategy.

The process employed in the development of this book can best be described as a "quasi-grounded-theory" methodology. As expected, the application of this methodology led to enhancement of the initial framework. We hope that this process will be replicated in the future, thus leading to even more comprehensive models in the comparative management field.

We are living in an interdependent world. Our students and managers need to acquire global rather than ethnocentric viewpoints. They need to learn how other environments and management systems are different from and similar to their own. We will be amply rewarded if this book contributes to this learning and the development of a "global" frame of mind.

Raghu Nath
Pittsburgh, PA
May 1987

Acknowledgments

Of necessity, a book such as this, which utilizes a broad framework, draws upon the prior work of many scholars from a variety of disciplines. In addition, I have benefited greatly from my conversations with leaders of business, government, and international organizations.

In particular, I must thank the authors who contributed to this book. Each did a masterful job of projecting the uniqueness of his or her region or country while staying within the broad guidelines provided by the framework.

Special thanks are due to S. Prakash Sethi, who encouraged me to develop the book. I have enjoyed working with Marjorie Richman, Barbara Roth, and others at Ballinger. They have been patient, understanding, and cooperative.

Finally, I must acknowledge contributions made by several of my doctoral students. Kunal Sadhu, in addition to coauthoring Chapter 8 with me, provided much needed assistance throughout this project. Amy Fried, Margie Jonnet, and Joyce Shelleman were helpful in copyediting various manuscripts. Won-Woo Park streamlined tables and figures and developed an outline for each chapter. And my secretary, Debbie Scott, cheerfully typed various versions of the manuscript.

CHAPTER 1

Comparative Management

Raghu Nath

PURPOSE

The purpose of this introductory chapter is fivefold: to describe comparative management and why comparative management is important; to identify various approaches to the study of comparative and cross-cultural management; to trace the major developments in allied fields such as organization theory, development, and change, strategic planning and management, and industrial organization and policy; to describe various orientations to the accumulation of knowledge; and finally to discuss the multistage process that underlies the development of this book and briefly outline the major elements of the framework that provided overall guidelines for the next six chapters.[1]

COMPARATIVE MANAGEMENT

Comparative management, defined broadly, focuses on the similarities and differences among business and management systems from different contexts. These comparisons could be profit versus nonprofit organizations, manufacturing versus service industries, small versus large organizations, successful versus unsuccessful companies, and developed versus developing countries. In this book, however, a limited but often used definition of comparative management is used: the study of organizations from different countries or cultures. Thus, in this book *comparative* and *cross-cultural management* are synonymous terms.

COMPARATIVE MANAGEMENT AND INTERNATIONAL BUSINESS

Comparative management is quite different from international business. Whereas comparative management is primarily interested in studying the similarities and differences among nations and management systems of different countries, international business is primarily concerned with the study of issues and problems that are related to the management of the multinational firm. Therefore, comparative management does not have as its major point of interest the special problems that arise with business activities across national boundaries. For example, the question of potential conflict between the nation state and the multinational firm, which receives major attention in international business studies, is not likely to be the central theme in comparative management studies (Robock and Simmonds 1983: 5).

These two concepts—comparative management and international business—are interrelated and overlapping. Therefore, the international manager may benefit greatly from comparative management studies.

REASONS FOR STUDYING COMPARATIVE MANAGEMENT

There are at least five major reasons for studying comparative management. First, we are living in an interdependent world. In 1978 about 30 percent of the world economic product ($2,000 billion out of a total of $8,800 billion) was generated by international business activity, most of which can be attributed to multinational corporations (MNCs) that operate in various countries of the world. It is important that managers of these firms be knowledgeable about these countries' cultures, political economies, and business practices. Even managers of primarily domestic firms are increasingly required to think in the global context. As the U.S. auto and steel industries have learned through experience, foreign competition can challenge an industry in its own backyard. Today no firm or industry is immune from foreign competition; all managers must think and plan in global terms.

Second, the comparative approach is inescapable. We measure and assess everything in relation to something, whether an implicit ideal or standard. The comparative approach is universal; it is not limited to management but has been applied to such disciplines as economics, sociology, psychology, law, education, religion, and literature.

Third, the study of different cultures or systems sharpens our understanding beyond the understanding that comes from knowing only our own culture. It develops an appreciation of and sensitivity toward diversity in human affairs, which is important in transacting business with people of other cultures.[2]

An example may illustrate this point. At a recent conference, I met with the director of the industrial development authority of a developing country. His organization has put together five major foreign direct investment projects involving many foreign firms. Although U.S. companies were technologically superior to European and Japanese firms that bid for the contracts, all five contracts went to non-U.S. firms, primarily because of the cultural insensitivity of the U.S. managers and their lack of knowledge of how business operates in that developing country. The development director indicated that delicate contract negotiations in his country are handled through informal channels, whereas Americans always pushed for formal contacts. This type of story is repeated many times in the literature. Hall (1959) in his book *Silent Language* cites many examples in which cultural insensitivity and lack of knowledge have been responsible for the failure of a foreign person in a new cultural environment.

Fourth, the study of comparative management widens the knowledge base by extending the range of variables over which a particular organizational or management phenomenon can be studied (Murdock 1965). For example, different cultures can be organized along a continuum on different variables. A given culture therefore represents only a limited range. By carefully selecting cultures, it is possible to considerably extend the range.

Fifth and finally, the most important reason for studying comparative or cross-cultural management is that it helps the individual to appreciate his or her own culture and environment. We often are not aware of our own culture and environment because we take them for granted. In fact, when the study of management was limited primarily to the United States, the role of environment or culture was completely ignored by scholars. As is discussed in the next section, it was the comparative management scholars who described the importance of culture and environment as crucial and critical factors in the study of management systems.

It is clear that the study of comparative management is important for every manager and student of management. Today's interdependent world requires managers to think globally and plan in a worldwide context. As Buckley (1985: 3), past chairman and chief executive officer of Allegheny International, states, "Globalism is the dominant business force today." The study of comparative management can help the international frame of mind that is central to this concept of globalism.

HISTORICAL REVIEW

Economic and organization scholars historically have looked for universal laws. Until recently, scholars in these areas have either ignored the roles of environment and culture or treated them rather superficially. The main thrust of work in these areas has been nomothetic—that is, looking for relationships that are universally applicable. Comparative management scholars were the first ones to identify the importance of environment in the study of business systems.

VARIOUS APPROACHES TO COMPARATIVE MANAGEMENT

Major thrusts in the comparative management literature can be broadly classified into four categories (Nath 1975; Negandhi 1983): the economic development approach, the environmental approach, the behavioral approach, and the open systems perspective. A fifth approach emphasizes the role of culture in comparative management and has begun to emerge in recent years.

Economic Development Approach

This approach developed during the 1950s and is best exemplified by the work of Harbison and Myers (1959). The basic premise of this approach is simple: Managerial input plays a significant role in achieving rapid industrial and economic development. This approach is basically a macroapproach, concentrating on examination of trends in management development. Its basic assumption underscores an inherent logic that propels nations toward industrialization. The underlying model postulates four stages along the developmental path that leads a society from an agrarian-feudalistic system to an industrial-democratic state. Harbison and Myers (1959) conclude that a specific management philosophy is compatible with each of the four stages of economic development and that all management systems eventually tend toward the participative or democratic (theory Y) management philosophy.

In many ways, this approach is a sophisticated form of universal management theory that emphasizes the inevitable applicability of a given management philosophy to *all* organizations in all cultures and societies.

In spite of their universalist tendencies, Harbison and Myers commissioned scholars to write in-depth chapters about selected aspects of carefully selected nations of the industrial world. Their pioneering work provided much needed legitimacy and impetus to the field of comparative management.

Environmental Approach

This is also a macroapproach, best exemplified by the work of Farmer and Richman (1965). The underlying assumption in this approach is that managerial effectiveness is a function of external environmental factors such as sociocultural, legal-political, economic, and educational. Whereas Harbison and Myers work was primarily focused on economic factors in the environment, Farmer and Richman conceptualized environment in a much broader framework. These authors also tried to operationalize environmental variables through the use of a delphi process, but this quantitative approach has not yielded any useful findings. Although some empirical studies have been conducted by students of Farmer and Richman, these studies have had rather limited impact. Another drawback of this approach is its overemphasis on external variables to the complete exclusion of internal organizational variables. According to Boddewyn (1966), a real danger exists—of letting environment crowd the comparative analysis. Care must be exercised not to throw the management baby out with the environmental bath or smother it in a blanket of social context. Nonetheless, this approach has provided a comprehensive framework for conceptualizing the general environment.[3]

The Behavioral Approach

The basic assumption of this approach is that management practices as well as effectiveness depend on cultural variables such as attitudes, beliefs, value systems, behavioral patterns, management philosophies, and so forth. Behavioral research in the United States has a long tradition of empirical work. Unlike the first two macroapproaches, variables in this approach are operationalized in terms of attitudes and value scales.

This approach attempts to explain behavioral patterns of individuals and groups in organizational settings. This is basically a microapproach, and authors have concentrated on its three different aspects:

1. National character profiles, which are linked with certain organizational behavioral variables (Davis 1971; Narain 1967).

2. Attitudes and perceptions of managers concerning key management concepts and activities (Barrett and Bass 1970; Haire, Ghiselli, and Porter 1966; Nath 1968; Ryterband and Barrett 1970; Thiagarajan 1968).
3. Prevalent beliefs, value systems, and need hierarchies in a given society (Davis 1971).

It is clear from this research that significant differences exist among cultures in terms of attitudes, beliefs, value systems, need hierarchies, and managerial practices. Differences also exist among the various subgroups (ethnic or occupational) within a given society. A major implication of this research is that care must be exercised when management practices are transferred from one culture to another.

The behavioral approach has had several drawbacks. A major shortcoming has been that most studies in this area have ignored the measurement of organizational effectiveness. Most of the research instruments were developed and validated in the United States. Except for a few studies, research in this area has used these instruments without validating them for different cultures. Finally, *culture* has never been explicitly defined in many of the studies, yet the differences found are attributed to cultural differences. In fact, these differences may be due to other contextual or environmental variables such as size, technology, location, economic, market, and political conditions.

Open Systems Perspective

This approach uses an open systems model in conceptualizing the organization and its interaction with the environment. Negandhi (1983) describes three kinds of environments: organizational, task, and societal.

The first, organizational environment, deals with such variables as size, technology, organizational climate, and human and capital resources of the firm. This layer of the environment is considered to be largely under the control of the managers.

The second, task environment, includes distributors, suppliers, employees, consumers, stockholders, government, and community. Negandhi and Prasad (1971) have conducted cross-cultural studies to show how this environment affects organizational patterns and effectiveness. Estafen et al. (1970) dealt with the interchange between the organization and the task environment in Spain, Chile, and Sweden. These studies have attempted to show the relationship between interaction at the boundary and its effect on organizational effectiveness as measured by profits, marketshare, and so forth. The third layer, the societal environment, is the macro environment as identified by Farmer and Richman (1965).

In terms of empirical research, Negandhi and Estafen have studied the effect of the task environment and the relationship between task environment and organization, and organizational patterns and effectiveness. This research has tended to treat the organization as a unit of analysis. The major drawback of this approach, however, is that variables are vaguely defined and therefore results have not had much credibility or predictive validity.

Role of Culture in Comparative Management

Although the importance of environment was recognized by early comparative scholars, their universalist stance inhibited the explicit consideration of culture in explaining business behavior. From the 1960s on, a great flood of work testified to the culture-bound nature of management theory.[4] Yet the methodological quality of most of the comparative management studies left much to be desired (Nath 1968).

Ajiferuke and Boddewyn (1970) reviewed twenty-two studies of comparative management that employed culture as an independent variable to explain differences in management practices among nations. Yet only two authors ventured a definition of the concept. In most studies, *culture* was used as a pseudonym for *nation*.

In recent years, there have been some promising developments in the cross-cultural and comparative management area. For example, Hofstede (1980) has operationalized *culture* in terms of four dimensions and described different countries and societies in terms of these dimensions. Kelly and Worthley (1981) used an innovative research design to separate the effects of culture from other environmental factors. As a result of a comprehensive review of literature, Triandis (1983) has isolated thirty dimensions of culture.

In spite of a few serious attempts to operationalize culture and its impact on organizational behavior in comparative management settings, most of the research in the comparative management area is still of the type where *culture* is very vaguely defined and cross-national differences are attributed to differences in culture. A random sampling of the research papers presented at the Academy of Management meetings for the last two years as well as of the articles published in leading journals indicates that a majority of comparative management research still suffers from serious design and methodological problems (Nath 1986).

MAJOR DEVELOPMENTS IN RELATED FIELDS

This section briefly reviews important developments in the related fields such as organization theory, development, and change; strategic planning and management; and industrial organization and policy.

Organization Theory, Development, and Change

The discipline of organization theory is most closely allied to the work of comparative management scholars. In fact, some have argued (Negandhi 1983) that the most productive approach is to have cross-cultural and comparative management fields join the organization theory area.

Many of the recent developments occurring in the organization theory area are especially relevant for comparative management, and many of the developments taking place in comparative management are relevant for organization theory. These two fields can enrich themselves by linking with each other (Nath 1975). Four major developments have taken place in the macro organization theory field that have important implications for comparative management studies.

First, and probably the most important, is the emergence of an open systems perspective. The shift from a closed to an open systems view can be traced to the pioneering work of Katz and Kahn (1978).[5] In the open-systems framework, organization maintains dynamic equilibrium with its environment. Thus, there is a constant exchange of energy between the organization and its relevant environments. This view is in contrast to the closed system approach,[6] which concentrates primarily on examining how internal variables affect organizational structure, behavior patterns, and effectiveness.

In addition to considering the interaction between the organization and its environment, many organization theorists have also described the organization in terms of its subsystem. For example, Emery and Trist (1963) divide the organization into social and technical subsystems. Kotter (1976), on the other hand, describes the organization system in terms of six subsystems (key organizational processes, employees and other tangible assets, formal organizational arrangements, the internal social system, the organization's technology, and the dominant coalition). Tichy (1983) divides the organization into three subsystems (technical, cultural, and political). Nath and Ready (1974) describe the system in terms of four subsystems (functional, informational, social, and political). Finally, Pascale and Athos (1981) describe the system in terms of seven S's (shared values, strategy, structure, systems, staff, style, and skills).

The second major development is the emergence of the contingency model. Whereas the system theorists stressed the significance of organization-environment interaction, the contingency theorists described the nature of this relationship and provided specific empirical evidence. Another major contribution of contingency theorists has been the shift from a normative to an analytical and descriptive framework. The prior theories (that is, the bureaucratic as well as the participative management model) were both normative theories, but the contingency framework evolved as a result of empirical studies conducted in the United States as well as Britain by such scholars as Lawrence and Lorsch (1969) and Woodward (1965).

The normative scholars believe that their models are applicable to all situations. Contingency theorists, on the other hand, proved that neither the bureaucratic nor the participative management model is appropriate for all situations. The basic premise of the contingency model is that the management system must be compatible with the nature of people, the nature of the task, and the nature of the environment. If the tasks are routine and involve well-established technology, the people are primarily dependent-type, and the environment is stable and certain, then the theory X style of management or the bureaucratic model is appropriate. On the other hand, if the nature of the task is nonroutine, creative, and complex and involves rapidly developing technology, the environment is changing and uncertain, and the people are independent-type (highly educated), then the appropriate management philosophy is theory Y or the participative management model.

Although contingency theorists recognized the importance of environment, most of the contingency variables that they considered were internal to the organizational system—the nature of the task and technology and the nature of people. In addition, environment was operationalized in terms of rather vague concepts such as certainty/uncertainty, complexity/simplicity, and changing/stable. Finally, the role of culture was ignored by the contingency theorists because they looked for universally valid relationships.

The third development is the recognition of the role of power and politics in organizations. For a long time, issues of politics and power were ignored by most organization and management theorists, but in the late 1970s some scholars in the organization theory area started addressing these issues. Pfeffer and Salancik (1974) were the first to seriously study this influence of power and policy in academic settings.[7]

Fourth, and the most recent development, is the role of culture in organizational systems. In the organization and management theory, belief in discovering universal management principles has been around from the beginning (Max Weber 1946; Taylor 1947; Fayol 1949). The apparent success of U.S. management methods in the post–World War II period further strengthened this belief in universal applicability of theories developed in the United States.

By the late 1950s, however, the universalist stance in management theory came under sustained attack. Corporations operating in several countries started experiencing difficulty in applying U.S. management practices to other countries (Duerr and Greene 1968). The AID technical assistant programs ran into difficulty because they failed to take into account the local values in administering the programs (Niehoff and Anderson 1964). Although practitioners in the government as well as business started questioning the applicability of U.S. management theory to overseas locations, the scholarly work continued in the ethnocentric tradition. Thus, management scholars and organization theorists continued to ignore the role of culture.

The precipitating event that finally brought the role of culture to the forefront in management theory was the rise of the Japanese management system during the late 1960s and early 1970s. By this time it had become clear that the performance of Japanese corporations in many industries far exceeded those of U.S. and European companies, and a number of scholars started studying the Japanese system. These studies[8] finally established beyond any doubt that the Japanese had not copied the U.S. system of management. In fact, they had evolved a management system particularly suited to their cultural and ecological environment, and this system was much more successful than the existing U.S. system of management. As a result of these findings, interest in the subject of culture has intensified to the point of becoming a fad. Although much of the writing and thinking on culture is superficial, a number of organization scholars are grappling with the issue of defining the role and concept of culture in meaningful ways so that useful research can be conducted. Noteworthy among these attempts is the special issue of the *Administrative Science Quarterly* (1983, vol. 28), the conference held at the University of Pittsburgh in October 1983, and writings of many scholars such as Deal and Kennedy (1982), Davis (1984), Schein (1985), and Nath (1986).

In addition to the four developments in the organization theory field, a major development has been the emergence of the field of organization development and change. Although the field of organizational theory had many rigorous studies, these failed to establish the usefulness of the field (Kilmann et al. 1983). It is through the implementation of organization development and change methods that the field has been useful to the world of management. The basic guiding model in organization development is that of action research—that is, research leads to action, and this in turn leads to further research. Although this field started with the development of microlevel techniques such as sensitivity training, team building, conflict resolution laboratories, and job enrichment, it later developed macrolevel intervention strategies. The most useful macrolevel work uses an open system perspective and deals with issues of politics, power, and culture. Some of the recent work in this area is by Michael Beer (1980), Pascale and Athos (1981), Peters and Waterman (1982), Tichy (1983), and Kilmann (1984). Except for Pascale and Athos (1981), most of these models have been developed in the context of a single culture—that is, the United States.

Strategic Planning and Management

This is a rather young field; most of the important developments in this field occurred in the 1970s and 1980s. The first major contribution of this field is to recognize the importance of environment and the notion that strategy is developed to achieve a fit between the organization and its environments. Chandler (1979) established that structure follows strategy in successful organizations. In recent years, Hax and Majluf (1984) enlarged this concept to include the entire management system.

The second major contribution of this field has been to define the environment in specific ways. In this connection, the work of Mitroff (1983) is significant because he developed the notion of stakeholders and the interaction between these stakeholders and the organization. Many of these stakeholders are from the environment. Thus, the stakeholders represent the relevant environments.

Industrial Organization and Industrial Policy

The third related field is that of industrial organization and policy. The first major work in this area is that of Porter (1980), who, in his *Competitive Strategy*, develops the notion of a worldwide competitive system. For example, in the case of automobile industry, he demonstrated that this industry can no longer be considered a national industry. Therefore, he predicted the development of a world-class car and the formation of joint ventures involving firms from different nations resulting in the final emergence of three or four worldwide megacorporations. An important contribution of this field is considering the world as a marketplace for many industries and alerting managers to think in global rather than national terms.

The second important contribution has come from the work of Reich and Magaziner (1982), who advocated the development of explicit industrial policy for the United States. Their argument is that because we are living in a global village, it is no longer possible for any nation (including the United States) to develop its policies in isolation from the rest of the world. Because the industrial policy in Japan and many other countries is explicitly and formally developed, the only viable option for the United States is to do the same. Their hypothesis is that the distinction between industry and national government is not viable in the modern age and that the relevant level for policy setting is the nation rather than an industry. Thus, decisions regarding industries to be targeted for growth and development must be decided by the national government in consultation with industry and labor. In this framework, competitors are other countries of the world.

Third, Ouchi (1984), in his book entitled, *The M-Form Society*, states that in Japan there are elaborate institutional arrangements that bring together financial institutions, industrial organizations, labor, and government to develop industrial strategy. According to Ouchi, integrated planning at the societal level is responsible for the Japanese success. The implication is that any other nation that wishes to compete with Japan has to develop a similar system at the societal level. In a different vein, Sethi et al. (1984) argue that a management system is embedded in a given culture and there has to be a fit between the national culture, environment, and the business system. Unlike Ouchi, who advocates copying Japan, Sethi et al. argue that the United States must develop a unique management system that is compatible with the U.S. culture and political system.

This review of comparative management and related fields has highlighted several themes. First, the world has become a single marketplace. Second, nations in this marketplace are interdependent. Third, the most useful approach is the open systems perspective in which the organizational and industrial systems are considered a part of the larger societal environment with which they continuously interact. Fourth, the nature of these interactions (collaborative versus conflictual) determines the productivity of these systems. Fifth, organization and environment can be conceptualized in terms of several subsystems. Finally, the strategy must be planned in the global context.

STRATEGIES FOR KNOWLEDGE GENERATION

Strategies for accumulating or generating knowledge can be classified in two ways: (1) the ideographic versus nomothetic and (2) the ethnocentric, polycentric, and geocentric. This section briefly describes the major characteristics of these strategies and discusses their advantages and disadvantages.

Ideographic versus Nomothetic Strategy

As outlined in the historical review section, the primary strategy used by both organization as well as comparative management scholars has been the universalist or the nomothetic approach. Contingency theorists have generally ignored the role of culture and instead have focused on such variables as technology (Woodward 1965), resources of customers, employees, materials, and finance (Hickson et al. 1974), and environmental stability (Burns and Stalker 1961). Most cross-cultural scholars, on the other hand, have treated culture as if it is synonymous with *nation*.

The ideographic strategy has been primarily used by anthropologists. Comparative and organization scholars have rarely used this approach. Therefore, Crozier's (1964) study of the French bureaucracy remains the classic example of this type of research. Because a good ideographic study requires a collection of detailed information obtained through a prolonged and systematic observation of a given culture or society, it tends to be very costly in terms of time and resources required.

Ethnocentric, Polycentric, and Geocentric Strategies

According to Hofstede (1983: 89),

Most present day management theories are "ethnocentric," that is, they take the cultural environment of the theorist for granted. What we need is more cultural sensitivity in management theories; we could call the result "organizational anthropology" or "management anthropology."

Management theories and frameworks developed in the United States and Europe have guided most of the research. Even the work reported in Harbison and Myers (1959) and performed by scholars of other nations was guided by the logic of an industrialization hypothesis developed by U.S. scholars. Because the concepts themselves are seldom tested to determine whether they are relevant to the other cultures, ethnocentric research has often led to misleading results.

According to Adler (1983), polycentric studies are individual domestic studies conducted in various countries around the world. This strategy considers each country and culture unique and studies them in terms of their own concepts and frameworks. The ideographic strategy mentioned above probably fits best into this category. This type of research can provide valuable in-depth information about a given culture. However, it is very difficult to compare such information across cultures because a common framework is lacking.

The geocentric strategy requires the development of a common framework by integrating inputs from different cultures or nations. This is what effective MNCs do in developing their international strategies. They gather data from the different countries in which they operate. After analyzing these data, a unified strategy is developed that provides a common framework for operation and control of subsidiary operations in different countries. Prahalad and Doz (1981) indicated that the MNCs with integrated strategies tend to be the most successful ones. Such an approach, however, requires a careful balancing act in terms of providing a sufficient autonomy to the subsidiaries and, at the same time, developing a common framework for worldwide operations. Developing a geocentric strategy in comparative research requires bringing together a carefully selected group of scholars from diverse cultures and countries. These scholars through careful discussion and debate could then develop a common framework. Having developed a common framework, the next step would be to conduct in-depth studies in each culture using this comprehensive framework. This is what Hofstede (1983) calls organizational or management anthropology. According to him, "It is unlikely to be a product of one country's style and intellectual effort; it needs by definition a synergy between ideas from different sources."

The geocentric strategy outlined above is very costly and would require the type of funding provided by the Ford Foundation during the early 1960s. Without such funding, it is not likely that geocentric research could be conducted.

In summary, most of the researchers in organizational, cross-cultural, and comparative management fields have followed nomothetic and ethnocentric strategies. For the most part, this type of research has completely ignored the role of culture in management systems. The attempt has been to establish and identify laws and relationships that are universal and therefore ignore cultural imperatives. In practice, frameworks and theories developed in the United States and Europe have been imposed on other cultures.

Therefore, we need geocentric strategy with sensitivity to ideographic considerations. If this is not possible, due to practical considerations such as lack of resources and funding, then it may be best to follow an ideographic strategy in the first stage followed by the development of a comparative framework in the second stage.

THE PLAN FOR THE BOOK

The best approach to comparative management is the geocentric strategy with sensitivity to ideographic considerations. Extensive funding is needed to implement this strategy so that a multicultural team of scholars can be assembled to develop a common framework. Each of these scholars then can study his or her own country, using the agreed on framework. And finally these individual country studies can be analyzed by a cross-cultural team of scholars to identify similarities and differences among countries.

Strategy Used for This Book

This book follows an alternative and practical strategy: It develops an in-depth study of carefully selected regions or countries using a comprehensive framework that allows for ideographic sensitivity. This is followed by a comparative analysis that identifies similarities and differences among these regions or countries.

In carefully selecting regions or countries and commissioning an in-depth study of each selected region or country, the book's approach is similar to that used by Harbison and Myers (1959) in developing their pioneering work. Because the economic development theory was dominant in the 1950s, Harbison and Myer's framework was highly biased in that direction. In addition, Harbison and Myers were influenced by the universalist viewpoint and employed a nomothetic strategy. In contrast, this book employs an open systems framework that is more comprehensive than the economic framework. We had no a priori hypotheses to be tested, and, in view of ideographic considerations, each scholar was free to develop whatever approach was appropriate for his or her region or country. Only after the individual chapters were completed was the final chapter reporting similarities and differences developed.

Multi-Stage Process

To implement the above strategy, a multi-stage process was followed. In the first stage, six regions or countries were selected to represent different

Table 1-1. An Open Systems Framework for Comparative
Management.

Systems	Subsystems	Some Elements
Environment	The cultural milieu	Cultural values and belief systems (Hofstede's dimensions), social norms and mores, myths and stories
	The sociopolitical context	Political parties, business/government relations, political/economic groups, policymaking bodies, unions and other advocacy groups
	The economic system	Stage of economic development, economic philosophy, banking system, capital markets, fiscal policy, factor endowment, income distribution, parallel economy
	The legal system	Nature of society, legal framework, type of laws, enforcement of laws
	Technology	Level of technology development, scientific/technical manpower, R&D expenditure, type of technology, developer versus copier
	Communication and transportation	Communication (press, telephone), transportation (highways, air system)
	The industry structure	Urban/rural, small versus large organizations, sectoral distribution
Business and management	Management philosophy	Prevailing management ideology, managerial style and orientation
	Organization structure	Type, degree of centralization and formalization
	Organization processes	Decisionmaking and communication processes
	Human resource management	Attitudes, practices, and policies
	Other policies	Production, marketing, financial, etc.
	Union/management relations	Conflictual versus cooperative, labor legislation
	Unions	Type, affiliations
	Other stakeholders	Consumers, church, environmental groups, etc.

stages of economic development and diverse economic, political, and cultural systems. These were North America (the United States), Europe (democratic and socialist states), Africa, Latin America, Japan, and China. Although this is not a comprehensive sample,[9] it includes a sufficient number of regions or countries to make it a representative sample along economic, political, and cultural dimensions.

In the second stage, a comprehensive framework utilizing an open systems approach was developed. In this framework there were two interacting systems: the environment and business and management. The environment was further subdivided into seven subsystems: the cultural milieu, the sociopolitical context, the economic system, the legal system, technology, communication and transportation, and the industry structure. Business and management system was divided into eight subsystems: management philosophy, organization structure, organization processes, human resource/personnel policies and practices, other policies (marketing, production, financial), union/management relations, unions, and other stakeholders. This framework (see Table 1-1) provided overall guidelines for the next six chapters (each chapter is focused on one region or country). Following the ideographic approach, each author was free to develop themes that were significant and important for his or her region or country.

In the final and third stage, the six regions or countries were analyzed to identify similarities and differences among them. The results of this comparative analysis along with some conclusions (their implications) and future directions are reported in the concluding chapter.

NOTES

1. A detailed outline of the framework is reported at the end of this chapter.
2. U.S. businesspeople have been criticized because of their lack of this sensitivity. The syndrome of the "Ugly American" is well documented in the literature.
3. Another scholar who has developed a comprehensive framework is Hans Schollhammer (1969).
4. For the view that management principles are highly culture bound, see Gonzalez and McMillian (1961) and Oberg (1963).
5. Some of the other open systems scholars are Dill (1958), Emery and Trist (1963), Miller (1955), Nath (1967, 1974), Negandhi (1973, 1983), Thompson and McEwen (1958), Thorelli (1967), and Von Bertalanffy (1950).
6. Some of these scholars are Caplow (1957); Harvey (1968); Hickson et al. (1969); Indik (1963); Perrow (1967); Woodward (1965); and the Ohio State University and the University of Michigan studies on leadership (Likert 1967; Stogdill 1965).

7. Others who have studied power are Mintzberg (1983), Kanter (1979), and Kipnis (1976).
8. Some of these are Vogel (1979), Ouchi (1981), and Pascale and Athos (1981).
9. For example, this sample does not include Middle East, South Asia, and Australia. It is hoped that subsequent works will include these regions and countries.

REFERENCES

Adler, N.J. 1983. "Typology of Management Studies Involving Culture." *Journal of International Business Studies* 14(2): 29–48.
Ajiferuke, M., and J. Boddewyn. 1970. "Culture and Other Explanatory Variables in Comparative Management Studies. *Academy of Management Journal* 35: 153–64.
Barrett, G.V. and B.M. Bass. 1970. "Comparative Surveys of Managerial Attitudes and Behavior." In *Comparative Management: Teaching, Research, and Training,* edited by J. Boddewyn, pp. 179–207. New York: New York University Graduate School of Business Administration.
Beer, M. 1980. *Organization Change and Development: A Systems View.* Santa Monica, Calif.: Goodyear.
Boddewyn, J. 1966. *Comparative Concepts in Management, Administration and Organization.* New York: New York University Graduate School of Business. Mimeo.
Buckley, R.J. 1985. "Making the World Safe for Enterprise." In *Highlights of the Second Partnerships for Development Dialogue Conference Human Resource Building,* edited by Raghu Nath, p. 3. New York: UNDP.
Burns, T. and G.M. Stalker. 1961. *The Management of Innovation.* London: Tavistock.
Caplow, T. 1957. "Organizational Size." *Administrative Science Quarterly* 2: 485–505.
Chandler, Jr., A.D. 1979. *The Visible Hand: The Management Revolution in American Business.* Cambridge, Mass.: Belknap Press.
Crozier, M. 1964. *The Bureaucratic Phenomenon.* London: Tavistock.
Davis, S.M. 1971. *Comparative Management: Cultural and Organizational Perspectives.* Englewood Cliffs, N.J.: Prentice-Hall.
———. 1984. *Managing Corporate Culture.* Cambridge, Mass.: Ballinger.
Deal, T.E., and A.A. Kennedy. 1982. *Corporate Cultures.* Reading, Mass.: Addison-Wesley.
Dill, W.R. 1958. "Environment as an Influence on Managerial Autonomy." *Administrative Science Quarterly* 2: 409–43.
Duerr, M.G., and J. Greene. 1968. *Foreign Nationals in International Management.* New York: National Industrial Conference Board.
Emery, F.E., and E.L. Trist. 1963. "The Causal Texture of Organizational Environments." *Human Relations* 18: 21–32.
Estafen, B.D., et al. 1970. "A Summary of the Systems Transfer Characteristics of Firms in Spain: A Comparative Study of U.S. and Spanish Firms." *Proceedings of the Twenty-ninth Annual Meeting of the Academy of Management,* pp. 61–68.

Farmer, R.N. and B.M. Richman 1965. *Comparative Management and Economic Progress.* Homewood, Ill.: Irwin.

Fayol, H. 1949. *General and Industrial Management.* Trans. by Constance Storrs. London: Pitman.

Gonzalez, F. and C. McMillan, Jr. 1961. "The Universality of American Management Philosophy." *Journal of the Academy of Management* 4(1): 33–42.

Haire, M., E.E. Ghiselli, and L.W. Porter. 1966. *Managerial Thinking: An International Study.* New York: Wiley.

Hall, E.T. 1959. *The Silent Language.* New York: Doubleday.

Harbison, F., and C.A. Myers. 1959. *Management in the Industrial World.* New York: McGraw-Hill.

Harvey, E. 1968. "Technology and the Structure of Organizations." *American Sociological Review* 33: 247–59.

Hax, A.C. and N.S. Majluf. 1984. *Strategic Management: An Integrative Perspective.* Englewood Cliffs, N.J.: Prentice-Hall.

Hickson, D.J., C.R. Hinnings, C.J. McMillan, and J.P. Schwitter. 1974. "The Culture-Free Context of Organization Structure: A Tri-National Comparison." *Sociology* 8: 59–80.

Hickson, D.G., D.S. Pugh, and D.C. Pheysey. 1969. "Operations Technology and Organization Structure: An Empirical Reappraisal." *Administrative Science Quarterly* 14: 378–97.

Hofstede, G. 1980. *Culture's Consequences: National Differences in Thinking and Organizing.* Beverly Hills, Calif.: Sage.

———. 1983. "The Cultural Relativity of Organizational Practices and Theories." *Journal of International Business Studies* 14(2): 75–90.

Indik, B.P. 1963. "Some Effects of Organization Size on Member Attitudes and Behavior." *Human Relations* 10: 369–84.

Kanter, R.M. 1979. *Men and Women of the Corporation.* New York: Basic Books.

———. 1979. "Power Failures in Management Circuits." *Harvard Business Review* 57(4): 65–75.

Katz, D., and R. Kahn. 1978. *The Social Psychology of Organizations,* 2d ed. New York: Wiley.

Kelley, L., and R. Worthley. 1981. "The Role of Culture in Comparative Management: A Cross-Cultural Perspective." *Academy of Management Journal* 24: 1964–73.

Kilmann, R.H. 1984. *Beyond the Quick Fix: Managing Five Tracks to Organizational Success.* San Francisco: Jossey-Bass.

Kilmann, R.H., K.W. Thomas, D.P. Slevin, R. Nath, and S. Jerrell, eds. 1983. *Producing Useful Knowledge for Organizations.* New York: Praeger.

Kipnis, D. 1976. *The Powerholders.* Chicago: University of Chicago Press.

Kotter, J. 1976. *Organizational Dynamics: Diagnosis and Intervention.* Reading, Mass. Addison-Wesley.

Lawrence, P.R., and J.W. Lorsch. 1969. *Organization and Environment.* Homewood, Ill.: Irwin.

Likert, R. 1967. *The Human Organization: Its Management and Value.* New York: McGraw-Hill.

Miller, J.G. 1955. "Toward a General Theory for the Behavioral Sciences." *American Psychologist* 10: 582–83.

Mitroff, I.I. 1983. *Stakeholders of the Organizational Mind*. San Francisco, Calif.: Jossey-Bass.

Mintzberg, H. 1983. *Power in and around Organizations*. Englewood Cliffs, N.J.: Prentice-Hall.

Murdock, G.P. 1965. *Culture and Society*. Pittsburgh: University of Pittsburgh Press.

Narain, D. 1967. "Indian National Character in the Twentieth Century." *Annals of the American Academy of Political and Social Science* 370: 124-32.

Nath, R. 1967. "Research Problems in Organizational and Comparative Systems." Paper presented at the Society for General Systems Research Symposium held at the annual meeting of the American Association for the Advancement of Science, 29 December, New York.

———. 1968. "A Methodological Review of Cross-Cultural Management Research." *International Social Science Journal* 20: 35-56.

———. 1975. "Comparative Management and Organization Theory: Linking the Two." *Organization and Administrative Sciences* 5(4): 115-24.

———. 1986. "Role of Culture in Cross-Cultural and Organizational Research." In *Advances in International Comparative Management* 2, edited by R. Farmer, pp. 249-67. Greenwich, Conn.: JAI Press.

Nath, R. and R.K. Ready. 1974. "Management Training and Developing Countries." In *The Making of the Manager: A World View*, edited by S. Mailick, pp. 392-416. New York: Anchor Press/Doubleday.

Negandhi, A.R., ed. 1973. *Modern Organizational Theory*. Kent, Ohio: Kent State University Press.

———. 1983. "Cross-Cultural Management Research: Trend and Future Directions." *Journal of International Business Studies* 14: 17-28.

Negandhi, A.R., and S.B. Prasad. 1971. *Comparative Management*. New York: Appleton-Century-Crofts.

Niehoff, A.H., and J.C. Anderson. 1964. "The Progress of Cross-Cultural Innovation." *Informational Development Review* (June): 5-11.

Oberg, W. 1963. "Cross-Cultural Perspectives on Management Principles." *Academy of Management Journal* 6(2): 141-43.

Ouchi, W.G. 1981. *Theory Z*. Reading, Mass.: Addison-Wesley.

———. 1984. *The M-Form Society: How American Team Work Can Recapture the Competitive Edge*. Reading, Mass.: Addison-Wesley.

Pascale, R.T., and A.G. Athos. 1981. *The Art of Japanese Management*. New York: Simon & Shuster.

Perrow, C. 1967. "A Framework for the Comparative Analysis of Organizations." *American Sociological Review* 22: 194-208.

Peters, T.J., and R.H. Waterman, Jr. 1982. *In Search of Excellence*. New York: Harper & Row.

Pfeffer, J., and G.R. Salancik. 1974. "Organizational Decision-Making as a Political Process: The Case of a University Budget." *Administrative Science Quarterly* 19: 135-51.

Porter, M.E. 1980. *Competitive Strategy*. New York: Free Press.

Prahalad, C.K., and Y.L. Doz. 1981. "A Approach to Strategic Control in MNCs." *Sloan Management Review* (Summer): 5-13.

Reich, R., and I. Magaziner. 1982. "Why the U.S. Needs an Industrial Policy." *Harvard Business Review* 60(1): 74–81.

Robock, S.H., and K. Simmonds. 1983. *International Business and Multinational Enterprises.* New York: Praeger.

Ryterband, E.C., and G.V. Barrett. 1970. "Manager's Values and Their Relationship to the Management of Tasks: A Cross-Cultural Comparison." In *Managing for Accomplishment,* edited by B.M. Bass, R.C. Cooper, and J.A. Hass, pp. 226–60. Lexington, Mass.: Lexington Books.

Schein, E.H. 1985. *Organizational Culture and Leadership.* San Francisco: Jossey-Bass.

Schollhammer, H. 1969. "The Comparative Management Theory Jungle." *Academy of Management Journal* 34: 81–97.

Sekaran, U. 1983. "Methodological and Analytical Considerations in Cross-National Research." *Journal of International Business Studies* 14(2): 61–74.

Sethi, S.P., N. Namiki, and C.L. Swanson. 1984. *The False Promise of the Japanese Miracle.* Boston: Pitman.

Stodgill, R.M. 1965. *Managers, Employees, Organizations.* Columbus, Ohio: Ohio State University Bureau of Business Research.

Taylor, F.W. 1947. *The Principles of Scientific Management.* New York: Harper & Row.

Thiagarajan, K.M. 1968. *A Cross-Cultural Study of the Relationships between Personal Values and Managerial Behavior.* Technical Report 23, NONR N0014-67A. Rochester, N.Y.: University of Rochester, Management Research Center.

Thompson, J.D. 1967. *Organizations in Action.* New York: McGraw-Hill.

Thompson, J., and W.J. McEwen. 1958. "Organizational Goals and Environment: Goal Setting as an Interaction Process." *American Sociological Review* 23: 23–81.

Thorelli, H.B. 1967. "Organizational Theory: An Ecological View." *Proceedings of the Academy of Management:* 66–84.

Tichy, N.M. 1983. *Managing Strategic Change.* New York: Wiley.

Triandis, H.C. 1982–83. "Dimensions of Cultural Variations as Parameters of Organizational Theories." *International Studies of Management and Organizations* 12(4): 139–69.

Vogel, E.F. 1979. *Japan as Number One: Lessons for America.* Cambridge, Mass.: Harvard University Press.

Von Bertalanffy, L. 1950. "The Theory of Open Systems in Physics and Biology." *Science* 11: 23–29.

Weber, M. 1946. *Essays in Sociology.* Edited and trans. by H. Gerth and C. Wright Mills. New York: Oxford University Press.

Woodward, J. 1965. *Industrial Organization: Theory and Practice.* London: Oxford University Press.

CHAPTER 2

North America

Douglas B. Allen, Edwin L. Miller, and Raghu Nath

THE CULTURAL MILIEU

Management and the managing process is not uniform across all national and regional cultures. In the words of Laurent, "There is no such thing as Management with a capital M and the art of managing and organizing has no homeland" (Laurent 1986: 96). As recently as a decade ago, faculties in many U.S. business schools thought that the West, and the United States in particular, had a monopoly on creative management thought and effective, efficient management practices. It was felt that if they were not invented in the United States, somehow management theorizing and management practices were not legitimate or relevant. Even a cursory review of the leading U.S. textbooks of that time could have led the reader to conclude that no one else in the world knew anything about the study and practice of management and that Western management thought and application were universal. Such an ethnocentric perspective is now recognized to be naive in light of the current foment occurring in management scholarship and in management practice.

Regional and national differences are not disappearing with respect to the practice of management, and this observation is being reaffirmed as a result of cross-cultural and comparative management research. For example, John Child (1981: 349) has written that although organizational principles of structure and technology are tending to become similar across cultures and nations, culture continues to influence people's behavior in the work setting. Despite the convergence of organizational structure and technology, leadership and managerial behavior remain culture specific and highly resistant to change.

Culture is an important force determining managerial attitudes and practices, and it does influence the practice of management. Coping with other cultures and trying to understand why and how culture influences behavior is one of the most crucial issues confronting the managements of multinational corporations trying to decide whether to establish an operation in one country rather than another. Two of the most difficult problems are (1) identifying which cultural factors are most important to the multinational corporation and (2) ranking the relative importance of the identified factors.

Culture is generally accepted as a determinant of behavior, and it is an essential tool for understanding the managerial process. Despite culture's acknowledged importance to comparative and cross-cultural management, controversy rages among scholars concerning an acceptable definition of the concept. It is not our mission to chronicle the debate surrounding culture nor list its many definitions. Acknowledging that there is disagreement regarding a precise defintion of culture, however, is it possible to provide a broad statement of culture and one that captures its substance? In a general sense *culture* refers to the way human beings understand the world in which they live. Ronen (1986: 17) writes that culture defines and expresses both attitudes and behavior. It represents a shared way of being, evaluating, and doing that is passed from one generation to another. Culture embraces the concept of morality, determining for each group what is right and what is wrong.

Culture is shared by all members of a particular group, and it is essential for the basis of social and communal life. In the words of Hofstede (1980: 27), the essence of culture is collective mental programming. It is that part of our conditioning that we share with other members of our nation, region, or group but not with members of other nations, regions, or groups.

Although culture remains at the center of attention, comparative management researchers have turned toward the use of nation or country as the primary unit of analysis when studying culture, and there are good reasons for concentrating on nationality. Hofstede (1980: 35) suggests three reasons for concentrating on the nation as an important variable for a comprehensive study of management and the management process. First, nations are political units influenced by their histories, their educational systems, legal frameworks, and labor and management systems. Second, nationality or regionality have strong symbolic value for citizens because people develop an identity associated with the places in which they were born, raised, and live. National and regional specific circumstances are perceived by people as reality, and hence, for these people, such perceptions are meaningful and important. Third, nationality contains a psychological dimension, too. Culture conditions the way that people from a particular region or nation organize and interpret certain stimuli.

The cross-cultural and comparative management field is relatively immature, and a variety of competing research emphases and paradigms are associated with theory development and model building. Researchers have used culture as an independent variable, a dependent variable, an intervening variable, and an explanatory variable. Adler and others have criticized the indiscriminate use of culture in cross-cultural and comparative management research because it has led to confusion in the field. Although research design and methodology are beginning to show some degree of rigor, one must still remain cautious about unequivocally accepting comparative management research findings. As knowledge and understanding have begun to accrue, investigators are beginning to recognize the importance of social, economic, and political forces as essential variables leading to a more comprehensive and valid body of cross-cultural and comparative management knowledge.

Culture influences organization design and structure as well as the means that organizations employ to influence the way employees think, behave, and manage. A fundamental question addressed by cross-cultural and comparative management scholars pertains to determining how culture impacts workers' behavior. Hofstede (1980) has completed one of the most important investigations of work-related values, and it provides the interested researcher with a valuable set of findings on that subject. His research is particularly impressive because of the rigorous objectives that he established in the design of the study. These objectives included the following: (1) the development of a commonly acceptable, well-defined, and empirically based terminology to describe cultures, (2) systematic collection of data from a large number of cultures (rather than just researcher impressions), (3) a thorough sampling of individuals' work-related values among fifty countries, and (4) a combination of multivariate statistical analyses and theoretical reasoning. Based on the data that were collected, Hofstede was able to isolate four dimensions of culture:

1. Individualism/collectivism,
2. Large/small power distance,
3. Strong/weak uncertainty avoidance,
4. Masculinity/femininity.

A brief description of each of these dimensions will follow. The first dimension, individualism/collectivism, is concerned with the nature of the relationships between an individual and his or her fellow human beings. Some societies view individualism positively; other societies view it with contempt and disapproval. A society that values individualism is one in which the ties between individuals are very loose. Everyone is expected to watch after his or her own interests, and individuals are left with a great deal of freedom to choose their own directions and activities. In contrast, a society that values collectivism is one in which individuals are expected to look after each other. People are born into collectives including extended families, and everyone is expected to look after the interests of the other members of his or her ingroup.

What are the implications of this dimension for management practice? In countries where collectivism predominates, individuals tend to interpret their organizational relationships from a moral perspective, and there is likely to be a psychological commitment and a sense of loyalty to the organization that transcends easy interpretation. There becomes a bond of responsibility that develops between the employee and his or her employer. Employees come to view their organization as their own; its successes become their successes and company failures become their failures. In those countries in which individualism predominates, individuals are likely to interpret their relationship with organizations from a calculative and individualistic perspective. The employee's commitment to the organization is tenuous and exists only to the extent that the individual feels that it is to his or her distinct advantage. The individual employee develops little commitment to the organization or need to respond to its demands. To some degree, the individual places his or her personal interest above the organization.

Power distance is the second dimension, and it is associated with the means that a society uses to manage the fact that people are unequal. People are born unequal, and they differentially exploit their physical and mental attributes. Some societies let individuals' inequalities grow to such an extent that over time the inequalities lead to differences in wealth and power, and these differences in wealth and power become institutionalized by society. No longer is the inheritance of wealth and power justified on the basis of physical and intellectual qualifications. Rather, it becomes accepted that the inequalities among people are attributed to kinship and birth order. Personal accomplishment is no longer a necessary and sufficient requirement for the distribution of power and wealth. As a general observation, societies have developed different criteria for the allocation of resources, and consequently certain members of the society are more unequal than others. A society that tries to downplay the inequalities of power and wealth as much as possible is classified as a low power distance culture. A society that has institutionalized differences in wealth and power as justified and not to be challenged is classified as a high power distance culture.

Power distance can be observed in the management and administrative processes of organizations, too. Power distance is related to the degree of centralization of authority, leadership, and decisionmaking. The strength of the relationship existing between the centralization of decisionmaking and autocratic leadership is rooted in the mental programming of the members of the society. For example, in organizations where superiors maintain high power distance, subordinates tend to emphasize dependence on their superiors. In this respect, superiors make decisions, and subordinates accept the decisions. In contrast, in low power distance societies, superiors maintain a lesser degree of power distance relative to their subordinates, and the subordinates prefer to participate in decisions that will affect the work performance.

Uncertainty avoidance is the third dimension, and it pertains to the means that a society uses to cope with the fact that time runs only in one direction. There is a past, there is a present, and there is a future, and societies deal with each time period differently. We live in a world in which the future is unknown, and uncertainty is associated with that condition of human existence. Some societies socialize their members into accepting that uncertainty is a fact of life and that there is little that one can do to alter that situation. Other societies socialize their members into trying to beat, influence, or control the future. A society that teaches its members to accept risk, to be tolerant, and to accept behavior different than their own can be classified as a weak uncertainty avoidance culture. Those societies that socialize their members into trying to beat the future are classified as being strong in uncertainty avoidance. Within those societies, there is a tendency to try and control the future by rules and procedures, and to the greatest extent possible there is an attempt to achieve the predictable. There is an intolerance toward the unpredictable or toward behavior and opinions that deviate from societal norms.

From an organizational and managerial perspective, uncertainty avoidance influences the degree to which an organization attempts to cope with the need to structure its activities. In strong uncertainty avoidance societies, the establishment of work rules and regulations are examples of organizational procedures designed to cope with uncertainty, and management tends to be relatively task-oriented and essentially job-centered.

When uncertainty avoidance is weak, there will be less emphasis on control, and employees are encouraged to accept ambiguity. There will be less attention and time devoted to the development of policies, practices, and procedures designed to restrict individual initiative.

Masculinity/femininity is the fourth dimension, it measures the division of roles between the sexes. Social role divisions are more or less arbitrary. The sexual role definitions of one society may vary significantly from those in another. Societies can be classified according to their inclination to minimize or maximize the social and sex-role divisions. Masculine societies stress such values as assertiveness, acquisition of money, and disregard for others. In a masculine-oriented society, the hero is considered to be a person who is a successful achiever and superman. In feminine societies, the dominant values for both men and women include such qualities as cooperation among people, conservation of the environment, the importance of the quality of life, and a belief that small is beautiful. The underdog attracts public approval, and individual brilliance is suspect.

Are there implications of this dimension for management? From an organizational perspective the masculinity/femininity construct seems to have a bearing on the importance that an individual attaches to earnings, recognition, achievement, and challenge. Thus an organization's reward system and management style will be affected by a society's orientation on this dimension.

The main finding to emerge from Hofstede's work is that organizations are heavily culture bound. This not only affects people's behavior within organizations but also influences the likelihood of successfully transporting theories of organization and management styles from one culture to another. Management and organizing are both culturally bound because they involve the manipulation of symbols that have meaning to the people involved. Meanings associated with these symbols derive from what an individual has learned from his or her family, school, work environment, and members of the society. As Hofstede (1980) has written, "Management and organization are penetrated with culture from the beginning to the end." Through a better understanding and awareness of a culture's values and the attitudes expressed by its members, one can better understand and interpret the behavior of organizations and the nature and operation of management in a given cultural setting. Ronen (1986: 20) concludes that people in different cultures create different solutions to the same problem, thus reflecting different definitions of the problem and approaches for resolving the problem.

How does the United States compare to its neighbor to the north, Canada? A brief review of Canadian and U.S. workers' values leads one to conclude there is a high correlation between the two countries.

United States and Canada

How similar are the two nations? Hofstede's findings are especially helpful because he has collected data on both countries.

On the individualism/collectivism dimension, both countries emphasize the importance of the individual. Canada and the United States can be classified as highly individualistic, with individualism viewed as a major contributor to the greatness of these two nations.

On the power distance dimension the data indicate that both countries tend to be relatively low in their use of power as a means to achieve one's goals and objectives. There is an inverse relationship between power distance and individualism. Both of these wealthy western nations combine low power distance with strong individualism. Such a relationship has an important effect on the management process as well as the day-to-day quality of life.

On the third dimension, uncertainty avoidance, the North Americans are about in the middle of the fifty countries included in Hofstede's study. Although the North Americans emphasize the development of means to cope with an uncertain future, they feel somewhat comfortable with a future that is unpredictable. In this respect, a mixed message permeates both societies and the means that organization use to influence the behavior of their members. On the final dimension, masculinity/femininity, the North Americans score toward the masculine end of the continuum. In many ways these data lead the researcher to conclude that although there are differences between the Canadians and Americans, what holds true for one country is similar to what exists in the other.

Are there other generalizations that can be drawn about the North American cultures and the United States in particular? Drawing on Hofstede's research, Ronen (1986: 181) describes the values and attributes of employees in U.S. corporations in the following terms:

The United States is high in pragmatism, emphasizing profit maximization, organizational efficiency, and productivity. It is individualistic and action-oriented, with a high tolerance for risk and a low uncertainty avoidance. Need for achievement is high, with stress on individual self-realization, leadership and wealth as life goals. Emphasis is on democratic leadership, favoring group decision making and participation, with a low score on power distance. One-way communication is disliked. The masculinity index score is moderate, with a preference for considerate, relations-oriented leaders. Americans believe in self-determination, resulting in decisions based on precise, accurate data, and an emphasis of planning. Rewards based on merit are considered appropriate because the individual is seen as being responsible for outcomes.

Harris and Moran (1979: 38) describe Americans in the following way:

> They approach activity with a concern with "doing," progress, change the external environment, while being optimistic and striving.
>
> Pace of life is fast, busy, and driving.
>
> Analytical techniques are stressed in planning.
>
> Responsibility for decisions lie with individuals who are affected by them and should make them.
>
> Achievement motivated and task centered.
>
> Person–person competition is evaluated as constructive and healthy.

Harris and Moran's observations are remarkably compatible with Hofstede's own findings on each of the four dimensions as measured in the North American society.

A society's myths and folklore help to provide additional insights about the nation's culture. The Horatio Alger stories and Chrysler CEO Lee Iacocca are two good examples. The Horatio Alger story illustrates an underlying value of individualism as a core dimension in the North American culture. Horatio Alger stories describe young people who, through hard work, rose to positions of success and prestige. Throughout his books, Alger stressed the importance of hard work as an avenue for achieving success. The message of his stories remains one of the cornerstones in U.S. society and is often cited as an example of what can occur through one's individual desire and determination to succeed.

The name Lee Iacocca is familiar to a large segment of North America because of his spectacular and highly visible role in the rescue of the Chrysler Corporation. To many, Iacocca represents a man of vision, a captain of business, and a successful achiever. Chrysler's recent success is interpreted as being the direct result of his hard work and leadership. Iacocca personifies the masculine or macho leader image typically associated with corporate America.

In the remainder of this chapter, we will concentrate on the U.S. legal, political, and economic systems. As we have noted, culture helps to shape these systems, and in turn they help to influence the management process as well as the principles of organization.

THE UNITED STATES ECONOMIC SYSTEM

What are some of the general observations that can be drawn about the economic system of the United States? Americans express a belief in free enterprise and the capitalist system. Ideally all means of production should remain in the private sector. However, current data present a different picture. For example, recent surveys indicate that the public sector comprises a larger percentage of the economy in the United States than in either West Germany or England. The U.S. economy is based on capitalist principles, but it is best characterized as a mixed economy or a blend between the private and public sectors.

Compared to many other nations of the Western world, the United States enjoys relative economic stability. However, there are other nations such as the Soviet Union that have had much more stability than the United States. Cyclical swings in the economy present problems for businesses because it is very difficult to predict the frequency and magnitude of the business cycles. History shows, however, that U.S. corporations have been able to withstand these dips in the business cycle regardless of their potential for destruction.

The income distribution in the United States has resulted in a large middle class. This means a relatively large market potential for most products, and, historically, this large market has resulted in the economy's movement toward a relatively closed economy. Consequently, most U.S. corporations have a strong domestic orientation, and this perspective has serious economic consequences for the economy. For example, over the last decade foreign firms have made their presence known throughout the United States and have caused economic and social disruptions.

Because of the existence of large domestic markets, relatively few transactions occur in a parallel (black market) economy. The widespread availability of almost all goods makes a parallel economy unnecessary. However, there are exceptions, and these include such newsworthy products as drugs and firearms. In addition, a variety of goods and services are sometimes exchanged informally and with secrecy. This is done as a way to avoid the attention of the U.S. Internal Revenue Service or state and local welfare agencies. Nevertheless, the United States and Canada are not known for a flourishing parallel economy.

A highly developed banking system helps to support the economy in the United States, and these financial institutions include multinational, regional, and local banks. Some of the multinational banks are very large, and according to *Fortune* (1986), forty-two banks report over $10 billion in assets. Furthermore, the top 100 commercial banks reported over $1.75 trillion in assets and $1.2 trillion in deposits and employed over 950,000 employees.

In recent years, banking laws have undergone drastic change. Indicative of this change has been the movement toward interstate banking.

Today, banks are able to acquire banks in other states, and this has resulted in frantic merger and acquisition activity among some of the country's large money center and regional banks. It is predicted that there will be concentration of banks and ultimately dominance by a limited number of large national banks.

Fiscal Policy

Two major fiscal policy issues involve the amount of the federal budget deficit and the balance of payments. Although the U.S. government stresses the importance of a balanced budget, actual performance has been the opposite.

The United States was in a very favorable balance-of-payment position for a number of years following World War II. In many ways it was the world's largest creditor country. This situation has been reversed in the last few years, leading to a relatively poor balance-of-payments situation. If the trend continues, it is very likely that the United States will become the largest debtor country in the world. In spite of the weakening of the dollar, the balance of payment deficit continues to be large, and many scholars have argued that a major structural adjustment is necessary to bring the balance of payments to a more favorable position.

THE SOCIOPOLITICAL CONTEXT

If the free enterprise system is to be maintained, Americans believe that the public and private sectors of the economy must be separated, and both government and business have promoted this belief. At the policy level and ideologically, the separation is supported by both political parties and the general public.

Occasionally, the federal government has intervened in the affairs of the private sector, and this has occurred because of federal regulation of particular industrial practices or by means of administrative action requiring compliance by industry. A wide variety of federal regulatory agencies have been established by the Congress. It is their purpose to enforce the legislation that Congress has enacted, and these regulatory agencies include the Federal Communication Commission, the Federal Trade Commission, and the Federal Drug Administration. For example, the Occupational Health and Safety Administration requires companies to follow specific occupational safety and health practices. Companies that fail to meet the mandated safety requirements can expect to receive fines and the prospect of possible cessaton of the unsafe production operations. As one would expect, business has vigorously objected to governmental intervention, and an adversarial relationship has developed between government and business.

There are two major political parties in the United States: the Democratic party and the Republican party. The Democratic party is generally perceived to be hostile to the interests of business, and the Republican party is seen to be generally supportive of business interests. Regardless of which party is in power, there continues to be an adversarial relationship existing between business and government. When the Republican party is in control of the Congress or the presidency, the hostility toward private enterprise is decreased but not eliminated. On the other hand, when the Democrats are in power, the conflict between business and government tends to increase. Scholars as well as business leaders have argued that the adversarial climate between business and government has been one of the major forces contributing to the United States' recent inability to compete successfully with Japanese business both within the United States as well as abroad.

U.S. corporations have traditionally avoided actively participating in the political process. However, that situation has begun to change. Industrial interest groups as well as the U.S. labor movement have begun to form political action committees designed to influence the political process. These political action committees offer financial support to those candidates for U.S. Congress or state legislatures perceived to be generally supportive of the particular committee's interests.

U.S. corporations and special industrial interest groups have established lobbies intended to influence members of Congress to vote in favor of the lobby's specific cause or welfare. Today there is considerable public interest in the process of shaping of federal and state legislation, and political action committees are trying to increase their influence within the political process. U.S. businesses have started playing an increasingly important role in the shaping of the political and legislative systems.

The U.S. Congress has been engaged in debate regarding differential treatment between domestic and foreign corporations. Until recently Americans felt that there was little or no need to differentiate between domestic and foreign-owned corporations. However, the unfavorable balance of trade and the difficulties that many large U.S. industries have been experiencing with respect to foreign competition have moved Congress to consider the need for greater regulation of competition. At the state level, some legislatures have imposed a unitary tax on foreign firms operating within their state boundaries. Although these taxes are being contested in the courts, increased attention is being directed toward the need to control foreign business activity.

The Sherman Anti-Trust Act of 1876 is one of the most significant laws affecting U.S. business. The intent of the Sherman Act has been to encourage free interplay of competitive market forces by preventing concentration of industrial power in a few companies. Antitrust legislation has been responsible for the breakup of several large industries including the petroleum industry. It can be argued that the threat of antitrust action by the federal government has been sufficient to discourage corporations from acquiring others as well as requiring the dissolution of proposed mergers. In its early days, the Sherman Act was used as an effective tool for controlling the expansion of the trade union movement as well. Recently professional sports have come under the scrutiny of the Sherman Act. The Sherman Anti-Trust Act represents one of the most controversial examples of government intervention and control of business activities.

Thurow (1983: 146–48) suggests that within the United States, antitrust laws have become outdated. According to him, much of the emphasis of antitrust thinking is based on price competition, and such reasoning does not adequately consider other competitive pressures including the demand for quality goods and service from the manufacturer. More specifically, he develops three dimensions to his argument: (1) Globalization of markets has made it irrelevant and dangerous for the U.S. government to limit the size of U.S. companies without regard to international competitors; (2) it is difficult to calculate an organization's share of the market; and (3) personal income in the United States has risen, and consequently a diverse set of markets has been developed. U.S. consumers have expanded their buying habits beyond purchases of necessities, and a relatively small percentage of disposable income is required to purchase the necessities of life. More and more income is being directed toward the purchase of discretionary goods.

As a result of the traditional emphasis on antitrust concerns, the United States government discouraged interorganizational cooperation among various industries. Between-company cooperation takes place in general business associations such as the chambers of commerce at the state and federal levels, the American Manufacturers Association, and industrial trade associations. These organizations provide services to their members in such areas as labor market analysis, updates on current events that are likely to affect business in general, and lobbying in the state legislatures and Congress.

Some of the most significant examples of federal influence on business have come about through the development and implementation of the nation's defense and foreign policies. Over the years, Congress has passed laws that prohibit U.S. businesses from selling sensitive technology to nations considered to be unfriendly to the United States. For example, without the express permission of the U.S. Department of Defense, it is illegal to sell any technology with defense implications to unauthorized governments. Until recently, the federal government has not vigorously implemented this policy, but that situation has drastically changed. For instance, the government closely examines the sale of almost all products to the USSR, and in several instances the department of defense has prevented the sale of computer equipment. The decision was justified on the basis of the equipment's potential military application. The United States has expressed its displeasure with South Africa's policy of apartheid, and the federal government prohibited the sale of certain goods to South African companies and the government.

Controlling the sale of agricultural products to the Soviet Union is an important way that the federal government controls foreign policy toward a particular government. Unfortunately, U.S. farmers have become the pawns in disputes between the USSR and the United States because they have been prohibited from selling grain to the Russian governments unfriendly to the United States. Defense and foreign policy considerations, therefore, have a significant and continuing impact on the commercial dealings between U.S. corporations and foreign nations, and in this respect, U.S. businesses may be the victims of decisions made at the national level.

INFRASTRUCTURE

Factor Endowment

The United States had at one time the world's largest pool of highly developed scientific/technical manpower. However, several countries have now achieved a comparable human resource base, and Japan is probably the best example. In Japan the quality of scientific and technical training is judged to be excellent, whereas the quality of education offered in U.S. high schools is seen as adequate at best. At the university level, the

United States continues to enjoy a leadership position because its world-class universities offer students cutting edge technologies. The quality of U.S. leadership in scientific education is attested to by the large numbers of students from countries throughout the world seeking admission to U.S. science and engineering programs.

Communications and Transportation

The U.S. communications network uses a wide range of technology. Satellite networks connect telephones and televisions with most parts of the world. The government operates a relatively reliable and speedy postal system. Private and government organizations vie for business in the overnight document delivery market, offering overnight delivery of small packages door-to-door almost anywhere in the country.

The rapid acceptance of the personal computer allows businesses of all sizes access to a variety of on-line databases and electronic mail networks. Today electronic data processing is revolutionizing the field of information management and communication between individuals within and between organizations. Furthermore, the communication mediums of telephone, television, and personal computer are merging into powerful new communication technologies that enhance office productivity.

The U.S. transportation system is one of the most extensive in the world. After World War II an expressway system was established throughout the country, and it links almost all portions of the nation. The system was originally established for national defense and the rapid movement of personnel and supplies from one area of the nation to another. Although the overall system is still a viable and effective means of transportation, portions of the system (as well as secondary roads and bridges) are in need of repair.

The air network effectively links most U.S. cities and towns, and almost all places in the United States can be reached from any other location within a few hours. In 1986, 392 million passengers were expected to fly on 19.2 million U.S. flights. The record number of flights in one day, according to *Fortune* (July 7, 1986), was 111,152.

Deregulation of the airline industry occurred during the late 1970s and early 1980s. This created an opportunity for the entry of an unprecedented number of new airlines. Since deregulation it has been reported that seventy-two new airlines have entered the marketplace and the number of flights and passengers has increased by about 50 percent. However, many of the new airlines have failed, whereas others have quickly expanded into serious competitors for the older, well-established airlines. The rapid expansion of air travel has put pressure on the entire air transportation system, including airports, terminals, baggage handling systems, and air controller facilities, and this rapid growth has resulted in facilities' being used beyond their intended capacity. Although most air safety experts consider air travel to be the safest means of travel, there has been some deterioration in the quality of service and an increasing potential for danger. Unfortunately, the number of reported airplane incidents of "near misses" has more than doubled since 1982. As in other areas of the world, concern over terrorist acts against airlines has led to tighter airport security and closer scrutiny of passengers and their luggage. These difficulties notwithstanding, the widespread availability of relatively safe and reliable air travel combined with an extensive road system communications network have resulted in the trend toward decentralization currently under way in much of U.S. business.

Technology

Coasting on its strong technological lead after World War II, the United States became known for its leadership position in a large number of technical fields including aerospace, electronics, computers, and heavy industry. A rapidly expanding domestic economy fueled by postwar consumer spending combined with new international markets created an extremely favorable business environment in the United States.

Strict U.S. patent laws have encouraged companies' investment in research and development because these laws provided federal protection for new innovations. U.S. patent protection has promoted innovation particularly among small potential entrepreneurs. Today foreign firms and individuals register their products in the United States to take advantage of patent protection.

In the high-technology industries as well, however, international competition is presenting unprecedented challenges. Korea and Taiwan are producing IBM Personal Computer clones that equal or exceed the performance of IBM's personal computer at a significantly lower price. The pressure in the area of IBM PC compatibles is so strong that *Business Week* (Lewis 1986) speculated that IBM might be forced out of the very market that it created. Meanwhile, the semiconductor chip industry in the United States is reeling under the pressure of Japanese companies that now control substantial portions of the world (and U.S.) chip market.

Automation (Robotic Technology)

The United States is a leading developer of robotics technology, and the early applications of robotics has occurred in such heavy industries as automotive manufacturing. In 1983 the Michigan Occupational Information Coordinating Committee forecasted that by 1990 the automotive manufacturing industry would be using between 50,000 and 100,000 robots. It is expected that the robotics industry will expand by approximately 40 percent annually over the next decade. However, growth will be limited by the ability of companies to invest faster and by limitations in the technology itself.

In many cases, the introduction of robotics has not led to replacement of workers by machines. Instead there have been changes in job requirements, and it is estimated that jobs created by the emerging robotics industry will involve about two-thirds white-collar (clerical, technical, and professional) jobs and one-third blue-collar (production) jobs. Furthermore, there will be an expanded need for engineers. Among those workers who are displaced, the vast majority will be relatively unskilled, and the realignment of the skill composition of the workforce will produce changes in worker training programs, increased social costs, and new roles for trade unions.

The creation of jobs requiring skilled employees has left a void between job requirements and the skill level of displaced workers. Unions and companies are responding to this realignment in the workforce by means of joint union company training programs for displaced workers. These training programs are the product of community, company, and union cooperation, and some of the most outstanding and successful programs have occurred in the automobile industry. In fact, the demand has been so heavy that training facilities have been operating twenty-four hours a day.

The retraining challenge will not easily be met and overcome. In many cases it will be impractical to train unskilled workers to fill the emerging high-tech jobs. The discrepancy between the skills possessed by displaced workers and the skills required by the new, emerging jobs may be too wide for the displaced workers to overcome. It is predicted that it will probably be necessary to train large numbers of workers to assume greater levels of technical and administrative responsibility in a stair-step fashion as the entire workforce is upgraded incrementally to handle the new job requirements. How long this undertaking will require and what suffering it will involve are questions without answers at this time.

BUSINESS AND MANAGEMENT SYSTEM

Industry Structure

The U.S. business sector is a complex network of over 4.8 million businesses ranging in size from General Motors (heading the 1985 Fortune 500 list with over $96 billion in annual sales) to hundreds of thousands of businesses with sales of less than $50,000 per year.

Mention of U.S. business often conjures up visions of giant enterprises. Although such businesses constitute a significant share of total U.S. business—the 1985 Fortune 500 industrial companies were responsible for $1.8 trillion in sales (about 25 percent of all business sales) and $69 billion in profits and employed 14 million people (about 13 percent of total workforce)—they are by no means representative of the overall business sector. Over half of the firms in the United States employ less than five people; 95 percent have less than 100 employees; and about two-thirds of U.S. companies have annual sales totaling less than $500,000.

Increasingly, attention is being focused on the smaller, more entrepreneurial companies as representative of the segment of the economy offering the highest potential for growth and future innovation.

Naisbitt and Aburdene (1985: 106), for instance, cite a recent study reporting that new business start-ups are occurring at an accelerating rate. As of 1985, businesses were starting at the rate of over 700,000 per year—twice the annual rate of the mid-1970s and eight times the rate of the mid-1950s. They identify three important factors behind this trend: decreasing job security in the larger corporations, new markets and new business opportunities created by the rapidly expanded information sector of the economy, and increased availability of venture capital for the funding of new projects. The result is that today small businesses are creating about 600,000 jobs per year—up from 93,000 in 1950.

Large corporations are trying to take advantage of the innovative atmosphere found in these smaller, entrepreneurial settings. International Business Machines (IBM), for instance, set up an entirely separate division in Boca Raton, Florida, with responsibility for the development of the IBM personal computer. Quoted by Naisbitt and Aburdene (1985: 64), John Akers, CEO of IBM, describes one aspect of IBM-promoted "intrapreneurship":

> We also encourage entrepreneurship internally by a policy of transfer pricing. Transfer pricing means that each plant is responsible for putting a firm price on

what it makes or does including sub-assembly work headed for another IBM plant. The plant has to deliver at that price and make a profit. If the price is too high, the receiver of that work is free to look elsewhere—either inside or outside the company—to obtain an alternate source. In other words, every step of our manufacturing process is compared to what is going on outside the business. Each step has to compete as a source of supply.

Naisbitt (1982: 11–38) identifies the shift from an industrial to an information society as his first megatrend. He sees the current shift as the latest in a series of technological revolutions that are occurring with increasing frequency. In 1830, over 70 percent of the U.S. workforce was employed on a farm. By 1900 that number had decreased to about 37 percent as the effects of industrialization were beginning to shape the economy. Today, less than 3 percent of the workforce is employed in agricultural jobs. Naisbitt observes that a similar transition is occurring in the industrial sector. Long heralded as the backbone of the U.S. economy, the industrial manufacturing sector is becoming less significant as an employer. As early as 1956, white-collar workers outnumbered blue-collar workers. Today only about 12 percent of the workforce is employed in manufacturing operations.

Naisbitt suggests that an important distinction must be made between the service and the information sector. Many studies tend to lump the two together as the service sector. This, according to Naisbitt is grossly misleading. It conjures up in people's minds a nation employing McDonald's employees and little else. Naisbitt suggests that if you take this service sector and extract the growing number of knowledge workers, you are left with about 10 to 12 percent of the workforce in the truly service-oriented jobs. This percentage has been fairly stable over the past twenty-five years.

The information sector is growing rapidly. Naisbitt calculates that 65 percent of the workforce is currently employed in the information sector of the economy (compared with 17 percent in 1950).

In *Megatrends*, Naisbitt (1982: 125–6) states that for the first time since the 1820s rural areas in the United States have begun to grow more rapidly than the cities. In fact, many of the nation's cities have experienced significant population loss. For example, the 1980 U.S. Census reported a ten-year loss in population of greater than 20 percent in such metropolitan communities as St. Louis, Buffalo, and Detroit. Although there is movement toward the rural areas, this does not mean that more people are seeking agriculturally related occupations. Companies are aware of the skill levels of those Americans choosing to live in the country. Jobs are coming to this highly trained and well-educated segment of the U.S. labor force. As people leave the cities for the rural areas of the country, they tend to bring part of the urban culture with them. Hence, rural and urban lifestyles in the United States are beginning to merge and economic distinctions are becoming less important.

For many businesses, the attraction of the rural areas include lower operating costs, lower labor costs, a union-free environment, local and state financial incentives, and a commitment to a strong work ethic. Companies located in rural areas are finding recruiting costs dropping because they are easily attracting highly qualified applicants who found rural areas to be much more desirable locations in which to live and raise their families. As such, businesses are seriously considering rural areas as possible locations for new plants.

Organization Structure

Large firms in the United States generally rely on some form of hierarchical organization. They probably use one or more of four common types: functional, product, geographic, or matrix structures.

A *functional* organization is most commonly used in companies specializing in a one-product category. It is characterized by a single general manager (usually referred to as president, chairman, or chief executive officer) occupying a position to which a variety of functional (manufacturing, finance, marketing, sales, and human resources management) heads report. Each function is organized as a separate department and positioned to provide its distinctive expertise to the entire organization where required.

A *product* organization is decentralized into product groups. Each will usually have its own general manager to whom a more or less complete complement of functional departments reports. Depending on the degree of decentralization adopted by a specific organization, some central services (such as finance and human resources) may be provided from a centrally controlled corporate staff.

A *geographic* organization is divided according to location of markets. A typical geographic structure in a U.S. firm might involve eastern, western, central, and southern divisions. In the case of multinational corporations, a single international division or a more complex continent- or country-oriented structure may be adopted. A geographic structure often is used in the sales and marketing functions along with product or functional organizations in other departments.

The *matrix* organization is best suited to handling high-technology and project-oriented tasks. In a matrix situation, a lateral product or project-oriented team will be headed by a project manager. Each member of the team effectively reports to two supervisors—a functional head and a project head. The matrix structure facilitates the effective coordination of both functional and project decisionmaking. It is recognized to be a difficult structure to manage well and requires more communication and coordination activity than the other simpler structures.

Small businesses in the United States are often less formally structured. The owner may serve as sole employee, a family may informally share responsibilities of running a small business, or an owner may simply direct the activities of a few workers on an ad hoc basis.

A *Business Week* special report (Jones 1986: 56–85) on "The Hollow Corporation" suggests that a new form of organization is emerging and may represent a step beyond the matrix. The network organization is "a small central organization" that relies "on other companies and suppliers to perform manufacturing, distribution, marketing, or other crucial business functions on a contract basis." The report cites Lewis Galoob Toys Inc. (1985 sales: $58 million) as an example of this increasingly popular form of organization:

> A mere 115 employees run the entire operation. Independent inventors and entertainment companies dream up most of Galoob's products, while outside specialists do most of the design and engineering. Galoob farms out manufacturing and packaging to a dozen or so contractors in Hong Kong, and they, in turn, pass on the most labor-intensive work to factories in China. When the toys land in the U.S., they're distributed by commissioned manufacturers' representatives. Galoob doesn't even collect its accounts. It sells its receivables to Commercial Credit Corp., a factoring company that also sets Galoob's credit policy. In short, says Executive Vice-President Robert Galoob, "our business is one of relationships." Galoob and his brother David, the company's president, spend their time making all the pieces of the toy company fit together, with their phone, facsimile machines, and telexes working overtime.

Naisbitt (1985) also describes the move from hierarchy to network organization. He says that "networks exist to foster self-help, to exchange information, to change society, to improve productivity and work life, and to share resources." He cites Marilyn Fergusen's description of networking as involving "conferences, phone calls, air travel, books, phantom organizations, papers, pamphleteering, photocopying, lectures, workshops, parties, grapevines, mutual friends, summit meetings coalitions, tapes, and newsletters."

Interestingly, Tichy (1983: 70–72) suggests that networking exists in all organizations. Informal relationships can be identified that serve as transaction and interaction modes for "influence, information, affect, goods and services." Although these relationships may exist on a purely informal basis and fail to appear on organization charts, they serve an important facilitating role in the organization's activity.

Role of Unions

In the United States there are two kinds of unions: craft and industrial. Generally, industrial unions bargain with large companies at the national level. A typical situation would involve national bargaining between representatives of the company and the union with the goal of arriving at a national labor contract. In addition to a national agreement, a supplementary local agreement is often negotiated between individual plants and local union representatives.

Craft unions, on the other hand, tend to negotiate at the local level, and the international union has limited involvement in the collective bargaining process. Representatives of the international union provide the local union leadership with support and expertise, but the local union manages its own negotiations.

From the days of Samuel Gompers, union/management relations in the United States have been generally adversarial. The union movement was often a response to perceived and actual company exploitation of labor. Employees were attracted to unions by claims that collective representation could increase their ability to interact with the company on an equal footing. Labor/management relations tend to be characterized by a high degree of suspicion and mistrust. At times, this resulted in long strikes. Perhaps more important, it has caused a sharp division between production workers and management. The result has been a negative impact on productivity and the quality of worklife of all employees — production workers and managers alike.

Historically, unions have served as a vehicle for improving the lot of the worker, primarily through directly negotiated improvements in pay, benefits, and working conditions. As the U.S. industrial sector developed over the past seventy-five years, increased productivity and world leadership in technology made it possible and easy for companies to agree to union demands for significant increases in monetary and nonmonetary compensation. Thus, unions were able to justify their value to workers on a fairly consistent basis. By the early 1980s this situation had dramatically changed. Many of the basic benefits and working conditions that had been important points of negotiation in the past were now taken for granted as part of the employee compensation package by union and company alike. Overseas competitors with lower labor costs have been putting heavy pressure on many U.S. industrial segments.

It is estimated that the average small car could be built in Japan for $1,500 to $2,000 less than it could be built in the United States. Labor cost accounts for about $500 of that difference, whereas management and organization of work (for which management and labor shared responsibility) account for at least another $500 or so. It has become clear that U.S. industry cannot support further automatic increases in its compensation structure if it is to retain or regain its competitive position.

From a numerical standpoint, unions have become smaller. In 1956, 34 percent of private, nonagricultural workers were organized; by 1980 that figure had declined to 24 percent (Freeman and Medoff 1984: 221). In the 1950s unions won over two-thirds of the representation elections, and their election involved about 1 percent of the total workforce. By the 1980s, trade unions were encountering great resistance in their organizing drives. Unions were winning about 5 percent of the representation elections, and this represented only .14 percent of the unorganized workforce.

These and other factors led to unprecedented results in many union bargaining sessions in the early 1980s. Record numbers of companies not only refused to grant automatic increases during their negotiations but actually sought and often obtained giveback concessions from the unions. These givebacks took on a variety of forms including wage decreases, wage freezes, elimination of automatic cost-of-living adjustments, reduction of benefits, and reduction or elimination of union-imposed work rules. Although the traditionally adversarial relationship between workers and managers made it more difficult for companies to convince their employees of often genuine financial distress, many companies were able to convince their employees that the plight they faced was serious enough to warrant the givebacks. In many cases, givebacks on the employee's part were at least partially offset by other types of company concessions such as increased worker participation in the management of the company, employee access to company books, various assurances of job security, profit sharing, and employee ownership programs.

Mills (1983: 95) suggests that the giveback period and the increased worker participation may have a permanent and positive effect on labor/

management relations in the United States. Today labor and management are more willing to work together closely, and employees are involved in a variety of decisionmaking situations.

Management Philosophy

Traditionally U.S. managers have emphasized the distinction between managerial activities and actual production activity. This distinction has been reinforced in the minds of most managers and workers by a strong distinction between the legally defined exempt and nonexempt workforce. Further reinforcement comes from the assumption that managers represent and guard the interests of the owners while workers are often stereotyped as pitted against those very same interests.

Management has retained certain decisionmaking prerogatives (such as the right to allocate resources and to hire and fire). This usually results in little or no participation of the person on the line in the direction and strategic decisionmaking of the firm. Information is often disseminated through the organization on a "need to know only" basis. The result is often less than desirable. An adversarial relationship between managers and employees is not uncommon in U.S. business, and increasing numbers of employees in recent years have felt alienated from their work.

Further problems in the traditional approach taken by many managers have resulted from an overemphasis on so-called rational decisionmaking techniques. Hayes and Abernathy (1980) in their article "Managing Our Way to Economic Decline" summarize the major arguments. They suggest that by measuring managers' performance and tying bonuses to quarterly performance figures, managers are encouraged to take a short-term outlook on profitability. They are inadvertently being rewarded for postponing medium- and long-term investment as they maximize each quarter's profit. Under these circumstances, less investment in research and development, preventive maintenance, and human resource development can be expected because the payoff of such investment is not realized until much later on when the manager may well have been promoted elsewhere in the organization leaving someone else to inherit the problems left behind.

As international competition has become more intense, U.S. managers have come to realize that some of these inefficient practices must be corrected. Increased emphasis has been placed in recent years on maximizing human resource utilization through development and involvement. Books such as *In Search of Excellence* (Peters and Waterman 1982) and *The New Competitors* (Mills 1985) emphasize the importance of people management in achieving effectiveness in organizations.

Emphasis on the importance of people management is not particularly new. In the late 1950s and early 1960s, Douglas McGregor (1960) from MIT suggested that U.S. business practice in general reflected assumptions about human nature, which he labeled theory X assumptions. Theory X managers assume that people are generally irresponsible, prefer nonwork activities, and must be directed (even coerced) to work. He contrasted this view with structural alternative theory Y assumptions, which hold that in an appropriate environment people will willingly work hard, can be self-motivated, and may even seek out responsibility. McGregor suggested that the assumptions that managers hold about people will heavily influence the style of management that they exhibit toward their subordinates. In turn, a self-fulfilling prophecy can result when employees respond to the expectations of the manager behaving as the manager expects. McGregor called for the adoption of a new style of management that reflected theory Y assumptions. He argued that by creating a positive work environment and aligning organization and personal employee goals, employees could work more productively and with greater job satisfaction.

At the time McGregor and others were promoting the human relations school of management, few businesses responded enthusiastically to this style of management. The U.S. economy was still benefiting from the substantial technological lead that it had maintained since World War II and was experiencing strong productivity improvement. This seemingly invincible combination led to complacency and overconfidence in many companies, a condition that remained until the early 1980s. For the first time, intense competition at home as well as abroad forced U.S. business to begin to reassess its approach to its operations.

In 1982 the United States faced an economic recession and unemployment levels of 9.8 percent, worse than at any time since the end of World War II. Some of the problems were caused by a general worldwide recession, but the problems were compounded by a growing inability of U.S. manufacturers to compete against offshore competitors. Labor costs in the United States were extremely high—twice as high as in Japan and as much as ten times the labor cost in many developing countries. Perhaps more significantly, the quality of many U.S. products was lower than that achieved by the international competition.

Japanese auto production rose in 1980 to 11 million vehicles. The U.S. produced 8 million vehicles that same year, making 1980 the first year that any nation had produced more vehicles than the United States since 1903 when France produced 13,000 vehicles and the United States built 11,200 (*Technology Review*, Aug.–Sept. 1982). Consumer electronics, single-lens reflex cameras, and many other products were hit extremely hard, and some goods disappeared almost entirely from the collective production portfolio of U.S. companies. The "Made in Japan" label that had been a sign of low-quality, cheap products in the 1950s and early 1960s became a signal of very high quality and value in the 1970s and 1980s. In many industries, "Made in USA" signaled lower quality and (often) higher price. The U.S. business sector suffered a collective loss of confidence with respect to its capability for competing in a changing world. At first, it was common to blame U.S. workers for the problems. Some analysts suggested that the U.S. work ethic was dead—that employees were no longer dedicated to quality and productivity. Japanese workers, on the other hand, were the products of a culture of excellence. Others focused blame for the lack of U.S. competitiveness in world markets on high energy cost, excessive government legislation, and strong unions.

These explanations were inadequate for explaining the magnitude of the U.S. economic difficulties. Oil prices, government regulation, union presence and other macroeconomic issues were just as much or even more problematic in Japan and Europe. For example, the argument that U.S. workers were inferior proved to be incorrect when Japanese and European companies established highly productive operations in the United States and did it with U.S. employees.

Matsushita-Panasonic, for instance, purchased the Quasar Division from Motorola in 1974. In 1974 under Motorola management, the plant averaged 1.3 major defects per television set, $16 million in annual warranty costs, and a 63 percent rework rate before products left the factory. Six years after the sale, Matsushita (at the same plant with essentially the same workforce) was averaging .0005 major defect per set, less than $1 million in annual warranty costs, and a 2 percent rework rate.

Mills (1985) describes the Sony television plant in San Diego as the first plant in the world to (occasionally) outperform Sony's Japanese plants. Honda, in Marysville, Ohio, has successfully produced motorcycles and automobiles that are reputed to rival the quality of similar Japanese-produced Honda products. A joint-venture between GM and Toyota has resulted in the production of Chevrolet Novas, and these automobiles have been judged to be equal in quality to their Japanese equivalents. Unfortunately, Nova suffers from an image problem because U.S. consumers are skeptical of the automobile's quality. GM and Toyota recently announced that Corollas will be produced on the same assembly line in order to supply additional vehicles to Toyota dealers in the United States. Other foreign companies have established or are establishing U.S.-based manufacturing operations as well.

Because of the competitive success of the Japanese and European companies, managers in the United States are taking a closer look at what can be learned from management practices in other countries. What they have found is a strong emphasis on human resources management and a system that fosters participation of line workers in a variety of decisionmaking and problemsolving roles.

One practice borrowed from Japan—quality circles—has been widely adopted in the United States. Quality circles are ad hoc groups of workers who gather together on a more or less informal basis to examine issues of concern in the workplace (generally quality or productivity problems). The resulting analysis and recommendations are forwarded to management for consideration and possible implementation. Although quality circles have been successfully integrated as an ongoing practice in some firms, many managements adopted them as a simple solution to complex problems and then discontinued them after experiencing disappointing results.

When quality circles have been successfully adopted, they have generally been recognized as part of a larger human resource management system and not as a solution in and of themselves. Successful implementation of QCs has generally involved not only an opportunity for workers to work on problems and forward recommendations to management but to also receive feedback on their ideas: whether they were accepted or rejected, the reasons for the action taken, and the actual result of the ideas used. With adequate feedback, employees are more likely to perceive the program as a genuine effort to involve the employees in important problemsolving activity and not a cosmetic facade intended to conjure up the illusion of employee participation.

Just-in-time (JIT) inventorying—a system widely practiced in Japan—received increased attention in the United States. General Motors, for instance, discovered that it could reduce its capital costs by about $300 million per year simply through the introduction of a JIT system. Interestingly, JIT systems must also be recognized as a part of a larger manufacturing system, if they are to be implemented successfully. In companies suffering from a variety of quality and supplier problems, JIT may represent a disastrous innovation. Problems that have been masked by cushions of inventory rapidly manifest themselves as the entire production process is finetuned to operate in a low or no inventory mode. The analogy used by Japanese companies is that of a river. As long as the river is high, you don't see the rocks, but when the river is low, the rocks are exposed and treacherous. To operate a JIT system, you must be alert for rocks and dedicated to removing them whenever they appear. This requires teamwork combined with a problemsolving orientation.

In the midst of intense observation of Japanese and European companies as possible models for U.S. management change, Peters and Waterman published *In Search of Excellence* (1982) and identified excellent U.S. companies, documenting their practices for others to emulate. Although controversial in academic circles, the book became the best-selling business book of all time as U.S. managers hungered for hope that the United States could again achieve competitiveness.

In the final analysis, *In Search of Excellence* was a primer on people management arriving some twenty-one years after McGregor's *The Human Side of Enterprise*. McGregor's book was published in a radically different era, an era in which the United States—far from being overconfident—was indeed "in search of excellence."

Management Style

In recent years increasing numbers of scholars have observed a trend in the United States toward a more participative style of management. Lawler has summarized the implications of this trend as shown in Table 2-1. He describes the old way—a control model of management—and the new way—a model based on commitment (see Hoerr, Pollock, and Whiteside 1986).

Although the effort on the part of U.S. business to move toward a participative style of management is increasingly noticeable, it will be many years before the majority of U.S. companies adopt the sweeping changes implied by a truly participative style of management. Eric Trist (see Hoerr, Pollock, and Whiteside 1986), commenting on the progress made in this direction in the United States, said that the new model of work relations is not yet the dominant one but that "I'd be sad if we weren't getting close to that point by the end of the century."

As U.S. management begins to regard the workforce as a resource rather than a liability, many U.S. managers are taking a new look at the role of their personnel departments. In the last ten years, the term *human resources manager* has replaced the formerly popular designation of *personnel manager*. In many companies, the name change may be the only change. But many other companies have begun to regard their human resources management staff as strategically critical to the company and

Table 2-1. The Organization of Work: A Comparison.

Former	Current
Managerial Assumptions About Workers	
Workers are lazy, irresponsible, and motivated only by money.	Workers are willing to accept responsibility to seek out challenging work assignments, and they are motivated by opportunities for responsibility, recognition, and personal and professional growth.
Principles and Assumptions About Job Design	
Work is fragmented, requiring minimum worker skills. The individual worker has little influence on productivity.	Work requires a broad range of the worker's skills and talents. Team work has become an important means for worker involvement and productivity.
Organization Design and Structure	
Organizations are designed hierarchically. Authority flows downward and management is responsible for making all decisions influencing work and worker involvement.	Organizations are designed with few layers of management. The worker is encouraged to participate in the management process.
Job Training and Employee Security	
Workers are expendable and easily interchangeable. Worker training is limited and concentrated upon the acquisition of a few basic skills.	The worker is an important resource possessing skills, an ability to think, and a desire to contribute. The worker's value to the organization appreciates over time.
Reward Structure	
Pay is related to job requirements. Job evaluation systems determine the worth of the job to the organization.	Pay is related to the worker's skills, acquired as well as required. Rewards include more than monetary compensation.
Labor Management Relations	
Adversarial relationships between organized labor and management. The union representing its members' interests challenges management on a broad range of work-related issues.	Cooperative relationships between labor and management. Sharing of information by management with union. Management invites union participation in a variety of company-related matters.

Source: Adapted from Hoerr, Pollock, and Whiteside (1986: 71).

contributing directly to the effectiveness of the organization (Fombrun et al. 1984: 51).

Too often in the past, the personnel department has been relegated to a variety of administrative and clerical tasks undertaken merely to keep track of people in the company. When business plans were formulated, the personnel department would (if they were lucky) receive copies of the strategic plan from which they would calculate workforce requirements.

A distinguishing characteristic of human resources management (HRM) is its strategic orientation in HRM, and it is noted that the HRM professional is confronted by a twofold challenge: (1) to develop viable processes whereby HRM contributions can and do occur in the strategic planning process and (2) to adopt and promote strategic thinking within the human resource function itself.

What are the variables that differentiate strategic human resource management from previous definitions of the personnel function? We believe that it is helpful to use Miles and Snow's strategic human resource management dimensions (Miles and Snow 1984). The following attributes appear to capture the spirit of the developing model:

1. Top managers of the human resource function possess at least a conceptual familiarity with all services needed to acquire, allocate, and develop managers and employees.
2. The function has a comprehensive understanding of the language and practices of strategic planning. Appropriate human resource representatives are participating in the planning process to assess the probable demand for their unit's services.
3. The human resource function pursues appropriate strategies of its own to match the organization's business strategy.
4. The function acts as a professional consultant to the line. In addition to their expertise in strictly human resource matters, the human resource specialists are knowledgeable about organization structure, management processes including communication and control, and organization change and development.

Other Stakeholders

Beer et al. (1984: 16) lists company stakeholders as shareholders, management, employee groups, government, community, and unions. Historically, it was the position of most U.S. companies that profitability and the maximization of return on investment were the appropriate means for satisfying the interests of their shareholders. More recently, however, increasing numbers of groups have purchased company shares as a way of influencing corporate policy. Such groups include consumers, churches and religious organizations, universities, as well as a variety of other special interest groups.

Some groups, for example, have taken a very strong stand as supporters of disinvestment in South Africa. Similarly, organizations such as the Sierra Club (concerned with environmental issues) and antinuclear groups have emerged to lobby for pollution control and the survival of the planet earth.

Many strategic management scholars such as Mitroff have argued that corporations need to carefully identify stakeholders and learn about their views. These views should provide significant input to the strategy formulation process.

Other stakeholders are receiving increasing strategic consideration as well. As mentioned earlier, the federal government continues to create a variety of regulations that may heavily influence the operation and profitability of a firm. Additionally, defense, energy, public programs, and many other policy areas can indirectly affect companies through their impact on the market for a company's product. Local community groups are also taking a more active role in a variety of issues related to the environment, safety, employment, and even product mix of resident enterprises.

CONCLUDING REMARKS

The United States does not have a monopoly on creative management thought and management practices. This has been a painful lesson for Americans to learn, and it is not clear that all U.S. managers and management scholars have come to accept this finding. Management does not occur in the abstract; it is played out within the cultural, social, legal, and economic subsystems of a country, and to understand the practice of management one must come to grips with the context within which management occurs. In this chapter we have highlighted some of the dynamics of American cultural, social, legal, and economic subsystems as they influence the practice of management.

The American approach to management is not universal, and what works well within the United States may not work well in other parts of the world. Likewise, what is appropriate in another culture may not be appropriate in the United States. Understanding the values and attitudes characteristic of a country's culture is essential to a more comprehensive understanding of the country's approach to management as well as the functioning of its social, legal, and economic subsystems. Americans emphasize the importance of the individual, a reluctance to use power in order to achieve one's goals and objectives, relative comfort with an unpredictable future, and an inclination toward masculinity. These values and attitudes color America's social, legal, and economic subsystems as well as the American approach to the practice of management.

REFERENCES

Adler, Nancy. 1983. "Cross-cultural Management Research: The Ostrich and the Trend." *Academy of Management Review* 8(3): 226–32.

Beer, Michael; Bert Spector; Paul A. Lawrence; D. Quinn Mills; and Richard E. Walton. 1984. *Managing Human Assets.* New York: Free Press.

Child, John. 1981. "Culture, Contingency and Capitalism in the Cross National Study of Organizations." In *Research in Organizational Behavior,* vol. 3, edited by L.L. Cummings and B.M. Staw, pp. 303–56. Greenwich, Conn.: JAI Press.

Fergusen, Marylin. 1980. *The Aquarian Conspiracy: Personal and Social Transformations in the 1980's.* Los Angeles, Calif.: Tarcher.

Fombrun, Charles, Mary Anne Devanna, and Noel M. Tichy. 1984. "A Framework for Strategic Human Resource Management." In *Strategic Human Resources Management,* edited by C. Fombrun et al. New York: Wiley.

"Fortune Service 500." 1986. *Fortune* M3(12) (June 9): 126–27.

Freeman, Richard, and James Medoff. 1984. *What Do Unions Do?* New York: Basic Books.

Harris, Philip, and Robert T. Moran. 1979. *Managing Cultural Differences.* Houston: Gulf.

Hayes, Robert, and William J. Abernathy. 1980. "Managing Our Way to Economic Decline." *Harvard Business Review* (July–Aug.): 67–72.

Hoerr, John, Michael A. Pollock, and David G. Whiteside. 1986. "Management Discovers the Human Side of Automation." *Business Week* (Sept. 29): 7a.

Hofstede, Geert. 1980. "Culture's Consequences: International Differences in Work Related Values." Beverly Hills, Calif.: Sage.

Jones, Norman. 1986. "The Hollow Corporation." *Business Week* (March 3): 57–59.

Laurent, Andre. 1986. "The Cross-Cultural Puzzle of International Human Resource Management." *Human Resource Management* 25(1) (Spring): 91–102.

Lewis, Geoff; Katherine Hafner; Dori Jones Yang; Scott Tice; and Kenneth Dreyfack. 1986. "The PC Wars: IBM vs. the Clones." *Business Week* (July 28): 62–68.

McGregor, Douglas. 1960. *The Human Side of Enterprise.* New York: McGraw-Hill.

Main, Jeremy. 1986. "The Worsening Air Travel Mess." *Fortune* (July 7): 50–55.

Miles, Raymond E., and Charles C. Snow. 1984. "Designing Strategic Human Resource Systems." *Organizational Dynamics* (Summer): 36–52.

Miller, Lawrence. 1984. *American Spirit: Vision of a New Corporate Culture.* New York: Morrow.

Mills, D. Quinn. 1983. "When Employees Make Concessions." *Harvard Business Review* (May–June): 103–13.

Mills, D. Quinn. 1985. *The New Competitors.* New York: Wiley.

Moore, Thomas. 1986. "What's Taking the Punch Out of Profits." *Fortune* M3(12) (June 9): 114–20.

Naisbitt, John. 1982. *Megatrends, Ten New Directions Transforming Our Lives,* New York: Warner Books.

Naisbitt, John, and Patricia Aburdene. 1985. *Re-inventing the Corporation.* New York: Warner Books.

Peters, Thomas, and Robert Waterman. 1982. *In Search of Excellence: Lessons from America's Best Run Companies.* New York: Harper & Row.

Ronen, Simcha. 1986. *Comparative and Multinational Management.* New York: Wiley.

Tichy, Noel M. 1983. *Managing Strategic Change.* New York: Wiley.

Thurow, Lester C. 1981. *The Zero-Sum Society: Distribution and the Possibilities for Economic Change.* Middlesex, England: Penguin.

"The U.S. since 1903 When France Produced Auto Production in France." 1982. *Technology Review* (Aug.–Sept.): 44–52.

CHAPTER 3

Japan

Nobuaki Namiki and S. Prakash Sethi

Japan's economic success has led many academics and businesspeople in the United States to believe that the Japanese business and management system (JABMAS) is the panacea for all that currently ails business firms in the United States, Canada, and Western Europe.[1] Some companies in these countries have attempted to adapt the Japanese management techniques in their operations in a hope to effectively compete with Japanese companies in the domestic and international markets.

There have indeed been many articles and books written about Japan that aim at introducing Japanese techniques into U.S. corporations. Most writings on Japan, however, have focused on one or two subsystems of Japan's system—such as management techniques, personal policies, business/government relations, and culture—often failing to provide full understanding of both the benefits and drawbacks of Japan's system. Any system has its benefits and drawbacks, which are measured in terms of the society's own value set and subject to tradeoff decisions made by the society. Because most societies have different value sets and priorities, transplanting a subsystem (such as management techniques) into another society may be unacceptable and have undesirable secondary effects. The question is not whether there are benefits to be derived from adopting Japanese management practices in the United States but whether the benefits justify the costs. This chapter analyzes the Japanese business and management system within its unique sociocultural and political context, not as a system of concepts and techniques, and attempts to identify the drawbacks and limitations of the system and the costs paid for the Japanese economic miracle.

THE CULTURAL MILIEU

The substance of the Japanese psyche can be summarized by the term *amae*—that is, a feeling of dependence (from *amaeru*, a verb meaning to depend and presume on another's love, to seek and bask in another's indulgence). It is not a pejorative term but a state of mind that describes a desire to be passively loved, a desire to be protected—as in a mother/child relationship—from the world of objective reality. Doi, a noted Japanese psychoanalyst, maintains that in the Japanese these feelings are prolonged into adulthood and shape character to a far greater extent than in the West (Sethi 1975: 38; see also De Mente 1975: ch. 1). The *amae*-based relationship between two adults assumes a degree of emotional attachment that may lead the dependee to resort to irrational behavior and avoid taking individual responsibility for his own actions, expecting the dependor to indulge him by protecting him. Because in Japan *amae* is vitally important to the individual's psyche and emotional stability, the entire social structure is set up to fulfill this need. *On* implies obligations passively incurred. One "receives an *on*"; one "wears an *on*." *On* are obligations from the point of view of the passive recipient (Benedict 1946: 116). *Giri* refers to a bond of moral obligation and debt that must be repaid "with mathematical equivalence to the favor received, and there are time limits (Yanaga 1965: 58). "*Giri* obligations often are mutual and reciprocal, especially within a collectivity" (Hall and Beardsley 1965: 95).

Ninjo refers to "human feelings" and includes all the natural human impulses and inclinations. Doi (1967: 330), however, maintains that for the Japanese *ninjo* is something more specific and means

specifically knowing how to *amaeru* properly and how to respond to the call of *amaeru* in others. Japanese think themselves especially sensitive to these feelings, and those who do not share that sensitivity are said to be wanting in *ninjo*.... *Giri*... refers to a bond of moral obligations.... Whereas *ninjo* primarily refers to those feelings which spontaneously occur in the relations between parent and child, husband and wife, or brother and sister, *giri* relations are relations between in-laws, neighbors, with close associates, or superiors in one's place of work.

Benedict (1946: 177–94), Hall and Beardsley (1965: 95), and Dore (1967: 113–52) maintain that the "circle of human feelings" and the "circle of duty" are mutually exclusive. For example, Beardsley states that "*Ninjo* refers to what one would like to do as a human being and equally to what one finds distasteful or abhorrent and of personal sentiment. *Giri* pertains to what one must do or avoid doing because of status and group membership (Hall and Beardsley 1965: 95). However, Doi contends that it would be erroneous to consider *giri* and *ninjo* as mutually exclusive: "They are not simply opposed but would seem to exist in a kind of organic relationship to each other. . . . [Furthermore] *ninjo* and *giri* indicate responses that have a close bearing on *amae*." The nature of *giri* relationships may be interpreted to mean that one is "officially permitted to experience *ninjo*," whereas in relationships like that between parent and child, *ninjo* occurs spontaneously (Doi 1973: 33).

Amae can also be used to describe the underlying reasons for the vertical one-to-one relationships typical of Japanese society. Although the recognition and pursuit of *amae* in Japanese society account for both its virtues and its faults, the supression or diversion of *amae* in human relations in the West explains the strengths and flaws of Western traditions. Doi also argues that these traits of mutual dependence and reciprocal obligations account for the fact that the attempt by occupation authorities to democratize Japanese society did not necessarily promote individualism, but by destroying the traditional channels of *amae*, contributed to Japan's postwar spiritual and social confusion.

Group Formation

The familiar Japanese social characteristics—variously termed *paternalism*, *groupism*, and *familyism*—originated in the strong tradition of *ie*, or household. But the term has a broader meaning in Japan, relates to any context (for example, the workplace), and is social in orientation (see Nakane 1967, 1972a, 1972b). Simply put, this is the Japanese sociopsychological tendency that emphasizes (in the sense of protecting, cherishing, finding needs for, or functioning best in) "us" against "them." In social organization, Japanese put far more emphasis on situational frame than on personal attributes. Thus, when a Japanese faces an outside group, he establishes his point of reference not in terms of who he is but what group he belongs to. According to Chie Nakane (1972b: 4–5), a distinguished cultural anthropologist,

the *ie* is a corporate residential group and, in the case of agriculture or other similar enterprises, *ie* is a managing body. The *ie* comprises household members (in most cases the family members of the household head, but others in addition to family members may be included), who thus make up the units of distinguishable social groups. In other words, the *ie* is a social group constructed on the basis of an established frame of residence and often of management organization. What is important here is that the human relationships within this household group are thought of as more important than all other human relationships.

The Thread of Personal Relationship and Veneration of Authority

The basic single-unit interpersonal relationship between two Japanese persons is *oyabun-kobun* (*oya*, father; *ko*, child), in vertical system. Members in a work-related group or in any Japanese organization are tied together by this kind of relationship. According to Nakane (1974; 4–5) (see also Bennett and Ishino 1963),

> The extension of this kind of dyadic relationship produces a lineage-like organization. The organizational principle of the *Oyabun-Kobun* group differs from that of the Japanese family institution in that the *Oyabun* normally has several *Kobuns* with more or less equal status, not only one as in the case of the household unit.... [Whereas] the Japanese father may discriminate in the treatment of his sons...the essential requirement of the *Oyabun* is that he treat his *Kobuns* with equal fairness according to their status within the group, otherwise he would lose his *Kobun* because of the unfair treatment....
> In this system, while the *Oyabun* may have several *Kobuns*, the *Kobun* can have but one *Oyabun*. This is the feature that determines the structure of the group based on the vertical system....
> Within the *Oyabun-Kobun* group, each member is tied into the one-on-one dyadic relation according to the order of and the time of his entry into the group. These dyadic relations themselves form the system of the organization. Therefore, the relative order of individuals is not changeable. Even the *Oyabun* cannot change the order. It is a very static system in which no one can creep in between the vertically related individuals.

The structure of a group in Japan, including the corporate group, is based on the accumulation of such relationships. When a class of university graduates enters a corporation, they are assigned to a section of a department for training after a short orientation period. A person will stay in a section for several years and then be transferred to another section within the corporation. Because most university graduates have economics or law degrees, they usually do not have any understanding of business operations. The number of Japanese universities with business departments is very small (Ueno 1972: 38–39).[2] Thus, most of the training is provided by managers who are at a level above those of the trainees. Moreover, because of the Japanese respect for seniority, *oyabun-kobun* relationships will be developed within this work-related group.

The concept of the *oyabun-kobun* or superior/subordinate relationship in corporate life has the following characteristics (Rohlen 1975: 197):

1. The senior manager is older than his or her junior, has worked longer for the company, and is in a position of relative power and security. This position enables the senior to assist the junior.

2. The senior is beneficially disposed toward the junior and befriends him or her.
3. The junior accepts the friendship and assistance of the senior.
4. These acts and related feelings are the basis of the relationship. There is no explicit agreement.
5. Ideally, the junior feels gratitude toward the senior for his or her beneficence, and this feeling is accompanied by a desire on the part of the senior to become a good older friend for the younger.

The relationship is developed not only by the social norms but also through time-consuming group-centered activities. Members of the work-related or office group do many activities together in order to promote an open and harmonious atmosphere: once- or twice-a-year trips, frequent drinking parties after working hours, monthly Saturday afternoon recreation, and so forth. Most of these activities are usually financed by the company. The activities also serve as a bridge between generations.

Notwithstanding, authority is absolute and greatly respected in a Japanese corporation or any group, mainly because of the customs, traditions, and the *oyabun-kobun* relationship between senior and junior employees (Rohlen 1974: ch. 5). In return for the devotion of subordinates to the master, the superiors are expected to exemplify the virtues of sagacity, benevolence, and purity (Tsurumi 1976: 220–21):

> Masters (leaders) who failed to demonstrate such qualities were belittled as "small men" in the eyes of observer-critics cultivated in the Confucian tradition. This moralistic standard by which the leaders were evaluated still lingers with Japanese institutions. Under this master–follower relationship, subordinates were not only expected, but obligated to help their master attain exemplary conduct; even such extreme forms of self-sacrifice as disemboweling themselves and thereby performing the "protest of death" were not unheard of. The merchant class emulated such ideologies of the ruling class of *Samurai*.

The superior must be a "warm leader" (in contrast to a "rational leader" in the Western context) and a guardian who looks after the best interests of subordinates. He or she is also expected to be flexible (or "mature") and willing to accommodate a subordinate's opinions, thereby giving subordinates a sense of participation.

Faction: Its Formation and Personal Ties

The vertical system of personal relationships, coupled with the Japanese need to belong, are the main bases for the formation of subgroups and cliques (*habatsu*) within a large group. This is true of political parties, government bureaucracies, large corporations, and newly emerging radical and dissent movements. Factions and cliques protect the interests of their members and also provide a system of checks and balances within an organization. At the same time surface group harmony is maintained and rigidly enforced until the group in power is challenged by another group. Membership in a faction depends on a combination or such factors as coming from the same university, marriage ties, or assignment in the same section or department of the company (Craig 1975: 11–15).

Factionalism is seen as an evil in Japan, especially for government bureaucrats. But it is tolerated because it has a positive function as well, particularly in communications within an organization. A faction promotes and sustains informal and personal relationships between juniors and seniors and facilitates a two-way communication. However, factions also provide for one-to-one relationships between a junior employee and his superior, a relationship far more important than larger, more formal group relationships. This is one of the reasons that bottom-up communications are inordinately slow in a Japanese bureaucracy: they must go through the entire chain, one link at a time. But it also tremendously facilitates lateral communication and coordination (Craig 1975: 14). The needs for coordination, easy two-way communication, and one-to-one relationships are some of the reasons that it is extremely difficult for Japanese companies to hire experts from outside at high levels of management; such experts simply cannot become part of the internal networks.

Factions and cliques provide one of the main underpinnings for faster promotions and increased individual rewards in corporate and government bureaucracies. Faster promotion is one of the major rewards for a Japanese employee under the lifetime employment and seniority-based wage and promotion systems, which make rewarding individual excellence difficult, especially in view of the widespread use of official retirement at age fifty-five for employees who are not promoted faster and do not obtain a top or senior management position.

Japanese Culture in Four Dimensions

Culture, according to Hofstede, can be explained in terms of the four basic dimensions—that is, individualism versus collectivism, power distance, uncertainty avoidance, and masculinity versus femininity (Hofstede 1983: 46–74). As discussed in the previous sections, Japanese value collectivism rather than individualism, such as emphasis on belonging to the organization and on loyalty to the group, collectivity orientation, and "we" consciousness. As to the power distance dimension, Japanese operate at both ends by maintaining a large power distance, such as recognition of status hierarchy, and also by allowing a small power distance, such as consensus decisionmaking.

On the uncertainty-avoidance dimension, Japanese tend to have high uncertainty-avoidance orientation. For example, the practices of lifetime employment and seniority-based wage and promotion are designed to reduce uncertainty in life and promote security. Conflict and competition are avoided, and group consensus and compromise are emphasized. They also value conservatism (that is, law and order) and do not tolerate persons who deviate from the social norms and mores. As to the masculinity versus femininity dimension, Japanese tend to operate at both ends. They maintain a high masculinity culture by differentiating to a large extent sex roles in society. The employment privileges, such as lifetime employment, are provided only to male employees. However, group performance rather than individual performance is considered important. They also have a people as well as "money and things" orientation. A corporation is expected to be paternalistic toward its employees.

THE SOCIOPOLICITAL CONTEXT

Business/Government Cooperation

Most observers of Japan's economic and political practices agree that there is a high degree of cooperation between Japanese business and government. Figure 3–1 shows the typical process for the formation of public policy and the roles of governmental agencies, political parties, and other economic and social groups. This close relationship has deep historical roots. From the beginning of the *Meiji* era, economic power has been shared between government and private business. The government deliberately set out to create industry in order to modernize Japan, often by building factories and then turning them over to private business. In the process, the government retained a large degree of control over business affairs (Davis 1972: 7; see also Halliday 1975). The growth of private monopolies and cartels has continued unabated, despite the passage of an antimonopoly law and the abortive efforts of the U.S. occupation authorities. The same identity of interests held when the Japanese political system sought to create a militarily strong Japan that required close cooperation with and supervision of business.

Japanese capital has continued to develop under the benevolent protection of the Japanese government because of the close ties between business and the government bureaucracy on the one hand, and business

Figure 3-1. Major Influences on International Policymaking in Japan.

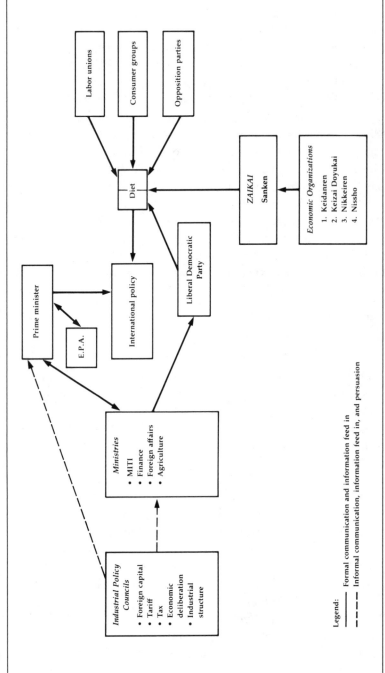

Legend:
——— Formal communication and information feed in
– – – Informal communication, information feed in, and persuasion

Source: Sethi (1975: 33).

and the Liberal Democratic Party (LDP) on the other hand. According to Jun Ui (1972: 281–91), a scholar who has done such work on pollution, Japanese economy is a classic example of state monopolistic capital where capital and state operate in a condition of complete mutual support.

Big Business and Government Bureaucracy

Japanese government exerts substantial influence over business through generous financial assistance and incentives (such as funds for R&D, export subsidies, and capital expansion) for industries and corporations that help achieve Japan's long-range industrial and economic policy, while protecting troubled industries and corporations. Administrative guidance issued by the government is usually followed and respected by the companies because the punishment for not following it is great (for example, denial of governmental financial incentives). Within the Japanese government there are six economic bureaucracies. Of these, the Ministry of International Trade and Industry (MITI) and the Ministry of Finance wield significant influence over the economic sector (Johnson 1982; Katabe 1984; 3342). The power of these bureaucracies is further enhanced by their discretion to interpret laws that are enacted by the Japanese Diet (parliament) and are more akin to policy statements.

The Japanese government selects and promotes industries, products, or technologies that are strategically important for Japan's national interest. The primary objective has been to build internationally competitive export industries, mainly because of Japan's poor natural resources. It is widely known that MITI has been a primary instrument in formulating and implementing such policies in Japan through a variety of financial and other incentives (Ministry of International Trade and Industry 1969: 62–66; see also Higashi 1983, Shinohara 1982: 3753). MITI and the Japanese government promoted such basic industries as shipbuilding, steel, and chemicals during the 1950s and the 1960s and have recently been assisting the development of supercomputers ("Where Japan Has a Research Edge" 1983; Uttal 1982; "Japan's Chip Makers" 1985; "Japan Focuses" 1985).

The Japanese government takes an active role in helping declining industries reorganize or rationalize the industrial structure without much pain. It assists them in many ways: (1) formation of cartels to rationalize output, (2) reduction of excess capacity through financial and other incentives, (3) reduction of excess labor force by helping arrange their transfer to expanding companies, (4) selection of surviving firms, and

(5) financial assistance for the employees retraining and education programs (Boyer 1983; Kanabayashi 1983).

The system of mutual support between business and government is further reinforced not only by regular and frequent contacts between the two but also by the fact that retiring civil servants expect to step into high-paying executive jobs with large corporations. This system of job switching, called *amakudari* (or heavenly descent), is widely practiced and just as widely criticized rhetorically. This practice is promoted by early retirement and low pensions for civil servants. Each ministry takes responsibility for placing its people with private industry, and a substantial number of government retirees move to corporations each year ("Heavenly Descent" 1974; "Occupational Mobility" 1974). The retirees can facilitate freer two-way communication between government and private business.

Big Business and Politics

Retiring bureaucrats with ambitions to achieve cabinet posts must first be elected to the Diet and therefore need business support for running an election campaign. Thus, money is another strong link between business and politics, and in Japan it is perhaps more prevalent, pervasive, and openly practiced than in most industrialized nations. There have been many scandals involving top politicians and "influential dealmakers" in Japan. The recent one is the Lockheed scandal, which involved former Prime Minister Tanaka and other top politicians. The long-time ruling party, the LDP, has about one-fourth of its membership coming from former civil servants who have had a long, close working relationship with big businesses and would be dependent on business funding for their electoral progress. Big business also has direct communication channels to the LDP leadership through clubs, the best known of which is *Itsukakai*, or Fifth-of-the-Month-Club.

Despite the appearances of democracy, Japan's political system is semifeudal in character; democracy is practiced more in form than in substance. The political parties are less concerned with politics and programs than they are with the accumulation of power and privileges for special factions and groups within the parties, organized around strong leaders and vying for political plums—for example, a ministership or premiership. The Liberal Democratic Party is an unstable coalition of more than half a dozen factions. Former Prime Minister Tanaka, who was involved in the Lockheed scandal and resigned from the LDP, has managed to maintain the largest faction in the LDP (Lerner 1981, 1983; "Illness of Japan's Kingmaker" 1985). Current Prime Minister Nakasone, who has been a close associate of Tanaka, includes so many members of Tanaka's faction in his cabinet that it is often called the "Tanaka cabinet" in Japan. Professor Yanaga (1965: 9) (see also Blaker 1976) says, "Wheeling and dealing, bribery, coercion, collusion, threats and violence (including assassination) are as much a part of Japanese politics as they are of Japanese life."

Policymaking Councils

Policymaking councils composed of political leaders and other experts from various segments of Japan's professional elite are for window-dressing purposes only. Although responsible for developing long-range policies, these councils initiate no action or recommendations and instead concentrate their efforts on discussing proposals made by various officials before sending them to the ministers. Official proposals are *never* rejected or changed by a council. Consumers, labor unions, and other groups have little to say in economic policy formulation because of their weak position in the Diet and also because few important decisions are determined or affected by the Diet (Sethi 1975: 31, 34).

The *Zaikai*

The primary influence of business on government in Japan is wielded through the *zaikai*, defined as "a politico-economic group of wealthy financial leaders who can exert tremendous influence on the government and politics (Sethi 1975: 34). The term *zaikai* is used to denote financial circles, or even more broadly, business circles—but always meaning big business. *Zaikai* leadership consists primarily of the top executives of four big business organizations, of which the most influential is *Keidanren*, or the Federation of Economic Organizations, whose board of directors consists of the presidents of the key organization and the elder statesmen of business, industry, and finance (Yanaga 1968: 32–35, 38–39).

One should not interpret the term to imply that big business in Japan always has a unified position on matters affecting it. Within the *zaikai* there are differences based on special interests, regional interests, attitudes toward the West, political leanings, and—most important—closeness to the seat of political power, that is, the LDP and the government. Similarly, the internal differences should not be misinterpreted to mean a lack of power and influence or inability to act on issues affecting business in Japan.

Organized business exerts a strong influence on virtually all aspects of government decisionmaking. This influence is openly acknowledged and recognized by all concerned. No legislation strongly opposed by the *zaikai* is introduced by the government or passed by the Diet. Japanese business therefore does not have to resort to lobbying in the sense that it is practiced in the United States because it holds a virtual veto over all important economic decisions.

Industrial Groups

In addition to the *zaikai*, there are also huge economic organizations, *zaibatsu* or *keiretsu*, consisting of oligopolistic firms. Until the end of World War II, they were called *zaibatsu* and consisted of ten family-controlled industrial giants. After the war, Allied occupation forces dissolved the *zaibatsu* to reduce the concentration in the economic sector and to promote democracy in Japan. However, these companies later regrouped, and the groups are now called *keiretsu* or industrial groups without existence of family control. Today, there are six industrial groups that were regrouped based on the old *zaibatsu*. They are Mitsui, Mitsubishi, Sumitomo, Fuji, Sanwa, and Dai-Ichi Kangyo. The first three groups are the direct successors of old *zaibatsu* and are considered to have stronger ties within the group than the other three groups. The latter three groups are tied through their main banks and also are successors of some former, smaller *zaibatsu* brethren (Sasaki 1981: 10, 12) (see also Hadley 1970; Bisson 1954).

Each group includes every industry in Japan. In one industry, for instance, at least six companies compete against each other. Normally, the industrial groups consist of many oligopolistic firms (member companies) plus numerous small- to medium-size companies. Member companies are all large in size, yet they keep close working relationships within the group. For example, member companies belonging to the Mitsui group are those that have a close relationship with the financing institutions that center around the Mitsui Bank, those that conduct large economic transactions with trading company of the same name, and those that are members of the group's policymaking organ – *Nimoku-kai* ("the Second Thursday Conference"). The *Nimoku-kai* is composed of the presidents of the participating companies and is responsible for making major decisions for the Mitsui group. There are twenty-three member companies in the group. Each member company with its subsidiaries and related companies represents one broadly defined industry. There is only one member company representing one industry in order to ensure of little competition within the industrial group. It is usually considered that each groups's leaders are the main bank and the trading company. Unlike the prewar *zaibatsu*, ownership control by a holding company is absent in these groups. However, group-member companies hold their shares mutually. These stockholdings are usually small, but cross-ownership by other companies in the group may be as high as 80 percent (Haitani 1976: 12) (see also Hadley 1970: 212–19). Coordination within an industrial group is further enhanced by personal contacts and interlocking directorates.

The intricate web of relationship of companies within an industrial group promotes businesses and cooperation within the group. The relationship is reciprocal: Firms belong to a group because of the substantial benefits that it offers, such as access to financial and capital markets, access to export market and distribution channels, and improved corporate image and status. Although bankruptcy rates for small firms are high in Japan, those for large firms are extremely low because of protection by the industrial groups. Only a handful of large companies have gone bankrupt during the last decade in Japan, mainly because of their lack of strong ties with a group and its main bank. There are only a few large companies that do not belong to an industrial group (such as Sony and Honda).

The six industrial groups explained above are sometimes called financially linked industrial groups. In addition, there are ten or so independent manufacturers' groups, also composed of numerous member companies and smaller, related companies. The examples are Toyota, Matsushita, and Nissan groups. Some of them belong to one or two financially linked industrial groups (Sasaki 1981: 10, 17).

Although a considerable degree of cooperation exists among member companies within an industrial group, to some degree, competition does exist between the industrial groups. However, competition that is considered potentially damaging to the Japanese economy is controlled by the Japanese government, notably the Ministry of International Trade and Industry (MITI).

Dual Structure

The Japanese economy is often called *dual structure* because large-size companies coexist with numerous number of small companies, and there are wide gaps in productivity and wages. Big businesses in Japan achieve much higher productivity and therefore provide much higher wages to their employees than small businesses do. Although the gaps in productivity and wages are also present in other industrialized nations, the gaps in Japan are much wider compared to those in other industrialized nations. Employees at smaller companies in Japan typically receive around 35 to 45 percent lower wages than workers at big companies, get considerably fewer fringe benefits, and enjoy no lifetime employment privilege (Sasaki 1981: 20).

Almost 98 percent of manufacturing companies in Japan have less than 100 employees and can be classified as small companies (Sasaki 1981: 17). Moreover, those numerous small- and medium-size companies are substantially controlled by large companies. Most of the smaller companies are subcontractors for the large companies. In 1971 it was found that almost 60 percent of small- and medium-size manufacturing companies were classified as subcontractors (Small and Medium Enterprises Agency 1975: 238). Each member company in an industrial group has developed many layers of subcontracting structure that has a hierarchy of parts suppliers. The smaller companies are, in other words, captives of the member companies and closely associated by ownership and financial control, making the smaller companies dependent on the larger for survival. Commonly, a big company even sends its own management teams to its captive companies (Broadbridge 1966; Yasuba 1976: 249–98).

This structure tremendously benefits the big companies. Because many large manufacturing companies in Japan are not integrated, they procure their parts from subcontractors who usually pay low wages to their employees and thus purchase them at a minimal cost. For automobile manufacturers, about 65 to 70 percent of the parts used to make a complete automobile are supplied by their subcontractors (Sasaki 1981: 21). Moreover, because of the dependency relationship, the manufacturing firms can depend on the subcontractors for quick delivery of these low-cost, high-quality parts. An example of such dependency can be found in the *kanban* or just-in-time system that is employed by Toyota Motor Company.

Japanese Sogo Shosha and Banks

Each industrial group has a bank and a general trading company. The bank serves an important integrative function for the group as the main source of capital resources. As explained earlier, Japanese companies belong to an industrial group because of the benefits of getting large financing from the main bank and of getting protection from the bank in case of financial exigencies. Most Japanese large companies rely on their group's main bank to finance rapid expansion and have considerably high debt-to-equity ratios. In return, these companies usually accept the bank's management personnel, who oversee them as the companies' top executives, thereby losing their management autonomy to, and allowing substantial control by, the main bank.

The trading company plays an equally important role of integrating the group through its diverse activities. There are more than 6,000 trading companies in Japan, but only the largest of them, usually the top ten, are called general trading companies, or *sogo shosha*. Examples are Mitsubishi Corporation, Mitsui & Co., and Sumitomo Shoji. They handle more than half of total exports and imports (Haitani 1976: 128). The primary function of the general trading companies is to conduct the marketing and distribution of merchandise for commission, mainly for the industrial group's companies. Also, they initiate development of new industries and organize new business ventures both domestically and internationally (Kojima and Ozawa 1984).

Another important function of the general trading companies is provision of credit to customers, particularly small businesses. They borrow heavily from the group's main bank and then provide credits to their customers for the purposes of providing operating funds for the borrowers, selling raw materials on credit, financing new equipment purchases on a long-term basis, and so forth. Although the major banks lend primarily to major corporations, trading companies conduct commercial financing for smaller companies. The trading companies also purchase equity shares of their customers, in order to develop or strengthen *keiretsu* relations (Haitani 1976: 129–30) (see also Kunio 1982).

The Social Costs of Close Business/Government Relationship

The close business/government relationship, coupled with the narrow national pursuit of rapid industrialization, have inevitably created costs to society and sacrifices of other social goals. Since World War II the national priority has been to reindustrialize and establish international competitiveness, and the goals of Japanese business have closely matched with those of the government and public at large. The result has been considerable destruction of the environment, ignorance of consumer and labor protection, and even abuse against individual stockholders because of the close relationship between business and government.

For example, Japanese individual stockholders have little power over the companies, although the Japanese Security and Exchange Act is almost identical to the United States' securities act. Most Japanese companies use paid professional thugs, called *sokaiya*, to intimidate shareholders at stockholders' meetings and deter them from asking embarrassing questions of management (Sethi 1978: 46–47) (see also Pearlstine 1976a; "Sokaiya Return" 1985). Most shareholders' meetings are over within fifteen to thirty minutes. Also, individual stockholders are usually the last ones to know of their companies' financial problems because the financial statements and accounting systems used by Japanese companies excel in obtuseness (Pearlstine 1974b).

In addition, the problem of pollution in Japan is more serious than in any other industrialized nation in the world. There have been a number of pollution-related incidents that attracted worldwide attention. The most famous incidents are Minamata disease, Itai-itai ("ouch-ouch") disease, and Yokkichi asthma. In all those incidents that started in the 1950s, the victims suffered for a long time (typically about twenty years) before they received adequate compensation and proper treatment, mainly because of the Japanese government's indifference to their plight and its narrow pursuit of industrialization (Huddle, Reich, and Stiskin 1975: 102–32).

Concern by large segments of the Japanese population about the considerable destruction of the environment and about the pollution incidents had increased substantially by late 1960s and early 1970s. Fish caught off nearby Japanese islands were no longer edible. Japanese were also concerned about their babies' health because of possible contamination through mothers' breast milk. The increased concern led the Japanese government to enact strict environmental protection laws in the early 1970s, some provisions of which were very similar to, or stricter than, those of the pollution-related laws of the United States.[3] The Japanese government promoted Japanese business for pollution clean-up through heavy governmental subsidies. It even helped finance R&D programs in pollution-control technologies. However, the problem still persists because the sociocultural and political factors that exacerbated the problem in the first place are very strong ("Nuclear Contamination" 1981; "Japan Says" 1981; "Forty-five Japanese" 1981; Stokes 1981; "Japanese Nuclear" 1981).

The Economic System

Under the protection and guidance of the Japanese government, Japan, after World War II, has transformed itself to one of the world's major powers. The growth of the Japanese economy in terms of total output averaged 9.5 percent a year from 1947 to 1973; it was then and still is unprecedented. Even after the oil shock in 1973, Japan's growth rate has remained higher than that of other advanced industrialized countries. By early 1980s the Japanese economy became almost comparable with the economies of other advanced countries, although it remains at an earlier stage of economic development. Compared with the economies of other advanced countries, the Japanese economy has higher employment in agriculture, higher share of gross domestic product (GDP) in manufacturing, and lower share of GDP in services (World Bank 1983: 153).

As explained earlier, the Japanese economy has been developing under the protection and guidance by the Japanese government, notably the MITI. It has selected target industries for development and has formulated and implemented the basic strategies for the industries and firms. It targeted heavy industries in the 1960s, and since the 1970s it has been promoting knowledge-intensive industries, such as computers, aircrafts, electronics, and information services. Therefore, it can be said that the Japanese economy is capitalistic but to a large extent is guided by the government. The government's efforts to develop the Japanese economy have been on export-oriented industries, mainly because of the lack of natural resource endowments. Until the late 1960s, when Japan had relatively low-cost labor, the export growth came mainly from labor-intensive industries. However, since the early 1970s, when labor costs rose sharply, the growing category of exports has been that of capital-intensive, high-wage, and skilled-labor–intensive goods such as steel and automobiles. R&D-intensive goods also showed significant growth. Specialized machinery, office products, telecommunications equipment, automobile, trucks, and household appliances showed particularly high export growth (Krause and Sekiguchi 1976: 409). Japan has accumulated large amount of trade surplus with its major trading partners, stirring protectionist sentiments, especially in the United States.

The rapid economic growth has brought about substantial increase in the standards of living of Japanese people. About 90 percent of Japanese population think that they belong to the middle class (Kosai and Ogino 1984: 108–09). However, Japan has some economic weaknesses. One major weakness in the Japanese economy stems from the government budget deficits that have been increasingly growing since the 1970s. Japan's accumulated debt has been considerably higher than that of the United States, as a percentage of the GNP. Because of Japan's high saving rate (in 1982 Japan's gross savings were about 32 percent of GDP, compared to 16 percent for the United States), its budgets deficits can be accommodated with little concern about inflation (Pepper, Janow, and Wheeler 1985: 46–47). Notwithstanding, the high debt had imposed constraints on Japan's fiscal and monetary policies, domestic financing markets, and the future economic growth.

INFRASTRUCTURE

Three aspects of the Japanese infrastructure are discussed in this section. These are transportation and communications, legal system, and technology.

Transportation and Communications

The Japanese railway system is well developed and is an example to the rest of the world. Major cities are connected via the airline system. The road system is comparable to most of the European nations but is not as good as that of the United States.

The telephone, telex, and other communication systems are excellent, both within Japan and between Japan and other countries. This is probably a major reason for the development of Tokyo as a major financial center.

Legal System

After World War II, Allied occupation forces made significant changes in the Japanese legal system. Many laws were enacted during the late 1940s, and some, such as antimonopoly laws and securities and exchange laws, were almost identical to those of the United States. After the occupation ended, however, most of the laws were significantly changed and relaxed, mainly to promote faster industrialization of the Japanese economy. For example, the antimonopoly law, which was enacted in 1947 and was highly restrictive, was considerably relaxed during the early 1950s (Hadley 1970). Interpretation of the law was also markedly relaxed; it has shifted from the strict per se philosophy (monopoly or restraint of trade per se is illegal) to a rule of reason (only the abuse of monopoly power and the unreasonable restraint of trade is illegal) (Henderson 1973: 51). The Fair Trade Commission (FTC) is a semiautonomous, quasi-judicial agency formed after the pattern of the U.S. federal agency and is supposed to enforce the antimonopoly law. However, the law is rarely enforced. Although the law permits formation of certain cartels (such as temporary, recession, and rationalization cartels), for economic reasons other cartels (special cartels) can be established without approval of the FTC. As a result, only a few cartels have been approved by the FTC, but numerous special cartels have been approved by the ministries, notably the Ministry of International Trade and Industry (MITI) (Caves 1976: 487). Moreover, the MITI can establish the guidance cartels that can regulate output, prices, and investment programs of various industries and firms targeted by the MITI for development. Furthermore, the MITI can provide various forms of tax incentives and subsidies to these industries. The tactics that have been used by the MITI to promote these industries have been to limit competition and promote bigness. These often conflict with the goals of the FTC and the antimonopoly law, but MITI usually prevails because of the overwhelming power of organized business and the powerful economic ministries (Haitani 1976: 135).

The cooperative relationship between the government and business often results in the sacrifice of consumer interests and interests such as environmental protection and stockholders, as discussed in the previous section. Practices of price fixing and hoarding by large businesses have been prevalent, especially for the consumer products (Sethi 1975: ch. 7; Zimmerman 1985: 136). Moreover, Japan is not a litigious society, mainly because Japanese culture values cooperation and compromise, and this is a major reason that it has taken so long to provide remedies to those injured.

Technology

It is well known that Japan has become a formidable industrial power by imitating and refining technology that it acquired from the West. Most Japanese industries have grown on imported technology. A significantly large portion of the techniques used by such industries as synthetic fiber, electronics, electric machinery, and automobiles are improvements made to imported foreign technologies (Sasaki 1981: 28). Also, technical innovation (or improvement) has been found more often in production processes than in products. Since the late 1960s labor costs in Japan have gone up sharply, and one of the major objectives of the Japanese government and industries has been to improve manufacturing efficiency, mainly through automation and robotics, with the assistance of computers. Japan builds almost half of the world's output of robots, most of which are used to automate domestic plants. The Japanese government, especially MITI, has supported the development of the computer industry through the provision of various tax incentives and subsidies, as well as protection of the domestic market from foreign imports. It also has promoted much collaborative research between government laboratories and private companies (Freigenbaum and McCorduck 1983).

In terms of absolute amounts of aggregate research expenditures in early 1980s, Japan ranked third after the United States and the Soviet Union. In terms of research expenditures as a percentage of national income, Japan ranked fourth after Soviet Union, West Germany, and the United States. In 1983 Japan spent a total of $24 billion on research and development expenditures ("Japan Focuses" 1985: 94). However, compared to the other advanced industrialized countries, Japanese government support for R&D expenditures has been modest. About 70 percent of Japanese R&D expenditures are supported by the industries, compared to about 50 percent in the United States.

Japan's traditional emphasis on applied research has slowly been changing toward a greater emphasis on basic research. Recently, Japanese companies have been setting up many research laboratories to work in such fields as ceramics, telecommunications, and biotechnology. However, one of the major obstacles to promoting scientific research is the lack of scientists. Japanese universities produce very few scientists compared to those educated in the United States and Europe ("Japan Focuses" 1985: 94).

THE BUSINESS AND MANAGEMENT SYSTEM

It is well known that Japanese companies use management techniques that are quite different from those practiced in the West. The Japanese management practices include decisionmaking by consensus, a highly ritualistic communication system for conflict avoidance and conflict resolution, lifetime employment, and seniority-based wage and promotion systems. It should be noted, however, that these practices are used primarily by large enterprises, although they may also be employed in medium and small-size enterprises in Japan.

Decisionmaking by Consensus

The Japanese decisionmaking process is that of consensus building, which is known as *Ringisei*, or decisionmaking by consensus.[4] Under this system any changes in procedures and routines, tactics, and even strategies of a firm are originated by those directly concerned with those changes. The final decision is made at the top level after an elaborate examination of the proposal through successively higher levels in management hierarchy, and results in acceptance or rejection of a decision only through consensus at every echelon of the management structure. The decision process is best characterized as bottom-up instead of top-down, which is the essential character of the decisionmaking process in U.S. corporations. *Ringisei* literally means "a system of reverential inquiry about a superior's intentions." However, the word in this context means obtaining approval on a proposed matter through the vertical, and sometimes horizontal, circulation of documents to the concerned members in the organization. The *Ringi* process may vary from one organization to another but usually consists of four steps: proposal, circulation, approval, and record. This typical procedure is described in a simplified form below (Sasaki 1981: 57–58).

When a lower- or middle-level manager is confronted with a problem and wishes to present a solution, a meeting is called for in that particular section by its section chief (*Kacho*). The members of a section may agree that the idea should be pursued, but they also may feel that it needs the overall support of the firm. The section chief reports this to his or her department head or department manager (*Bucho*) and consults with the head. If the department head expresses support for the section's proposal, the time-consuming activity of getting a general consensus starts.

First, a general consensus among the persons who will be directly and indirectly involved with the implementation in a department is sought. Then an overall but informal consensus in the firm is sought. The department head may arrange a meeting with the other departments concerned. Each department sends one department head, one section chief, and perhaps two subsection chiefs (*Kakaricho*, sometimes called *supervisors*). They are the ones who would be involved in the implementation stage. Thus, if there are four departments involved, sixteen to twenty persons will attend the meeting. If the opinion of specialists or experts on the shop floor is needed, it will be represented. In fact, the meeting is mainly aimed at exchanging information among the involved persons in order to implement the plan. Through the discussion, some other information and materials may prove to be needed. In that case the initiator and his consonant colleagues, under the leadership of the section chief, formally and informally go from section to section and from department to department to collect the necessary information and prepare the documents to be presented at the next meeting. This prior coordination is vital for the *Ringi* system to be effective.

After a number of meetings, the department judges will have attained an informal agreement from all the other departments concerned. The procedure up to this point is called *Nemawashi*, meaning informal discussion and consultation before the formal proposal is presented. This is the moment when the formal procedure starts.

First, the initiator and his colleagues under the section chief's supervision write up a formal document of request, the *Ringi-sho* (*sho* means document), which outlines the problems and the details of the plan for its solution. Also enclosed are supportive information and materials. The *Ringi-sho* is then circulated among various successively higher echelons of management for approval. Each responsible manager or executive affixes his or her seal of approval. The number of seals can reach ten or twelve. The *Ringi-sho* finally goes up to the top management for formal authorization and the final "go-ahead."

The *Ringi* process can be divided in two broad categories: the *Nemawashi* process, or decisionmaking by consensus, and the *Ringi* process, or formal procedure to obtain authorization ("Japanese Managers" 1977: 131–32). Once a proposal is accepted during the *Nemawashi* stage, it is seldom opposed or rejected at the *Ringi* stage. Scholars have labeled the *Ringi* system "consensual understanding" (Fox 1977: 79) and a "confirmation-authorization" (Hattori 1978: 12) process of decisionmaking. The *Ringi*, in this context, is used to confirm that all elements of disagreement have been eliminated at the *Nemawashi* stage. It ensures that responsibility is assumed by all who have affixed their seals of approval.

It is apparent that the shortcoming of the *Ringi* system is its excruciatingly slow pace. However, the process ensures the high degree of commitment by involved parties, which in turn speed up the implementation (Drucker 1971: 111–13). Another shortcoming of the *Ringi* system is that it is primarily designed to manage continuity but to avoid uncertainty. When a fast-changing environment and uncertainty arise, new information is avoided or processed slowly and must be internalized because new information is considered as representing a threat to group cohesiveness (Sethi and Namiki 1984: 450–51).

Consensus Decisionmaking and Internal Communication

The process of communication within a Japanese organization is very much akin to the mating dance of penguins.[5] Communicators resort to both verbal and nonverbal communication. A great deal of ritualistic communication precedes and follows any substantive discussion. Thus participants fully know and understand who is going to say what, and to whom, before it actually takes place. Yet all concerned would be quite offended if the ritualistic behavior were not strictly observed. A great deal is made of forms and gestures, leaving the listener to interpret the meaning of what is being said.

The communication process, however, is quite different when it takes place within each group and between two or more groups. A group is defined here as members working together in an office, section, or department who have face-to-face, intimate, and less structured relationships among themselves. The size of the group varies according to the company. This is the group that plays an integral role in initiating a proposal, in getting coordination from other groups to promote informal consensus among the concerned groups, and in writing up a *Ringi-sho*. On the other hand, employees who are in different offices or departments may not have similar relationships and personal ties among themselves, in which case their relationships are more functional, formal, and vertically structured. For ease of analysis, the former group will be referred to as the primary group and the latter as the secondary group. According to Nakane (1974: 12), "Since the groups are highly institutionalized, it is easy to recognize the hierarchical order among them; and this is the only acceptable pattern among the Japanese for communication that takes place between individuals and between groups who otherwise have weak relations or none at all."

There are many differences between the behavior patterns of the two groups. When a primary group holds a meeting, the subject to be discussed is gone into at length. The atmosphere is highly informal. It engenders a feeling of comaraderie and encourages all primary group members to talk freely. There is an intimate and familiar feeling of participating in a democratic process that makes members of lower status feel comfortable. The first part of the meeting consists of discussing factual information pertaining to the issue. Gradually the members begin to sense the direction of the group's opinion. Exposition rather than argument is the nature of the discourse. An understanding and acceptance among members is appreciated. After this is done the members try to adjust or arrive at a new line based on the points of disagreement.

Direct conflict is avoided. If a member wishes to present his opinion, he does so by prefacing it with "I happen to know someone who thinks that..." or "Let me say this, but I'm just thinking out loud." This gives him a way out, if he sees that what he says is radically opposed by other members. What he wants is a situation of understanding and acceptance by his fellow members before he lets his own opinion be known. Occasionally a heated argument does take place. When this occurs, one of the more prestigious members tries to reconcile the two sides, or one of the middle- or lower-status members injects some sort of comic relief. After working very hard toward acceptance by all, everyone knows that consensus is near when 70 percent of the members are in agreement. At that point the minority concedes and is willing to support the decision. Primary groups believe that there must be a basic accord, and that if they try their best they can come to a unanimous conclusion. In this way the decision will be implemented with a high degree of cooperation.

The secondary groups, on the other hand, are the formal, more ritualistic organs of the company. Their meetings are all ceremony and mark the final stage of reaching a decision. Although the members are also members of various primary groups, when they become members of a secondary group they change their behavior accordingly. Each member represents a particular group and must act exactly as that group tells him to. If something unexpected arises, he may have to ask that the meeting be suspended so that he can confer with his members to ascertain how they want him to handle the new situation.

The real power sources at these meetings are the "men of influence," sometimes called the "black presence." They always remain behind the scenes and can be found in every field and every large or influential group in Japan. Over a period of time they have managed to establish effective personal relations with influential members of various groups. The Japanese term for these influential men is *Kuromaku* (a term from the traditional *Kabuki* drama meaning "black curtain"). Figuratively, it connotes power behind the throne. Perhaps the two most influential behind-the-scenes power brokers in business and politics in Japan are Yoshio Kodama and Kenji Osano, who were involved in the Lockheed scandal in 1976 (Halloran 1976: 1, 8). The relations among such men are established through common bonds of age, school, or workplace. If these contacts are lacking, a relationship can be developed through a mutual compatibility evolving in the course of various meetings attended by both.

These "men of influence" rarely meet together. Instead they use informal channels to relay information among themselves. Their intercommunication is even more open than that among members of a primary group because they can always say that they are stating their group's opinion. Once they have reached a decision, they write the scenario for

the coming meeting. By the time the meeting is convened, each partici-
pant has been well rehearsed for the drama about to unfold. There is
even a scenarist, who sits next to the chairman to make sure that the
meeting goes exactly as planned. If a minor figure who was not given
any lines presents a contrary opinion, it is listened to politely: the chairman thanks him for his opinion and says that it will be considered. This
is a face-saving way of ignoring him. Actually, the scenarists want situations like this to arise, so that the process will appear democratic. The
dissenter is well aware of his powerlessness in the hierarchy, and his
purpose is expressive rather than communicative. And because he is
given a chance to express himself, it is easier for him to accept the final
decision. In Nakane's (1974: 19–20) words: "It is thus a highly political
procedure. The power and the authority of both a formal and an informal
hierarchy are effectively employed."

There is some similarity between the decisionmaking process of secondary groups in Japan and that of the top sector of the U.S. government and the Supreme Court. Highly ritualized activities do occur, but
they are restricted to very special areas or occasions. On the other hand,
there is no hint in the United States of a primary group entity. Americans tend to be much less open in disclosing themselves to other members of a group.

Organizational Structure in Japan

Japanese corporations adopt various forms of organizational structure,
such as functional, divisional or matrix. However, formal organizational
structure is only secondary in importance in Japan. In the United States
or other countries, the organizational structure is often defined in terms
of communication, authority, and work flow. It is the company's pattern
of relationships and formal arrangement of roles and relationship of people so that work is directed toward meeting the goals of the company.
As explained in previous section, operations of Japanese companies are
significantly different from those of companies in the West. Decisionmaking by consensus encourages initiatives for change from the lower
rather than the top management, diffuses sense of responsibility to all
members involved, and makes top management delegate its authority to
the group. Internal communication is also based mainly on personal relationships and factions rather than on the formal arrangement. The internal working of a Japanese corporation is therefore strongly influenced
by Japan's traditional cultural traits such as groupism, rank consciousness,

and vertical interpersonal relations. The processes, rather than the formal organizational structure, are the essence of the form in Japan (Davis and Lawrence 1977: 55–56).

Role of Middle Management

Middle managers perform an essential role in the *Ringi* system. However, how well a middle manager performs this role depends largely on his or her personal relationships and ties with other managers—links that lubricate the flow of information in the organization. Consensus, before a decision is taken, requires a flood of information, and much of the information that is relevant is produced at the place of implementation (Sasaki 1981: 77). Thus the demand for information pulls the decision process down toward the implementation level, while the need for the decision process to be exposed to corporate strategies pushes it upward. The equilibrium point of these two conflicting demands is generally found at the middle-management level. The system is effective only if the middle management is competent in bridging the gap between lower and higher levels of management, so that personal relationships with other people in the organization become critically important. In Japanese firms middle managers acquire these attributes through a system of job rotation from one function to another, life-time employment, and related training programs. Figure 3–2 and Figure 3–3 show a typical organization chart with seniority system and typical office outlay, respectively, in a Japanese corporation. One department occupies a large room in which employees of all levels sit at desks arranged in much the same order as the organization chart. It takes about thirteen to fifteen years to become a section chief. During this period employees may be transferred around in the department and in other departments, so as to make them generalists rather than specialists in the U.S. or Western sense. The system also encourages personal ties that enhance the efficiency of information flows.

Japanese middle managers therefore perform the essential role of closing the gap between decisionmaking and its implementation in their activity domains. The closeness of the decisionmaking to the implementation results in a high level of morale and motivation among middle and lower managers.

Role of Top Management

Under the Ringi system, presidential or top-management leadership is expected to cope mainly with crisis situations or with abrupt and clear-

Figure 3-2. Organizational Structure and Seniority Order.

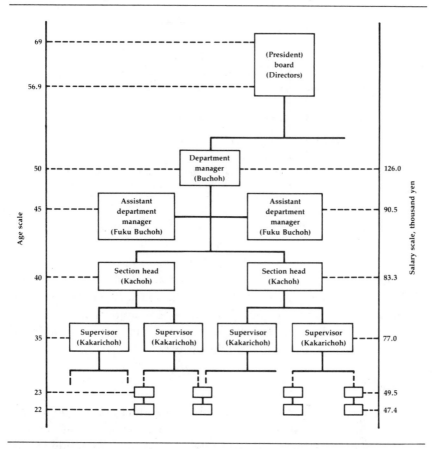

Source: Sasaki (1981: 73–74). Reprinted by permission of the Pergamon Press, Ltd.

cut changes in the direction of the firm. Once the general direction of the firm is communicated to the middle- and lower-management echelons, both operational decisions and incremental changes are entrusted to the initiatives of the lower- and middle-level managers. Most of the working hours of the top management in Japanese corporations are occupied with establishing and maintaining "private" relations with responsible men in policymaking positions in other corporations and government departments. This is accomplished through regular and frequent, formal and informal contacts that are demanded by the sociopolitical environment in Japan and is evidenced in the close cooperation between the Japanese government and private industry (Tsurumi 1976: 228–30) (see also Drucker 1981). For some Japanese companies that operate in rapidly

Figure 3-3. Typical Office Floor Plan: One Department in One Room.

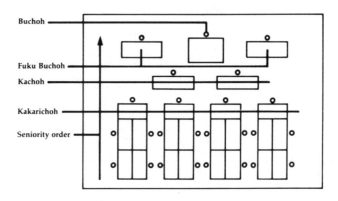

Source: Sasaki (1981: 73-74). Reprinted by permission of the Pergamon Press, Ltd.

changing markets, their leadership style has been similar to that in U.S. corporations and radically different from the traditional norm. Autocratic leadership style or top-down decisionmaking has become popular, although slowly, as many Japanese companies face rapidly changing environments in both domestic and international markets ("Japan's Autocratic Managers" 1985: 56-64) (see also Ohmae 1982: 26).

Personnel Policies

Most large Japanese corporations employ personnel policies quite distinct from those of the West: lifetime employment; seniority-based wage and promotion systems; in-company training on more than one job or function by rotation; and company-oriented rather than trade- or profession-oriented unionization.[6] All these practices are found in some degree in Western countries, including the United States—for example, in civil service and public-sector employment where salary increments are based largely on years of service; in the recognition of seniority in union contracts; in tenure in judiciary and academic institutions; and in company-based unions. However, in Japan these practices have been used for a very long time and their use is more widespread, culturally accepted, socially encouraged, and officially sanctioned.

Lifetime Employment

Lifetime employment creates a high degree of employee stability and, coupled with other management practices and personnel policies, gen-

erates tremendous employee loyalty for the company with all that it en-
tails. A company can invest money in the training of an employee, confident that once trained, he or she will not be hired away by a competitor.
A Japanese enters a company right after graduation from school and stays
in the company until the official retirement age of fifty-five to sixty. His
job security is virtually guaranteed unless he is accused of misconduct.

The origin of lifetime employment can be traced to the family tradition
of the old *zaibastsu*, according to which a youth entered the firm as an
apprentice and ended up being a trusted manager or founder of a new
branch. The bureaucratic structure of government and early state-owned
enterprises provided another influence for adapting the old master/vassal
system. Furthermore, after World War I socioeconomic conditions made
such an arrangement both feasible and desirable. The present form of
the lifetime employment system, which includes both blue-collar and
white-collar workers, emerged after World War II, when workers and
unions tried to improve employment security because of the crisis atmosphere of the postwar period (Richardson and Ueda 1981: 31–32).
Then in the 1950s this kind of job security became an established practice primarily in large firms, mainly because it was the most effective
means to make employees identify their own interests with those of the
corporation. Tsurumi (1976: 221) observes that the job security offered
by lifetime employment is "not a product of Japanese paternalism, but
a necessary economy to all persons in the firm."

The success of the lifetime employment system depends on the ful-
fillment of a dual set of expectations that are deeply rooted in Japanese
traditions and cultural norms. For the worker there is the expectation
that he will be able to stay with his chosen firm and intends to do so.
This intention is conditioned by the fact that he will be within the norm
of Japanese occupational life and that he has a good deal to gain financially by staying on. For the employer there is the expectation that the
worker will stay, provided that he is offered standard wages and conditions of employment. Social conditions and cultural norms impose a
sense of obligation on the employer, who is expected to provide work
for his employees and take care of them. Moreover, he stands to face a
tremendous loss of worker morale, not to mention union resistance, government pressure, and public ill will, if he deviates significantly from
the social norm (Dore 1973: 35).

However, the privilege of lifetime employment is not extended to
every employee but only to selective categories of employees. Largely
because of the ambiguous nature of the employment relationship, there
is confusion over what percentage of Japanese employees are covered by

lifetime employment. Estimates by various scholars put this number at between 25 and 40 percent of all employees, with the upper range more representative of employees in manufacturing industries. Female employees are usually excluded from the lifetime employment privilege and therefore occupy the lowest-paid jobs in the industry ("Japan's Secret" 1985: 54–55). Also, because only a large company has enough resources to provide lifetime employment, an employee in a smaller company does not have such a privilege. As mentioned in the industrial group section, these employees at smaller companies receive substandard wages and almost no fringe benefits.

The remaining workforce is divided into two groups: experienced recruits or midterm employees who did not join the company right after school graduation, and temporary workers. The temporary workers include manual workers and part-time, seasonal, subcontracted workers. An employee who retires at age fifty-five to sixty loses lifetime employment status right after retirement and may be hired as a temporary worker. Figure 3–4 shows the composition of the workforce in a typical Japanese firm.

Seniority-Based Wage System

Under the seniority-based wage system the remuneration of a worker is determined primarily on the basis of the number of years that he has spent with the company. This is subject to age and level of education at the time of entry (OECD 1977: 19). The seniority-based wage system is the dominant practice in Japan. Although the income difference between younger and older workers is greater in larger firms, wage differential according to age and length of service are prevalent in all enterprises, regardless of size. Figure 3–5 reflects the relationship between age, seniority, and the expenditure pattern of a typical Japanese worker. Wages rise and decline on the basis of length of service and also neatly coincide with the peaks and valleys in the expenditures of the worker and his family and his life cycle. Because an experienced employee is very valuable to a company, it is important that the company makes every effort to make his transition from one stage to another in his life cycle as smooth as possible.

The apparent drawback of the seniority-based wage is the difficulty in rewarding creativity and performance. However, the seniority-based wage system takes away the often destructive individual competition among employees and promotes a more harmonious group relationship

Figure 3-4. Employee Composition of a Japanese Firm.

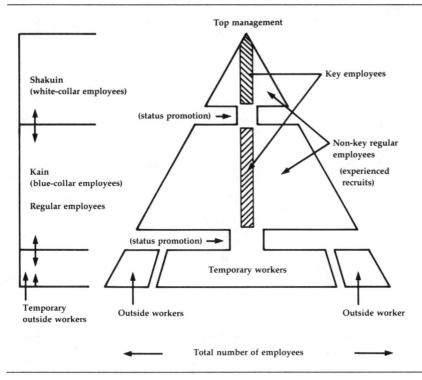

Source: Sethi (1975: 64).

in which each employee works for the benefit of the entire group, secure in the belief that he will prosper with the group and that, in due time, he will acquire the benefits that accrue for long and faithful service. The seniority-based wage system assures that longer experience makes an employee more valuable. Within the *ie* (group or community) framework, a supervisor must be more than a technically superior worker. He must be able to maintain order in the group and look after its wellbeing. Thus the older manager acts as the symbol of group strength and continuity. He also functions as the opinion leader and consolidates the community. He acts as the elder statesman and assists group members in all aspects of their lives, including non–job-related activities such as arranging marriages, settling family disputes, and so on. Middle managers contribute to the achievement of community purpose by educating, training, and controlling the young and by acquainting them with the rules of the community. "These abilities correspond to a skill

Figure 3–5. Relationships among the Seniority-Based Wage System, Family Expenditure Patterns, and the Life Cycle.

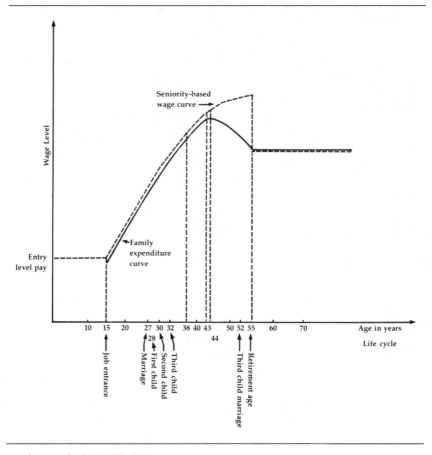

Source: Sethi (1975: 70).

of seniority. . . . Seniority-based skill is not a simple manual skill, but an overall mental and physical skill originated in a community" (Tsuda 1973: 25).

The prerequisites for maintaining the seniority-based wage and lifetime employment systems are a high economic growth and the resulting company expansion so that the company can absorb the expanding cadre of middle- and upper-level managers within it or into newly created subsidiaries. However, under the slow-growth economy since the late 1970s, "excess" middle- and upper-level managers have been accumulated in Japanese companies.

The bloated middle in the organization has many undesirable effects on the company and employees. It further slows down an already cumbersome decisionmaking process because many more employees need to be involved to reach a consensus. Also, it can demoralize younger employees by not allowing them faster promotion and an opportunity to reach the top management level by their retirement.

Some companies are reducing some of the excess middle-level managers through early or "voluntary" retirement. The others are even resorting to sideline excess middle-level employees without specific job responsibilities for the purpose of pushing them out. These employees are often called *madogiwa-zoku,* or those who sit along windows. They get paid, but they are given no work (Shimbun 1981). This is a clear message that the employee is not wanted and implicitly asked to resign voluntarily.

In-Company Training by Rotation

A Japanese employee keeps on training as a regular part of his job until he retires; at the same time he is trained not only in his job but in all other jobs at his job level. On-the-job training by rotation promotes tremendous flexibility in the Japanese workforce and also helps make of each middle or upper manager a generalist with the broader perspective and experience of the company's business and the wider human contacts and friendships that are vital for generating consensus in the *Ringi* decisionmaking process.

Because of lifetime employment, an employee seldom gets an opportunity to work outside his corporate group. Generally speaking, mobility between firms is almost nonexistent, whereas mobility within a firm is almost unlimited.

Management development by job rotation enables the firm to reassign production and office workers more freely and makes the employees, because of their job security, more receptive to organizational changes and the introduction of new technology or machinery (Whitehill and Takezawa 1978: 26–28). Wider experience within the firm tends to nurture the goals of the total firm rather than those of specific subunits in the firm. It can produce high-quality general managers. The job rotation system allows an employee to build wider interpersonal relationships that may result in freer information exchange. Finally, widespread use of on-the-job training in large companies tends to diminish an employee's capacity to work effectively if he does move on to another corporation. Thus it discourages employee mobility between competing firms.

Company-Oriented Unionization

Japanese unions are usually organized on a company basis, as opposed to the craft or industrywide unions common in the United States. The company union gives both management and workers an identity of purpose and provides an environment in which there is greater cooperation for the achievement of common goals. The company-oriented unions (hereinafter referred to as enterprise unions) have certain distinct characteristics. Membership extends to both blue-collar and white-collar workers with regular employee status. White-collar employees up to the level of section chief are included. Union officials consist solely of company employees. The union is regarded as an autonomous organization whose sovereignty is recognized within the whole union power structure (Van Helvoort 1979: 130–31). An enterprise union negotiates independently with its own employer, except for a short period of collective bargaining with the affiliated federation, the so-called spring labor offensive.

Labor disputes are resolved quite differently than in the West. First, there is the societal pressure toward consensus. Second, there is the tendency for industrial action to be taken in a demonstrative form—to make the public aware, as it were, that the workers feel that the employer has failed to do what he should to meet their needs. Third, the union, being mindful of the extent to which its members' interests are bound up with the enterprise, is likely to refrain from any action likely to prejudice its long-term future (OECD 1977: 25–26; "With Economy" 1983).

However, the recent trend toward automation and robotics has been causing strains in the company-union relationship. Robotic-based automation has allowed greater use of unskilled laborers who can be lower-paid part-time employees. Consequently, Japanese companies have been reducing the size of the permanent workforce through early or voluntary retirement and fewer new recruits, while increasing the size of the temporary workforce (Martin 1986: 22). Older workers, in particular, suffer because of automation. They are finding their skills obsolete, are frequently being reassigned, and are pressured to take early retirement. Enterprise unions, especially those in automobile and electronics industries, have become more militant in protecting their members (Saga 1983: 21; "A Spark" 1983: 96).

JABMAS in International Markets

Japanese business and management system (JABMAS) has important influences on the behavior of companies operating in international markets. It is understandable that many large Japanese companies are often reluctant to invest overseas until they are forced to by foreign as well as Japanese governments, due to the dedicated workforce, "captive" parts suppliers, and benevolent political environment in Japan. It should be noted that Japanese overseas investment patterns differ in one major respect from those of the other industrial nations. Nearly a half of foreign investments is made by small- to medium-size companies, whereas large portion of overseas investments is made by large corporations in the other industrial nations (Ozawa 1979: 26). Smaller-size parts suppliers that produce labor-intensive, low-technology goods have lost cost advantage to those in developing countries with low labor costs. Large Japanese companies, instead of buying parts from foreign suppliers, tend to encourage their parts suppliers to make foreign direct investment into low-wage countries.

There is another reason for their aversion to making foreign investments. As explained previously, the Japanese management system largely depends on maintaining and protecting highly exclusive members (lifetime employees) in a corporation. Permanent employees, who are subject to highly selective screening processes and are considered elite in the society, strongly resist accepting outsiders, both foreigners and Japanese, who do not join the firm right after graduation. Moreover, the highly centralized decisionmaking by consensus requires interpersonal relationships and communication skills that can be gained only by lifetime employees in the company. This is one of the reasons that Japanese multinational companies tend to send much larger numbers of expatriate managers to their foreign subsidiaries compared to other multinational corporations, in order to facilitate smoother decisionmaking at the headquarters in Japan (Tsurumi 1976: 189–93, 260–61; Ozawa 1979: 212).

Also, most Japanese companies operating overseas tend not to adapt into the local environment and create tensions locally, especially in Asian countries (Manglapus 1976). The Japanese expatriate managers fully realize that his fortunes depend on remaining familiar with the nuances of conditions in the home office. They tend to isolate themselves from the local culture and care little to learn anything about it because they become outsiders to the Japanese home office if they are too identified with the local culture (Sethi 1973: 14).

CONCLUSION: FUTURE IMPLICATIONS OF JABMAS

The Japanese business and management system (JABMAS) has been well suited to the Japanese cultural and sociopolitical context, and Japan has succeeded in building internationally competitive, export-oriented industries. Many Japanese manufacturing corporations have captured a large share of markets in the United States and other countries, and Japan has also become a major financial center in the world. The spectacular performance, however, has been attained with great social costs — such as environmental destruction and ignorance of consumer protection and of worker safety and health. The side-effects have become intolerable, and partial remedies have been provided during the last decade. Also, the success of Japanese corporations has greatly increased the standards of living and at the same time raised the expectations of the population, especially those of the younger generations. Many employees, especially younger ones, are less interested in long working hours and totally dedicating themselves to the employer because they are getting less satisfaction from their efforts at the workplace. Instead, they are expecting even higher standards of living, less work time, more leisure time, and more time for their families ("The High Price" 1986: 52–53; "The Company Man" 1986: 57).

In other words, Japan has been shifting the priorities from industrial advancement and international competitiveness to better quality of life, although extremely slowly. The changes in the Japanese environment are forcing JABMAS to adapt to these changes. Moreover, there are changes in the international environments to which JABMAS needs to adapt ("Will Japan" 1986: 47–58). One is the changing nature of competition in the international markets. Japanese companies usually excel in manufacturing efficiency, delivering high-quality products at low costs. However, competitive advantages in some industries have been lost to other advanced developing countries with lower wages, notably South Korea. Some Japanese companies have been opting for greater automation and robotics to further increase productivity. Other firms have increased their efforts to promote innovation, which is ill-suited to JABMAS in its traditional form. Some large companies encourage innovation by creating small entrepreneur-type subsidiaries. Moreover, realizing that an innovative process may not develop in large companies, some large companies are supporting, and conducting business with, small-size entrepreneurial firms, particularly in electronics, computer software, telecommunications, and biotechnology (Yoder 1986) (see also Lohr 1983; Christopher 1983; "The Exodus" 1981). These new companies have opened new opportunities for capable Japanese employees, especially for workers with high-technology skills. They are finding it easier to change jobs and demand skill-based wages rather than seniority-based wages. In the process, the new trend is likely to weaken the traditional bonds between corporations and workers.

Another factor that is likely to influence JABMAS in the future is the internationalization of Japanese companies and markets. As trade deficits with Japan have increased during the last decade, many countries have been pressuring Japanese companies to produce locally and demanding Japan to open its own markets. As discussed in the previous section, JABMAS is not well suited for operating overseas and is likely to create tensions with the local environment, mainly due to the needs to maintain the corporate values. However, Japanese large companies have recently started to experiment with hiring foreigners and accepting them into the system, in an attempt at internationalizing the home office (Wysocki 1986: 1, 12).

Japanese management system has been slowly changing in response to the changes in the corporate system and its own society and in its relationships with the other countries. Japan has a largely homogeneous society and a stable set of values. The system is averse to change, especially change introduced from without. However, any social or economic institution must change in response to a changing environment in order to survive and grow. Therefore, JABMAS's success in both domestic and international markets depends on adapting itself to changing environments in its own country and to the changing external environment of other countries.

NOTES

1. The ideas on the Japanese business and management system (JABMAS) have been discussed in Sethi, Namiki, and Swanson (1984). The discussion on Japanese culture, business/government relations, and management practices are substantially derived from Sethi (1975) and Sethi and Namiki (1984).
2. Sixteen percent (or 62 out of 389) of colleges in Japan had departments of business administration, and only 7 percent of the total college student population was registered in those departments in 1972.
3. For an exhaustive treatment of the environmental law in Japan, see Greasser, Fujikura, and Morishima (1981). For a citizens' environmental protection movement, see McKean (1981).
4. The discussion in this section is derived substantially from Sethi (1975: 51–56).
5. The discussion in this section is derived from Sethi (1975: 56–59).

REFERENCES

Benedict, Ruth. 1946. *The Chrysanthemum and the Sword*. Boston: Houghton Mifflin.

Bennett, John W., and Iwao Ishino. 1963. *Paternalism in the Japanese Economy: Anthropological Studies of Oyabun-Kobun Patterns.* Westport, Conn.: Greenwood Press.

Bisson, T.A. 1954. *Zaibatsu Dissolution in Japan.* Berkeley, Calif.: University of California Press.

Blaker, Michael K., ed. 1976. *Japan at the Polls: The House of Councillors Election of 1974.* Washington, D.C.: American Enterprise Institute for Public Policy Research.

Boyer, Edward. 1983. "How Japan Manages Declining Industries." *Fortune* (Jan. 10): 58–63.

Broadbridge, Seymour. 1966. *Industrial Dualism in Japan.* Chicago: Aldine.

Caves, Richard E. 1976. "Industrial Organization." In *Asia's New Giant,* edited by Hugh Patrick and Henry Rosovsky, pp. 459–523. Washington, D.C.: Brookings Institution.

Christopher, Robert C. 1983. "Changing Face of Japan." *New York Times Magazine* (March 27): 87–90.

"The Company Man May Be an Endangered Species." *Business Week* (May 12): 57.

Craig, Albert M. 1975. "Functional and Dysfunctional Aspects of Government Bureaucracy." In *Modern Japanese Organization and Decision-Making,* edited by Ezra F. Vogel, pp. 11–15. Berkeley: University of California Press.

Davis, Paul A. 1972. *Administrative Guidance in Japan—Legal Considerations.* Bulletin No. 41. Tokyo: Sophia University Socio-Economic Institute.

Davis, Stanley M., and Paul R. Lawrence. 1977. *Matrix.* Reading, Mass.: Addison-Wesley.

De Mente, Boye. 1975. *Japanese Manners and Ethics in Business.* Tokyo: Simpon-Doyle.

Doi, Takeo. 1967. "Giri-Ninjo: An Interpretation." In *Aspects of Social Change in Modern Japan,* edited by Ronald P. Dore, pp. 327–34. Princeton, N.J.: Princeton University Press.

———. 1973. *The Anatomy of Dependence.* Tokyo: Kodansha.

Dore, Ronald P., ed. 1967. *Aspects of Social Change in Modern Japan.* Princeton, N.J.: Princeton University Press.

———. 1973. *British Factory–Japanese Factory: The Origins of National Diversity in Industrial Relations.* Berkeley: University of California Press.

Drucker, Peter. 1971. "What We Can Learn from Japanese Management." *Harvard Business Review* (March–April): 111–13.

———. 1981. "Behind Japan's Success." *Harvard Business Review* (Jan.–Feb.): 87.

"The Exodus That Shook the Establishment." 1981. *Business Week* (Dec. 14): 118.

"Forty-five Japanese Workers Are Reported Exposed to Nuclear Radiation." 1981. *New York Times,* April 26, p. 6.

Fox, William M. 1977. "Japanese Management Tradition under Strain." *Business Horizons* (Aug.): 79.

Freigenbaum, Edward A., and Pamela McCorduck. 1983. *The Fifth Generation.* Reading, Mass.: Addison-Wesley.

Greasser, Julian, Koichiro Fujikura, and Akio Morishima. 1981. *Environmental Law in Japan.* Cambridge, Mass.: MIT Press.

Hadley, Eleanor M. 1970. *Antitrust in Japan*. Princeton, N.J.: Princeton University Press.

Haitani, Kanji. 1976. *The Japanese Economic System: An Institutional Overview*. Lexington, Mass.: Lexington Books.

Hall, John Whitney, and Richard K. Beardsley. 1965. *Twelve Doors to Japan*. New York: McGraw-Hill.

Halliday, Jon. 1975. *A Political History of Japanese Capitalism*. New York: Pantheon Books.

Halloran, Richard. 1976. "Five Japanese Had Key Roles in Pushing Lockheed Bids." *New York Times*, March 1, pp. 1, 8.

Hattori, Ichiro. 1978. "A Proposition on Efficient Decision-Making in the Japanese Corporation." *Columbia Journal of World Business* (Summer): 12.

"Heavenly Descent." 1974. *Japan Times*, March 29, p. 15.

Henderson, Dan Fenno. 1973. *Foreign Enterprise in Japan: Laws and Policies*. Chapel Hill, N.C.: University of North Carolina Press.

Higashi, Chikara. 1983. *Japanese Trade Policy Formulation*. New York: Praeger.

"The High Price Japanese Pay for Success." 1986. *Business Week* (April 7): 52–53.

Hofstede, Geert. 1983. "National Cultures in Four Dimensions." *International Studies of Management and Organization* 13(1–2)(Spring–Summer): 46–74.

Huddle, Norie, Michael Reich, and Nahum Stiskin. 1975. *Island of Dreams: Environmental Crisis in Japan*. New York: Autumn Press.

"Illness of Japan's Kingmaker Roils Politics and Weakens Prime Minister Nakasone." 1985. *Wall Street Journal*, May 29, p. 32.

"Japanese Managers Talk How Their System Works." 1977. *Fortune* (Nov.): 131–32.

"Japanese Nuclear Plant Closed for Six Months for Not Reporting Spill." 1981. *Wall Street Journal*, May 20, p. 30.

"Japan Focuses on Basic Research to Close the Creative Gap." 1985. *Business Week* (Feb. 25): 94–96.

"Japan's Autocratic Managers." 1985. *Fortune* (Jan. 7): 56–64.

"Japan Says Nuclear Mishap Exposed Fifty-six to Radiation." 1981. *New York Times*, April 22, p. 5.

"Japan's Chip Makers Aim for New Products." 1985. *Wall Street Journal*, Nov. 29, p. 12.

"Japan's Secret Economic Weapon: Exploited Women." 1985. *Business Week* (March 4): 54–55.

Johnson, Chalmers. 1982. *MITI and the Japanese Miracle: The Growth of Industrial Policy, 1925–1975*. Stanford, Calif.: Stanford University Press.

Kanabayashi, Masayoshi. 1983. "Japan's Recession-Hit Companies Make Complex Arrangements to Avoid Layoffs." *Wall Street Journal*, Feb. 17, p. 32.

Katabe, Masaaki. 1984. "Changing Roles of the Sogo Shoshas, the Manufacturing Firms, and the MITI in the Context of the Japanese 'Trade or Die' Mentality." *Columbia Journal of World Business* (Fall): 3342.

Kojima, Koyoshi, and Terutomo Ozawa. 1984. *Japan's General Trading Companies: Merchants of Economic Development*. Paris: OECD.

Kosai, Yutaka, Yoshitaro Ogino. 1984. *The Contemporary Japanese Economy*. Armonk, N.Y.: Sharpe.

Krause, Lawrence B., and Sueo Sekiguchi. 1976. "Japan and the World Economy." In *Asia's New Giant*, edited by Hugh Patrick and Henry Rosovsky, pp. 383–458. Washington, D.C.: Brookings Institution.

Kunio, Yoshihara. 1982. *Sogo Shosha: The Vanguard of the Japanese Economy*. Tokyo: Oxford University Press.

Lerner, Urban C. 1981. "Tanaka, Former Japan Leader, Wields Big Power Despite Corruption Charges." *Wall Street Journal*, May 6, p. 30.

———. 1983. "Jail Term Requested in Tanaka Trial." *Wall Street Journal*, Jan. 27, p. 36.

Lohr, Steve. 1983. "Japan's New Nonconformists." *New York Times*, March 8, p. 27.

Manglapus, Raul S. 1976. *Japan in Southeast Asia: Collision Course*. New York: Carnegie Endowment for International Peace.

Martin, Bradley K. 1986. "Japanese Working Poor Hit Tough Times." *Wall Street Journal*, April 21, p. 22.

McKean, Margaret A. 1981. *Environmental Protest and Citizen Politics in Japan*. Berkeley: University of California Press.

Ministry of International Trade and Industry. 1969. *Tsusho Sangyo-Sho Nigunen Shi (Twenty-Year History of MITI)*. Tokyo: MITI.

Nakane, Chie. 1967. *Kinship and Economic Organization in Rural Japan*. New York: Humanities Press.

———. 1972a. *Human Relations in Japan*. Tokyo: Director General of the Public Information Bureau.

———. 1972b. *Japanese Society*. Berkeley: University of California Press.

———. 1974. "An Interpretation of Group Cohesiveness in Japanese Society." Paper presented at the regional seminar, Center for Japanese and Korean Studies, Berkeley, University of California, March 1.

"Nuclear Contamination Found in Japanese Soil." 1981. *New York Times*, April 19, p. 7.

"Occupational Mobility—Not Yet." 1974. *Japan Times*, March 16, p. 1.

Ohmae, Kenichi. 1982. "Japanese Companies Are Run from the Top." *Wall Street Journal*, April 26, p. 26.

OECD. 1977. *The Development of Industrial Relations Systems: Some Implications of Japanese Experience*. Paris: Organization for Economic Cooperation and Development.

Ozawa, Terutomo. 1979. *Multinationalism, Japanese Style: The Political Economy of Outward Dependency*. Princeton, N.J.: Princeton University Press.

Pearlstine, Norman. 1974a. "In Japan the Sokaiya Rise to the Rescue at Firms Meetings." *Wall Street Journal*, May 29, pp. 1, 25.

———. 1974b. "Tarnished Image: Global Trust in Firms in Japan Is Damaged by a Major Collapse." *Wall Street Journal*, June 19, pp. 1, 24.

Pepper, Thomas, Merit E. Janow, and Jimmy W. Wheeler. 1985. *The Competition: Dealing with Japan*. New York: Praeger.

Richardson, Bradley M., and Taizo Ueda, eds. 1981. *Business and Society in Japan: Fundamentals for Businessmen*. New York: Praeger.

Rohlen, Thomas P. 1974. *For Harmony and Strength: Japanese White-Collar Organization in Anthropological Perspective*. Berkeley: University of California Press.

———. 1975. "The Company Work Group." In *Modern Japanese Organization and Decision-Making*, edited by Ezra F. Vogel, pp. 185–209. Berkeley: University of California Press.

Saga, Ichiro. 1983. "Japan's Robots Create Problems for Workers." *Wall Street Journal*, Feb. 28, p. 21.

Sasaki, Naoto. 1981. *Management and Industrial Structure in Japan*. New York: Pergamon.

Sethi, S. Prakash. 1975. *Japanese Business and Social Conflict*. Cambridge, Mass.: Ballinger.

———. 1978. "An Analytical Framework for Making Cross-Cultural Comparisons of Business Responses to Social Pressures: The Case of the United States and Japan." In *Research in Corporate Social Performance and Policy*, vol. 1, edited by Lee E. Preston, pp. 27–54. Greenwich, Conn.: JAI Press.

———. 1983. "Drawbacks of Japanese Management." *Business Week* (Nov. 24): 14.

Sethi, S. Prakash, and Nobuaki Namiki. 1984. "Japanese Style Consensus Decision Making in Matrix Management: Problems and Prospects of Adaptation." In *Matrix Management Systems Handbook*, edited by David I. Cleland, pp. 431–56. New York: Van Nostrand.

Sethi, S. Prakash, Nobuaki Namiki, and Carl Swanson. 1984. *The False Promise of the Japanese Miracle*. Boston, Mass.: Pitman.

Shimbun, Nihon Keizai. 1981. *Salary-Man: Document #2*. Tokyo: Nihon Keizai Shimbun, Inc. In Japanese.

Shinohara, Miyohei. 1982. *Industrial Growth, Trade, and Dynamic Patterns in the Japanese Economy*. Tokyo: University of Tokyo Press.

Small and Medium Enterprises Agency. 1985. *Chusho Kigyo Hakusho, showa 50-nen ban (White Paper on Small and Medium Enterprises, 1975)*. Tokyo: Ministry of Finance.

"Sokaiya Return to Japan's Annual Meetings, Raising Questions, Stirring Corporate Concern." 1985. *Wall Street Journal*, July 15, p. 16.

"A Spark of Militancy in the Land of Loyalty." 1983. *Business Week* (Sept. 5.): 96.

Stokes, Henry Scott. 1981. "For the Japanese, Sudden Misgivings about Nuclear Power." *New York Times*, May 16, p. 3.

Tsuda, Masumai. 1983. "Lifetime Employment and Seniority-Based Wage Systems." Paper presented at the International Symposium on the Japanese Way of Management and International Business, Tokyo, Nov. 27–28. Sponsored by the Japan Management Conference Board.

Tsurumi, Yoshi. 1976. *The Japanese Are Coming: A Multinational Interaction of Firms and Politics*. Cambridge, Mass.: Ballinger.

Ueno, I. 1972. "The Situation of Management Education in Japan." In *Management Education*, pp. 38–39. Paris: Organization for Economic Cooperation and Development.

Ui, Jun. 1972. "The Singularities of Japanese Pollution." *Japan Quarterly* (July–Sept.): 281–91.

Uttal, Bro. 1982. "Here Comes Computer, Inc." *Fortune* (Oct. 4): 82–90.

Van Helvoort, Ernest. 1979. *The Japanese Working Man: What Choice? What Reward?* Vancouver, Can.: University of British Columbia Press.

"Where Japan Has a Research Edge." 1983. *Business Week* (March 14): 116.

Whitehill, Arthur M., and Shin-ichi Takezawa. 1978. "Workplace Harmony: Another Japanese 'Miracle'?" *Columbia Journal of World Business* (Fall): 26–28.

"Will Japan Really Change?" *Business Week* (May 12): 47–58.

"With Economy Troubled, Japan's Unions Are Likely to Seek Smaller Pay Rise for '83." 1983. *Wall Street Journal*, Feb. 24, p. 31.

World Bank. 1983. *World Development Report 1983*. New York: Oxford University Press.

Wysocki, Jr., Bernard. 1986. "How Foreigners Hired by Japanese Adjust to a New Way of Life." *Wall Street Journal*, March 24, pp. 1, 12.

Yanaga, Chitoshi. 1965. *Japanese People and Politics*. New York: Wiley.

———. 1968. *Big Business in Japanese Politics*. New Haven, Conn.: Yale University Press.

Yasuba, Yasukichi. 1976. "The Evolution of Dualistic Wage Structure." In *Japanese Industrialization and Its Social Consequences*, edited by Hugh Patrick, pp. 249–98. Berkeley: University of California Press.

Yoder, Stephen Kreider. 1986. "Japan's High-Tech Whiz Kids Thrive and Breathe Life into Country's Industries." *Wall Street Journal*, March 17, p. 22.

Zimmerman, Mark. 1985. *How to Do Business with the Japanese*. New York: Random House.

CHAPTER 4

Europe

Moshe Banai and Cyril J. Levicki

Within the literature on comparative management there is universal agreement that contextual variables affect how businesses can be managed. However, there has been no agreement about which contextual variables are important, which are less so, in what way they influence management behavior and organizational effectiveness.

Farmer and Richman (1965) claim that managerial activities are a direct result of environmental and contextual variables that are specific to each country in which the firm is implanted. The contextual variables that Farmer and Richman consider important are education, sociology, legal and political inputs, and the general economy. Negandhi and Prasad (1971) agree with Farmer and Richman's choice of contextual variables but add a further variable, which they call management philosophy. They define *management philosophy* as management attitudes toward employees, consumers, suppliers, stockholders, government, and community (Negandhi and Prasad 23). They argue that if those four general variables proposed by Farmer and Richman were the same for any two firms in any one country then both firms should have similar management behaviors and hence be equally effective—and then point out that this is not the case. The management philosophy variable explains the differences between firms' performances. According to Negandhi and Prasad management philosophy is an independent variable, so they did not specify whether environmental factors affect management philosophy. However, management philosophy might be an intervening variable.

Child (1981) argued that there are three schools of thought, each emphasizing different elements in the contextual variables. The first is the contingency school, which emphasizes the level of industrialization (Dore

1973). The second school is the culture school, which emphasizes the development of social institutions, such as the democratic process, elite recruitment, and labor movement (Hofstede 1980). The third school that Child discussed is capitalism, which emphasizes the ownership of the means of production (that is, the degree of capitalism vesus socialism). Child's focus on political philosophy highlights an important element that has not yet received sufficient attention from researchers.

The disagreements among the schools suggest that the major scholars in the field have had difficulty in isolating independent from dependent variables and in defining the actual range of variables that are involved in studies of comparative management. In order to define precisely the relevant variables and the relationships between them, descriptive studies are needed that may enable us to examine the relevant variables. In this chapter, the variables that are considered are sociopolitical and include both capitalist and socialist models. The chapter also examines legal frameworks, education, economic and technological systems, and the cultural and sociological framework.

The variable of culture must be distinguished at both the national and organizational levels. For example, Hofstede's (1980) four dimensions of culture refer to the national culture as do some religious values and social morals. Organizational culture is marked by leadership, legends, myths, rites, and rituals as well as the previous history of the company (Nystrom and Starbuck 1984; Schein 1984; Adler and Jelinek 1986). In this chapter national culture is included in the group of environment variables that are regarded by the three models outlined above as independent variables. Organizational culture is included in the group of business and management systems variables that are regarded as a dependent variable, such as structure, technology, organization philosophy, and different aspects of organizational policy- and decisionmaking. It should be emphasized that this chapter will go no further than a descriptive analysis of the variables mentioned above.

SOCIOPOLITICAL SYSTEM

History

The origins of European countries can be divided into the southern tribes with Gallic and Roman origins and the northern tribes such as the Goths, Danes, and Vikings. Russia's population origins are mainly Nordic and Slavic and date from as late as the ninth century (Kochan and Abraham

1983; Shoemaker 1985). Most European nations have a history of monarchic and imperial systems dating from the early Roman empire through Charlemagne to the British empire of the eighteenth and nineteenth centuries followed by the Napoleonic expansion of France.

Although the monarchical tradition is strong, over the past two centuries a revolutionary movement has also been strong. Two revolutions of note were the French revolution of 1779 and the Russian revolution of the early twentieth century, and these revolutionary movements were accompanied by the unification of many minor Italian and German states. By the beginning of the twentieth century, the scene was set for the major influences on Europe during the twentieth century—World Wars I and II.

Economic and Political Coalitions

The primary result of World War II, which may be considered to be the major consequence of World War I, was the division of Europe into democratic, mainly republican, states and soviet socialistic republics or satellites. Within the democratic system the most important emergent group has been the European Economic Community (EEC), consisting of France, West Germany, the United Kingdom, Italy, Belgium, the Netherlands, Greece, Denmark, Ireland, and Luxemburg.

Among the important features of the EEC is the Common Agricultural Policy (CAP), which is the farming policy of the market. CAP displays the remarkable power exercised by a small minority of farmers over the allocation of economic resources. The agriculture policy was created by the administrators of the ECC in order to satisfy the political needs of French, German, and Italian governments. It consists of a major subsidy program for goods that cannot be sold profitably by farmers in a free market of agricultural goods (Kerr 1977: ch. 5; Hudson, Rhind, and Mounsey 1984: 12). The results of this policy have been the accumulation of large stock of milk, wine, and grain. These have become known as the butter mountains and wine lakes of the EEC (Swann 1985: 218) and are symbolic of the power exercised by the farming community.

Of further interest in the EEC policy is the European monetary system (EMS). This links the various currencies of the members of the common market through a European currency unit (ECU) so that free trade without excessive currency fluctuation may take place among them (Kerr 1977: 145; Swann 1985: 198). The EMS was a major step in the dream of the founders of the Common Market to create a solid unified political coalition.

Six European countries do not belong to the EEC and have a special free trade agreement. Members of the European Free Trade Association (EFTA) are Austria, Finland, Iceland, Norway, Sweden, and Switzerland (Van Meerhaeghe 1980). The remaining countries of western Europe (Portugal, Spain, and Turkey) are currently in negotiations to join the EEC in order to enjoy the preferential trade and tariff agreements of the market.

Following the establishment of the EEC in 1948, the USSR, Bulgaria, Czechoslovakia, Hungary, Poland, and Romania responded in 1949 by creating the Council for Mutual Economic Assistance (COMECON). It was later joined by East Germany and Albania (the latter was expelled in 1961). The Mongolian People's Republic became a member in 1962 (Sobell 1984).

The communist sector may be considered advanced industrially in world terms, although the net per capita income of most inhabitants of communist countries is about half that of their capitalistic counterparts (see Table 4–4). Lane (1978: 174) considered that most communist countries are operating a system of state capitalism. Within the marxist system all capital property is owned by the state, and only a minimal level of personal private possession is permitted. Within the various communist countries there are differences in the levels of personal wealth allowed. For example, a higher level of private property and enterprise is permitted in Czechoslovakia, Hungary, and East Germany than in the USSR.

Within the communist system, political power is channeled through the communist party, and frequently economic priorities are subsumed under political dialectic. As such, power accrues through the party (Lane 1978: 230; Shoemaker 1985: 52). In addition to the political economic subdivision of Europe, there is yet another subdivision that is purely political: the North Atlantic Treaty Organization (NATO) and the Warsaw Pact. NATO was established in 1949 as a reaction by the West to the blockade put on West Berlin by the Russians. NATO has changed its objectives according to the political situation and has been used since 1967 to maintain détente. NATO members are Belgium, Canada, Denmark, France, West Germany, Greece, Iceland, Italy, Luxemburg, the Netherlands, Norway, Portugal, Spain, Turkey, the United Kingdom, and the United States (Myers 1980; Hartley 1983; Hunter 1984).

In reaction to the move made by West Germany to join NATO, a countervailing communist pact was established in 1955. The Warsaw Pact includes Bulgaria, Czechoslovakia, East Germany, Hungary, Poland,

Rumania, and the Soviet Union (Clawson and Kaplan 1982). This coalition is used by the Soviets as leverage for bargaining in international diplomacy (Larrabee 1984). It also gives the Soviets a tighter control over its satellites, as was demonstrated in Hungary (1956), Czechoslovakia (1968), and Poland (1981). A summary of the different economic and political classifications of Europe is presented in Table 4-1.

Economic development in the communist block has been slow in comparison with Western Europe. Defining World War II as the zero point, however, the communist countries started further behind than the capitalist states. With this in mind their growth rates appear to be comparatively good (Lane 1978: 288). In this regard Albania has proven to be very remiss in its attempt to grow, and Yugoslavia and Bulgaria have never really made the progress promised by their political regimes. The USSR itself is energy rich, and some of its characteristics resemble those of a petrocurrency state—that is, it balances energy exports against many of its import needs (Shoemaker 1985). Much of the internal trade of the Soviet satellites is centralized through the Russian system. The levels of human capital and skills are relatively low compared to the rest of Europe, although the degree of secondary education available has increased rapidly since the Russian revolution. Economic stability is good within the Communist block partially because Russia dominates the banking system of satellite states. Russia normally issues credit to cover the deficit balances of the satellites of the communist system. In recent years Russia has encouraged a parallel economy, particularly in the agricultural sector where peasants and other farmers are allowed to sell their products on small local and private markets (*The Economist* 1986: 62). In contrast to the communist system the free European states have a system of private property. For example, in the United Kingdom 60 percent of gross domestic product is created by the private sector (Prest and Coppock 1982). The major contrast with communist system is the belief in the private contract system and in private property. The motivation and need for contracts is created by the fact that profit accrues to individuals. This is in contrast to the communist system of state direction of contracts that are irrevocable and founded on party interest rather than on private interest.

Capital and wealth accumulation take place privately in the capitalistic states. Although defense and other infrastructural interests are centralized and state controlled, they still normally use only 40 percent of GDP. Government influence is exerted within the free system but only concerning matters that the state legitimately regards as its own, such

Table 4-1. Economic and Political Classification of the European Countries.

Political	Economic			
	EEC	*COMECON*	*EFTA*	*Nonaligned*
NATO	Belgium, Denmark, France, Greece, West Germany, Italy, Iceland, Luxembourg, Netherlands, United Kingdom		Iceland, Norway	Portugal, Spain, Turkey
Warsaw Pact		Bulgaria, Czechoslovakia, East Germany, Hungary, Poland, Rumania, USSR		
Neutral			Finland, Sweden, Switzerland	
Nondeclared			Austria	Albania, Yugoslavia

as defense, education, and social welfare. This contrasts, of course, with the Russian system, which regards everything as being within the state's realm of interest.

Labor Markets and Unionism

Another difference between capitalistic and Communist Europe are labor unions. European labor unions were formed with the aim of a total social transformation. Historically they sought and achieved major political goals such as the rejection of feudalism and the right to vote. Today, most of the free democratic nations have highly developed labor union systems that usually are allied to the left wing and socialist parties and thus help draft social legislation. In addition, they keep their traditional role in the collective bargaining with employers but only as second to their legislative role. Hence, the labor union strength appears to wax and wane according to two major variables: (1) healthy economic conditions and (2) the political power of the allied party. Within the communist sector the labor unions are a subject of the party system. A statistical description of the European labor force is presented in Table 4–2.

THE CULTURE MILIEU

Geography and ecology may provide some of the explanations for the cultural unity of Europe as well as the type of technical and economic leadership that emerged during the nineteenth century. Geographical features such as varieties of landscapes, mildness of the climate, wealth of natural resources available, and a central location enabled Europe to receive influences from both Asia and Africa and minimized the dangers of insular stagnation.

Ethnology and Language

Europe may be divided, ethnologically, into four main culture regions – the Atlantic Fringe, the Mediterranean, the Carpato Alpine West-Plain Climax, and the East-Plain Caucasus. The classification of the European countries presented in Table 4–3 shows the states that may be included under each of the four ethnological and cultural spheres mentioned above and the level of homogeneity of their languages.

Table 4–2. Labor Force, Unemployment, and Unionized Workers in Europe, 1984.

Country	Labor Force (in millions)	Percentage of Unemployed	Percentage of Unionized Workers
USSR	148		
Poland	17.5[a]	–	–
Romania	10.5[b]	–	–
Yugoslavia	10.1	14	–
East Germany	8.9	–	87.7
Czechoslovakia	7.5	–	–
Hungary	4.9	–	–
Bulgaria	4.1[b]	–	–
Albania	0.60	–	–
West Germany	27.6	7.2	28
United Kingdom	27.6[a]	13.1	40
France	23.8	10.1	20
Italy	23	10.4	40–45
Turkey	18.1	16.5	10–15
Spain	13.3[a]	21.9[a]	25[b]
Netherlands	5.9	12.5[a]	33
Portugal	4.5	10.6	45
Sweden	4.4	3.1	90
Belgium	4.0[a]	13.6	70
Greece	3.7[c]	10.0	10–15
Switzerland	3.0	0.9[a]	20
Austria	2.9	4.5	58
Denmark	2.7	10.3	65
Finland	2.6	6.2	80
Norway	2.0	3.9	66[a]
Ireland	1.3	17.0	36
Luxemburg	0.2[b]	1.5	–
Iceland	0.1	1.3	60

a. 1985.   b. 1983.   c. 1981.
Source: The World Factbook (1986).

Religion

Noncommunist Europe has state-recognized religious systems. The Christian ethic is of prime importance, particularly the protestant work ethic. This contrasts strongly with the communist system where the church

Table 4–3. Primary European Ethnic Culture Areas.

	Language	Country
The Atlantic Fringe	Celtic and English French Netherlandish Scandinavian	England,[a] Ireland[a] France,[a] Belgium, Switzerland Holland,[a] Belgium Denmark,[a] Iceland,[a] Norway,[a] Sweden[a]
The Mediterranean	Iberian Italic Balkan	Spain, Portugal[a] Italy,[a] Sicily,[a] Sardinia,[a] Malta[a] Cyprus, Greece,[a] Albania,[a], Bulgaria, Romania, Yugoslavia, Turkey[a]
The Carpato Alpine–West-Plain Climax	German West Slavic West Urgic	West Germany,[a] East Germany[a] Czechoslovakia,[a] Poland Hungary[a]
The East Plain and the Caucasus	East Slavic West Finno Permian	USSR (Blareyzia, Ukrania) Poland[a] Finland

a. Linguistically homogenous nations.

is not approved of, nor encouraged, by the state. Christianity is the most common religious belief system throughout most of Europe. The main exception is the Islamic area in the Balkans and the Turco-Tatar area in the southeast. It should be noted that even within the communist states, where for several decades regimes have attempted to reduce the influence of religion, Christianity remains a powerful influence. For example, the Catholic religion was a major driving force behind the revolutionary Solidarity movement in Poland.

The three major branches of Christianity are Catholicism, Protestantism, and Orthodoxy and are linked respectively with the Latin, German, and Slavic cultures. A people's religion is frequently closely related to its ethnic consciousness, and this is true in the European sectors. For example, in Ireland Catholics rage against assimilation in the form of the Protestantism of the English mainland. In Finland, Protestantism is lined up against the Orthodoxy of Russia's religion of marxist ideology (Shoemaker 1985: 57).

Cultural Change

Culture change in Europe has certain features. The rate of change of cultural tradition is most rapid in west central Europe in an area bounded by an approximate quadrilateral whose corners are London, Paris, Milan, and Hamburg. The more traditional country cultures are in the eastern, northern, and southern regions. The dynamic population growth of these centers and their higher standard of living have created an influx of ambitious and socially mobile peoples. The less dynamic populations have either moved away from these centers or not ever migrated toward them. In the eastern, northern, and southern regions there have been comparative gradual declining standards of living and a more preserved traditional culture. In other words, the geography of material poverty coincides with the geography of ethnic traditionalism.

The Dual System of City versus Country Values

Most European countries contain highly developed urban societies, but the lifestyles and values of people living in towns are not those of urban groups anywhere in the world. The migration from country to town throughout Europe was a migration of ideas and values, and there is a strong tradition of preindustrial village values throughout European towns, particularly in the suburbs of those urban centers.

Hofstede's Four Dimensions of Culture

Hofstede (1980) identified and measured four operational dimensions of culture—power distance (PD) and uncertainty avoidance (UA), which are measured from high to low; individualism (IND) measured against collectivism; and masculinity (MAS) measured against femininity.

Table 4–4 is taken from Hofstede's (1980) clusters describing the different European cultures—Anglo, Germanic, Middle Eastern, Nordic, and Latin European. Although the table is taken directly from Hofstede's work, it isolates his measures for the European countries that are included in this study.

The table presents the different value systems that Hofstede used. Hofstede's thesis was that value systems are consequences of some regional facts and artifacts—such as climate, man's interaction with nature, the use of technology, historical events, the modernization of agriculture, the level of urbanization, the level of literacy, social mobility, national wealth, the political system, and the size of population. Hofstede used the correlative findings from his studies to substantiate his thesis, but the relationship between value systems and environments' constituencies have not yet been validated in independent studies. In this chapter we are not assuming that value systems are dependent variables. Rather, we are using them as the independent variables that are a part of

Table 4–4. Regional and National Scores of the Four Dimensions of Culture.

Cluster	Country	PD	UA	IND	MAS	Characteristics
Anglo	Great Britain	35	35	89	66	Low to medium PD
	Ireland	28	35	70	68	Low to medium UA
						High IND
						High MAS
Germanic	Austria	11	70	55	79	Low PD
	West Germany	35	65	67	66	Medium to high UA
	Switzerland	34	58	68	70	Medium IND
						Medium to high MAS
Near	Greece	60	112	35	57	High PD
Eastern	Turkey	66	85	37	45	High UA
	Yugoslavia[a]	76	88	27	21	Low IND
						Medium MAS
Nordic	Denmark	18	23	74	16	Low PD
	Finland	33	59	63	26	Low to medium UA
	Netherlands	38	53	80	14	Medium to high IND
	Norway	31	50	69	8	Low MAS
	Sweden	31	29	71	5	
Latin	Belgium	65	94	75	54	High PD
Europe	France	68	86	71	43	High UA
	Italy	50	75	76	70	Medium to high IND
	Portugal[b]	63	104	27	31	Medium MAS
	Spain	57	86	51	42	

a. The study in Yugoslavia was not conducted in the same organization as in all other countries.

b. Originally, Portugal was clustered among the South American Latin countries.

Source: Hofstede (1980).

the overall environment that affects all organizations and organizational behavior.

Although Hofstede's (1980) study covered a wide range of countries, it did not include any Communist countries except Yugoslavia. This restriction was imposed on him because the company through which he obtained his sample did not operate in Eastern Europe. Table 4–5 represents an attempt to predict the possible outcomes of a study that would use Hofstede's four dimensions of culture in those countries. It does make use of the way that Hofstede reasons about Yugoslavia. That has been taken as his proxy prediction for other communist block countries. East Germany will probably follow its sister country and would score

Table 4–5. Predictions about the Scores of East European Countries on the Four Dimensions of Culture.

Cluster	Countries	Characteristics
Germanic	East Germany	Low PD Medium UA Medium IND Medium MAS
Balcanic	Albania Bulgaria Romania Yugoslavia	High PD High UA Low IND Low to medium MAS
West Slavic	Czechoslovakia Poland (West)	Low PD Medium to high UA Medium IND Medium MAS
East Slavic	USSR Poland (East)	Low PD Medium UA Low IND High MAS
West Urgic	Hungary	Low PD Medium to high UA Medium IND Medium MAS

low on power distance, medium on uncertainty avoidance, medium on individualism, and medium on masculinity. The Balkans (Albania, Bulgaria, and Rumania) probably will shadow the scores of Yugoslavia and display high power distance, high uncertainty avoidance, low individualism, and low to medium masculinity.

For the East Slavic group of countries (USSR and the Eastern part of Poland) predictions are much more difficult because we have no clear indications of trends. Various descriptions of life in these countries lead us to expect low power distance measures, medium scores of uncertainty avoidance, low levels of individualism, and high masculinity. In this respect, the USSR may be similar to the United States except for the differences in levels of individualism, which is high in the United States and may be low in the USSR.

The West Slavic and the West Urgic clusters of countries (Czechoslovakia, West Poland, and Hungary) present a combination of the Germanic clusters and the East Slavic cultures. Hungary and Czechoslovakia were at one time a part of Prussia, which later became Austro-Hungary. One could predict that these countries would display a low level of power distance, a medium to high level of uncertainty avoidance (possibly lower in Hungary and higher in Poland), a medium level of individualism, and a medium level of masculinity.

These predictions are all based on historical events and the geography mix that we are including. There are insufficient data with regard to management values and attitudes in those countries to substantiate these predictions. Thus, we recommend that they should be treated as hypotheses and used cautiously.

ECONOMIC SYSTEMS

Economic Performance

The first major industrial revolution took place in Great Britain. Although it is commonly assumed that technological breakthroughs were the catalysts for the change from an agrarian system into an urban village and town society, the need to organize workers—and not merely the capacity of machinery and engines to use higher quantities of labor—also inspired the early revolution. The British industrial revolution was the spearhead through which England created the British empire. The industrial revolutions of France, Prussia, and other major countries in Europe were much slower in getting under way.

Both World Wars I and II were catalysts for great technological breakthroughs, but there were further economic results from World War II. It is frequently theorized that Great Britain's relatively poor economic performance since World War II is related to the fact that Britain, in winning the war, found its resources depleted but its technological and economic infrastructures not sufficiently destroyed as to render them unusable. Consequently, the British rebuilt their industrial base after World War II using factories with poor equipment and old-fashioned technologies. On the other hand, France and particularly Germany had to rebuild the whole of their industry and infrastructure from scratch. This enabled them to incorporate the very latest and innovative breakthroughs that had taken place in the relatively unscarred United States. This explanation may account for the much higher rate of economic growth of Germany and France in comparison to Great Britain since World War II. Italy, too, although frequently stricken with political anarchy, has also maintained a better rate of growth than the United Kingdom. In addition, more assertive postwar leadership of the governments of the three countries may have contributed to their faster growth rate. Other countries in Europe, such as the Netherlands, the Scandinavian group, and other members of the EEC, seem to have steered a middle course between the somewhat tired postimperial performance of Great Britain and the energetic postwar revival of France and Germany.

The communist block ended World War II with somewhat different agendas and problems than the Western democratic states did. First, many communist countries felt themselves under the powerful communist influence of Russia for the first time and, for some of them, unwillingly. It seems reasonable to speculate that economic motivations were not high. Furthermore, centralized systems on a gigantic scale such as practiced in Russia have never been proven to be optimal in economic terms, although communist party members might assert that they are optimal in political-economic terms. The differences between the economic development of the communist countries compared with their Western democratic counterparts may be examined by reference to Table 4–6.

Examination of Table 4–6, especially the columns with per capita income and gross national product, shows that the communist block countries have made far less economic progress, measured in personal income terms, than the free democratic states. This is also demonstrated by the high levels of population still working in the agricultural sector. Farm mechanization is, in this regard, the counterpart to industrial revolutions in urban center.

The distribution of the factors of production throughout Europe is uneven. It is contingent on physical factors and acquired human resources. For example, Germany, up to World War II, founded its power on the iron and coal resources of the Ruhr. Since the war these resources have become less relevant to economic well being, and Germany's resource base may be considered to be more its human capital than its mineral wealth. Switzerland, which has never had any important natural resources, has one of the highest standards of living in the world as a result of the acquired technological and services management skills of its sophisticated and well-educated population.

Natural Resources

Europe possesses a wide variety of useful minerals. However, in relation to the ever increasing requirements of the advanced industrial nations within Europe, most European state economies depend on imports of raw materials.

Table 4–6. Gross National Product, Per Capita Income, Export and Import to and from the World, and Percentage of Population Employed in Agriculture of European Countries.

Country	GNP ($ Billion)	Per Capita Income ($)	Export ($ Million)		Import ($ Million)		% of Population in Agriculture
			1980	1985	1980	1985	
Communist block							
USSR	734,300	5,730	32,431	31,124	38,789	38,650	20
East Germany	89,249	8,000	4,196	4,160	5,270	3,642	10
Czechoslovakia	87,601	5,800	5,366	4,643	5,440	4,466	12
Rumania	45,536	5,350	12,056	9,324	14,257	7,354	40
Yugoslavia	38,979	2,300	8,977	10,641	15,101	12,163	30
Bulgaria	26,000	2,625	2,090	1,623	2,621	3,076	23.2
Hungary	18,631	4,180	8,648	8,543	9,229	8,228	20.6
Poland	14,400	4,670	7,217	5,664	9,734	5,607	30
Albania	2,380	830	239	158	250	208	60
Western Europe							
West Germany	655,500	9,450	192,861	183,911	188,002	138,489	6
France	568,690	7,179	116,014	101,674	134,874	107,754	8.3
United Kingdom	505,610	6,309	110,078	101,249	115,733	108,956	1.6
Italy	350,038	6,914	77,676	79,020	99,472	91,040	10
Spain	182,760	4,180	20,719	24,245	34,077	29,963	17
Netherlands	122,448	9,749	73,942	68,216	78,039	65,072	6
Switzerland	105,060	14,408	29,643	27,447	36,355	30,698	7
Sweden	89,500	14,821	30,892	30,198	33,434	28,287	5.6

Table 4-6 continued.

Country	GNP ($ Billion)	Per Capita Income ($)	Export ($ Million) 1980	Export ($ Million) 1985	Import ($ Million) 1980	Import ($ Million) 1985	% of Population in Agriculture
Belgium/ Luxembourg	81,162/ 4,470	9,827/ 9,643	64,654	53,658	71,863	56,197	5/ 0.7
Austria	66,800	8,280	17,508	17,234	24,452	20,970	13.8
Turkey	58,260	1,000	2,914	6,423	7,668	12,392	61
Denmark	54,600	11,018	16,975	17,068	19,409	18,222	7
Norway	53,400	13,630	18,560	19,856	16,926	15,558	8
Finland	50,600	10,477	14,161	13,635	15,615	13,242	11
Greece	35,700	4,590	5,183	4,562	10,581	10,135	29
Portugal	22,490	1,930	4,637	5,693	9,334	7,666	24.4
Ireland	16,960	4,750	8,498	10,357	11,142	10,028	26
Iceland	2,100	9,100	918	815	999	905	23

Source: Direction of Trade Statistics (1986); *Countries of the World* (1985).

Coal resources in important economic quantities are situated within Britain, Belgium, the Netherlands, France, West Germany, Poland, Czechoslovakia, and the USSR. Petroleum and natural gas are available in very limited quantities within Europe. Most are concentrated within the Soviet Union, Rumania, and Albania, as well as the North Sea controlled by Great Britain and Norway. Western Europe is still highly dependent on energy supplies from the Arabian Gulf countries and members of the OPEC cartel.

Sources of uranium for use in nuclear reactors have been discovered in several European countries including France and the Soviet Union. Lesser amounts have been found in parts of central and eastern Europe.

The largest known iron reserves are in the Soviet Union. These reserves are more than sufficient for the needs of the USSR and its European satellites. Iron reserves in other European countries are fairly low, although France, Sweden, and Germany do have economically viable levels of reserves. Overall, iron needs are larger than the reserves.

Europe is relatively well supplied with water. The mountains and upper level areas of Europe collect large quantities of surface water that supply rivers and lakes. The water table is normally not far below the surface in the lowlands, and wells and springs are widely available in these areas.

Monetary and Fiscal Policies

International and national trading systems are supported by a highly developed and sophisticated banking system. Although the democratic states have important private-sector banking corporations, almost all have a central bank that is an arm of the government. Within the EEC France has a government-owned banking sector. Italy and Germany use the central banks as the leading edge of government fiscal and monetary planning policies. In the United Kingdom the Bank of England is a more subtle force of indicative planning, although monetarily a government instrument. It is very largely used as a controller of money supply, the main political instrument of the current conservative government. The Labor governments that controlled the period before Margaret Thatcher gained power in the United Kingdom used both monetary policy and fiscal (incomes and wages control) programs to balance the economy.

Within the communist block there are strong instruments to carry out the national and party political economic will. They are less efficient, in some respects, than their free democratic state counterparts because economic decisionmaking is usually subservient to political parameters. Within the USSR itself, all monetary transactions go through the state bank (Granick 1960: 236).

The system of financing corporate growth has played a major part within the free democratic states' industrial development. The development in the United Kingdom of the joint stock company, with limited liability for shareholders, enabled corporations to raise very large amounts of capital and to share the risk of corporate development. The counterweight to this has been the conservative attitudes of the banking system in the United Kingdom, which is highly risk adverse. This may be contrasted with the banking system of Western Germany, which has played a major part in that country's enormous economic resurgence since the war. Banks have been the major providers of capital for industrial development, and because bankers are able to make long-term investments in their corporate customers, companies have been able to carry out long-term strategies. In the United Kingdom capital funds come from stock market and share offerings, in which investors frequently look to short-term three-month and one-year returns on investment in order to make judgments, appraisals, and reinvestments. In France, where the banks are substantially owned or controlled by the government, there has been, like in Germany, a much longer-term view taken of the need for capital and loans to private corporations. A similar model has guided industrial development in Italy.

Trade

Europe is a leader in world commerce and accounts for more than 50 percent of total world trade (*Direction of Trade Statistics Yearbook* 1986). Although the basis of trade between European countries with each other and with the rest of the world (see Table 4–6) was originally based on regional specialization, much of the import and export trade is now influenced at the government level by national and supernational policy decisions. Many of these have evolved from international agreements within Europe itself, such as the European Economic Community (EEC) or *Comecom*, the communist block equivalent in economic trading agreement terms of the EEC.

In the political section mentioned above reference was made to the imperial pasts of Britain, France, and Germany. It should be noted that the inheritance of the imperial age still accrues wealth and income to those states, from the colonies that they still control or the colonial states that are still strongly influenced by the culture of their previous imperial masters. The EEC has now developed major political as well as economic unions that would safeguard Europe against the repetition of the catastrophe of World War II. The economic sectors of the EEC agreements are meant to regulate political needs in order to protect the poorly developed French and German agricultural sectors. The parallel major objective of the EEC in trade agreements is to remove entirely all trading barriers for industrial and commercial goods and services between all the member states. It also aims to create a common tariff barrier against the rest of the world. The economic rationale of this system is that such a large and highly developed mature economic union will give each of these corporations and states within the union such large advantages of trade that they will then be efficient enough to overcome any tariff barriers of their non-EEC customers and competitors.

Since the 1960s the COMECOM states have changed their policy and now aim for a greater degree of openness toward trading with both EEC and other western states. EEC members conduct a vigorous two-way trade with the United States.

LEGAL SYSTEMS

There is a major difference in the legal systems of the USSR and the democratic Western states. Noncommunist countries have a tradition of relatively conservative legal systems based on Romano-Germanic law, whose influence spread throughout Europe (Renee and Briley 1985: 106). Romano-Germanic law is based on three important areas and traditions. The first is that of natural law. Natural law refers to what is fair or just based on concepts of private rather than public property systems. The second premise on which Romano-Germanic law is founded is the supremacy of private property and private law over and above public law. Once again this safeguards the rights of the individual against the state. The third major branch of Romano-Germanic law is custom or common law. This is law that is based on what has been traditionally accepted as right over many years. Frequently it is enacted in courts by judges who recognize and make judgments about traditional behaviors or trends toward accepted behaviors.

In general the European peoples are not litigious. This is probably due to the relative stability of their populations and cultures, which results in their having a clear understanding of what is acceptable in any one society. This may be compared with the relatively litigious U.S. society where the constant renewal of new immigrant populations means that no common cultural inheritance will enable people to understand each other without the intervention of law. More law means more litigation.

The Romano-Germanic legal tradition has generally created strong patent laws with a high regard for the sanctity of intellectual property. It is well protected and respected.

The USSR has had a different legal history. Indeed, it could be said that the USSR had no legal traditions. The Russian state came into being with invasions from the Scandinavians in the ninth century. The developments during that period through to the nineteenth century created a tradition of tyrannical absolutist regimes and a peasant and serf system where the rule of the ruler or the local lord was the law. Power was the real law, and it was idiosyncratic and particular to the local governor or the tyrant. There was no traditional law or belief in natural law (Renee and Briley 1985: 165).

After World War I for the USSR (and after World War II for the other communist block states) the concept of socialist law became prevalent. The prime premise of socialist law is that all property is vested within the state and that only very limited private property accruing to the individual is permissible. Within a communist regime the state is regarded as all powerful because it holds only temporary power. It holds that power until people within the state have been cleansed of their old ways and all have a socialist mind. When that state arrives, politics are no longer necessary because people can govern themselves and will not need governments or state power to intervene (Shoemaker 1985). These beliefs have important consequences for concepts about monopoly and antitrust legislation, the rights of private intellectual property, patent law, private property, and individual rights.

Because all power and property is vested in the state, monopoly antitrust concepts are not regarded as problems. This contrasts strongly with the Western states, which are less fearful of monopoly than the United States but still are cautious about the dangers of monopoly powers' being vested in any one firm.

Most of the Western states have antitrust legislation on the books, although almost all use it judiciously—that is, some monopolies are accepted as long as profits are not excessive and the government is able to exercise regulatory control. Indeed, some monopolies are state owned (such as coal in Great Britain, electricity and gas in France, and oil in Italy).

It may be possible to argue that Europe's higher acceptance of monopoly and cartel-like arrangements is also based on its concepts of natural law. The tradition of natural law within Europe has been an acceptance of elite rule. The feudal traditions in Great Britain and the aristocratic rulers of Italy and Prussian states are examples of the belief in different classes of human beings. Rulers were special and had greater rights than the ruled. As such they also could inherit rights to monopoly power vested in ownership of property. For many years a prime source of income for British kings came from the sale of monopoly rights to aristocrats.

In summary, therefore, the contrast between the communist block countries and the Western states is marked. The latter have a strong tradition of respect for natural law founded on Romano-Germanic principles. The former have very little tradition of law, although since the communist revolution they have developed a greater respect for a socialist set of laws founded on a belief that the state is supreme.

INFRASTRUCTURE

Transportation and Communication
Europe has one of the world's best transportation systems. Networks of airline routes, canals, highways, railroad lines and rivers are available all over Europe except for parts of Russia and Scandinavia. . . .

Communication in Europe is much the same as in the United States. Modern communication systems which include radio networks, newspapers, space communication satellites, mail and telephone and telegraph services, link almost all parts of Europe with each other and with the other continents (*World Book Encyclopedia* 1983).

Technology

Wars have always inspired great technological breakthroughs. Both World War I and World War II were catalysts for the development of land and air transportation. The major technological breakthroughs that came from World War II were (1) synthetics and plastics, which replaced traditional raw materials; (2) radar, which led to the postwar surge in electronic technological equipment, television, and computers; and (3) jet propelled engines, which led to faster air transportation for passengers, and satellite for intercontinental communication.

In these advanced sectors of the economy four factors are crucial: the relatively small market of every European country (except for the USSR), which makes it financially difficult to sustain projects to the stage of commercial viability; the unwillingness of governments to pay indefinitely for expensive projects; the smaller European market in military weapons; and the difficulty of countering the sales capacity of the Americans

(Minshull 1985). The industries that have suffered most from these problems are aircraft manufacturers and the electronic and electrical engineering industries. Less affected have been the telecommunication and the nuclear industries. In fact, West Germany and Sweden export more telephone and telegraph equipment than the United States, and the Netherlands and Belgium almost match U.S. exports (Linvill 1984).

The Soviet Union lags behind in its application of new technologies, such as in its use of computer-based information systems (CBIS). Between 1965 and 1985, almost 7,500 CBISes were built throughout the Soviet Union. About 3,300 are at the enterprise level, a few hundred are ministry-level systems, and most of the rest are for process control. Thus, out of the approximately 44,000 industrial enterprises, only 7.5 percent have their own CBISes. When compared to the 580,000 enterprises, organizations, and institutions that the Soviets say need computers in management applications, the number of CBIS appears small. About one-third of Soviet enterprises with more than 500 employees have CBIS, however, so CBISes cover a disproportionately large percentage of overall production (McHenry and Goodman 1986).

Most West European enterprises of this class in the EEC had some comparable applications running on their own mainframes by 1978. However, European users have generally had more computers, larger configurations, greater reliability, better support systems, and more access to time sharing.

INDUSTRIAL STRUCTURE

The mass production techniques of twentieth-century industry have led to basic structural changes in industry. The small workshops of the nineteenth century have become the large factories and the giant corporations of today.

The key to structural changes lies in the economies of scale that can be achieved by mass production, integration of the means of production, and large-scale capital investment in research and technology in industry. The large units may be typified by giant corporations such as Royal Dutch Shell, ICI, Unilever (U.K.) Siemens, or VEBA of West Germany.

The United Kingdom and West Germany have the largest units, reflecting their more mature and sophisticated industrial structure. However, dismantling of tariffs and increased production and movement throughout the EEC have created direct competition and the need for growth. Direct government intervention created a spate of mergers in all Community countries, particularly in France.

A quick look at the *Fortune* 500 demonstrates that although the U.S. companies are the largest, the United Kingdom, the Netherlands, and West Germany have the largest companies in the EEC. Energy, chemicals, motor vehicles, and electrical goods are the sectors that produce the most large companies. ENI in Italy and British Coal in the United Kingdom are the largest state enterprises. These two countries have considerable state intervention.

All industry in the EEC is not controlled by large companies; much of the industrial structure is small and fragmented. For example, although some giant companies dominate the industrial structure of Italy (Fiat, Montedison, Pirelli, Snia Viscosa, Finsider, and ENI), Italy in general was characterized during the 1960s by a predominance of small production units, many family firms, and the survival of small workshops.

A similar structure characterizes France, which is dominanted by giants like Renault (cars), Rhone-Poulenc (chemicals), and SNA (aerospace). Other European countries have a smaller number of large corporations.

Industry

Traditionally, some of the population has been employed in coal and iron mining, but the increase in the rate of mechanization during the last decade has led to a decline in the number of people employed in these industries (Lenel 1981). Lignite is produced in East Germany, West Germany, Czechoslovakia, and the Soviet Union. In addition European countries produce a fair proportion of the world's bauxite, copper, lead, and zinc (Kogut 1986).

Europe produces half of the world's steel output (Carlsson 1981). Steel is used in heavy machine tools and manufacturing, as well as motor vehicles and aerospace construction. There is a small civil airplane industry represented by the Airbus consortium between France, West Germany, United Kingdom, the Netherlands, and Spain (Hartley 1981). Within Europe the major aerospace industries are located in the United Kingdom, France, West Germany, Italy, Netherlands, and Sweden (Hochmuth 1986). Within the Soviet Union the aerospace engineering and building industry is self-contained.

In the European community, 5 percent of the population is engaged in the motor vehicle and motor-vehicle parts industry (Young 1986). The major car producers are West Germany, France, the United Kingdom, Italy, and Spain (Adams 1981).

Chemical industry organizations are concentrated in Western Europe around Rotterdam, parts of Germany, France, Italy, and Great Britain. The industry uses deposits of salt phospher and sulphur (Boisot 1986).

Fishing industries are important for Iceland, Norway, and the USSR. Fishing is a recognized industrial sector within Great Britain and in Spain.

The timber and wood industries are important in Sweden, Norway, Finland, and the Soviet Union (Gobbo 1981). Handicraft industries have had a revival in the advanced industrial nations in recent years, although these have not reached a significant level of GDP. They may be regarded more as part of the movement toward the basic values that have been manifested in the United States, Japan, and other advanced industrial nations in recent years.

Agriculture

Arable land in Europe covers almost 30 percent of the total area (compared with 20 percent in the United States and 10 percent in the Soviet Union). The percentage varies sharply within individual countries, ranging from more than 60 percent in the Netherlands to less than 3 percent in Norway. Western Europe is a major producer of cereals, roots, edible oils, fibers, fruit, and livestock products. Europe overall accounts for more than four-fifths of the world's rye output, two-thirds of the potato and oats output, and two-fifths of the world's total wheat supplies.

The organization of agriculture production also varies widely. Within the Soviet Union most farming is organized for the state under collective controls. It is estimated that about a quarter of all agricultural output in the Soviet Union is produced from private plots (Nove 1977: 122). Collective systems are also employed in Spain. In the democratic western states, the private property system means that agricultural industries are privately owned. Although these agricultural holdings, particularly within Germany, France, and Italy, were held in small parcels, in recent years there has been a tendency toward consolidation and the growth of larger units.

Reference again to Table 4–6 above, particularly the column showing the percentage of the population engaged in agricultural industries, demonstrates that there is a strong correlation between that proportion of the population involved in agriculture and the level of industrial development and per capita income of a country. For example, in the United

Kingdom, where less than 2 percent of the population is engaged in agricultural sector is very high. This may be contrasted with Turkey, which has 61 percent of its population involved in agriculture but a national per capita income level of $1,000 per annum. An example within the communist block would be Albania with a 60 percent agricultural sector and a per capita income of only $830 per annum. An exception to the correlation mentioned above is Iceland, which has 23 percent of its population involved in agriculture but a high per capita income of $9,000 per annum. This is accounted for by the fact that many Icelandics are involved in the forestry and fishing industries, which are included under the agriculture statistics.

BUSINESS AND MANAGEMENT SYSTEMS

General Philosophy of Management

Management philosophies can be classified in terms of five dimensions (Kluckhohn and Strodtbeck 1961: 12). These are

1. An evaluation of human nature classified as evil, mixed, or good;
2. The relationship of man to his surrounding natural environments (subjugation, harmony, domination);
3. Time orientation (past, present, future);
4. Orientation with regard to activity (being, being in becoming, doing);
5. Relationships among people (lineality, collaterality, individualism).

Management philosophy in Europe has a particular profile. The five elements of this profile are as follows:

1. Human nature in both the communist and noncommunist sectors may be regarded as mixed in nature. Korman and Locke (1986) criticize the assumption in the U.S. literature that people in organizations behave benignly; in Europe it always has been assumed that people are a mixed bag of both good and bad. Further, the assumption is that the good can be encouraged and the bad discouraged by the use of the appropriate incentives. The history of different trends in management science indicates a lack of agreement on what exactly acts as an incentive on this mixed bag of human beings in organizations.

2. The relationship between man and nature in the European context results in the former's mastery over the latter. The level of pollution in both the East and the West is high and indicates how nature has been

exploited and mastered for short-term results. Iceland offers an interesting contrast to the rest of Europe in that environmental hazards there are controlled and a greater degree of harmony with the environment is achieved by its people than elsewhere in Europe.

3. Time horizons throughout Europe tend to be spread on a continuum from the past into the present. Attention paid to the future frequently extends to only the next quarter or at most the financial year. Some of this short time horizon may be attributed to the strong and powerful effect of bankers and other financial controllers on stockmarkets and bourses, who frequently tend to look at very short (between three months and one year) financial time horizons. This, in turn, affects managers, who must perform according to stock market expectations. The pressure for a short time horizon also mounts when planning in organizations is based on crisis management and looks at the most recent problem and the shortest-term solution.

4. Human activity all over Europe consists mostly of a state of nature going from being to becoming. Although most people attempt to maintain stability, they also have achieved personal and organizational changes. This may be contrasted to the U.S. systems, which are oriented toward carrying out action and in which change has a value for itself.

5. Hofstede (1980) found that most West European countries (other than Greece, Portugal, and Turkey) displayed a high or an above average level of individualism (see Table 4–4). Yugoslavia from the eastern block shows a low level of individualism. It can be predicted that people in eastern block countries will display a high level of collectivism.

Recruitment and Promotion of Managers

Lawrence and Lorsch (1967) found that organizations need two types of managers: The first is a functional specialist who carries out specialized roles in the firm; the second is an integrator who is able to synthesize the different interests of functional departments in order to achieve an optimal balance in the interest of the firm overall.

There appears to be three major patterns of management recruitment and promotion within the European system, which reflect on Lawrence and Lorsch's theory (1967). The first type, of which a typical example is the United Kingdom, is one where eventual managers are usually recruited within functional specialization (accounting, engineering, operations). Throughout their management careers very little attention is paid to teaching these functional specialists general integrated skills (Granick

1972). Consequently, when they eventually are promoted into jobs that require, because of their high level in the hierarchy of the firm, a degree of integrative capacity, these managers are generally found to be deficient in the necessary skills. When these managers recognize the danger of their lack of integrated skills, they respond managerially by opting for decentralized management systems that temporarily remove from them the need for an integrated philosophy of the firm. The eventual effect of these behaviors is to create a suboptimal decisionmaking structure.

A second pattern using Lawrence and Lorsch thesis may be based on the German example. In this case managers, or potential managers, are usually recruited, as in the first pattern, as functional specialists. However, during their career as functionalists they are given generalized training that enables them to acquire integrated skills. Thus, by the time that they are actually promoted into jobs that require integrative managerial qualities, they are fully trained and prepared to undertake those integrative roles. As a result of this more organizationally conceptualized training system, the decisionmaking processes in this pattern are more attuned to optimal results than the first pattern mentioned above. Managers within this pattern are able to create decisionmaking structures that may be either centralized or decentralized. Managers' choices will depend on criteria that are relevant to the successful operation of the firm rather than on a lack of managerial skills to carry out the best structure. Hence, the German system contains far more centralized structures because the managerial skills exist to run these unified units. However, decentralized organizations are created when it is functionally more desirable to do so (for example, when special products of an innovative nature have to be produced).

One of the ways in which German managers are assisted in becoming better integrated thinkers stems from the German codetermination industrial democratic system. Within this process, companies are required to seek out and take into account the opinions of workers down to very low levels in the hierarchy (Burmeister 1977; Woodgate 1979). This, in turn, has forced lower- and middle-level managers to become accustomed to take into account many different views at all levels of the hierarchy before coming to their decisions. At the same time general managers keep in touch with narrow functionalized views.

The Scandinavian countries may be considered to be similar to the German pattern, with functional differentiation progressing with the use of expertise at the individual level toward an integrated organizational structure. The Scandinavian countries may be differentiated from the German because of a slightly more egalitarian society with less respect for titles or class origins.

Educational qualifications are important in Scandinavia, and people specialize considerably. Top positions in organizations tend to be reserved for performers from specialized areas who also display well-rounded problemsolving capabilities.

Scandinavian managers tend to be younger than those in the United Kingdom or France or Germany, which may account for the fact that their financial rewards are not very much above the levels of skilled operatives in their workforces and are noticeably lower than similar management ranks in Germany or France.

Many Mediterranean countries vary from the second pattern above—that is, most recruits to an organization go in as functional specialists and are selected for promotion to integrative-level roles on the basis of their functional skills. However, one of the extra criteria of selection is a noneconomic one. In the case of the Mediterranean countries the criterion usually is whether or not the promotee is a member of the tribe, group, or family that holds power and control of that organization (Ferrarotti 1959). In the case of the Mediterranean countries therefore, the result in terms of managerial effectiveness is suboptimal.

The Russian system could be considered to belong to this second pattern. It also may be considered to be a variation of the theme because promotion from functional to integrative management roles usually is based not only on managerial skills but also on ideological purity and membership of the communist party (Granick 1960). As such it may be considered to constitute a noneconomic selection process that renders the Russian version of this pattern suboptimal in its effect on organizational effectiveness.

The third pattern, of which France may be considered to be a typical example, is the one where the functional managerial role and the integrative role are never combined. Managerial appointments within functional roles reserved for one generally lower-class type of manager, and the integrative managerial roles are reserved for another higher-class person who has been groomed throughout his or her career to take the powerful integrative decisionmaking roles at the top of the organization (Granick 1972). Within France itself these are generally the managers who are trained within the Grandes Ecoles (Suleiman 1979). The superiority of the high level training of the integrative managers within such systems has led to strongly centralized organizations with relatively high levels of achievement. However, these levels of effectiveness are still lower than those in pattern two, where the functionalists have developed themselves into integrators. The degree of effectiveness is less than that in pattern two because a dysfunctional effect is experienced when the functionalists and integrators always belong to separate groups. Thus, no matter how good the integrators may be, they cannot overcome their lack of practical, functional experience.

Planning and Decisionmaking

This subject has been probably studied more than any other management practice in Europe. In order to encompass all this material separate paragraphs have been devoted to major European countries.

The United Kingdom. Most British organizations are highly decentralized (Child and Kieser 1979). This results from the education system in England, which tends to divide students at a young age into classes. Many higher-level managers receive their education at private schools and later go on to Oxford or Cambridge University. In contrast, most middle managers are educated at comprehensive schools and go to the redbrick, ordinary, and technologically oriented universities (Granick 1972).

The higher-management roles tend to go to people who have not been educated technologically to understand the details of the operations of the organizations. As a result they tend to decentralize decisionmaking at the operational level to middle managers (Graves 1973). A further consequence of this phenomenon is that important decisions are avoided because the higher-level managers are rarely competent technologically to appraise entrepreneurial opportunities. Risky decision-making is avoided. Furthermore, what would be a lower-level risk for a non-British firm appears to be riskier for a British firm because the managers do not know what data to collect or how to organize it to obtain for themselves a proper decisionmaking paradigm.

France. It is important to understand that the way that the French financial and administrative infrastructure is constructed gives a high level of capacity control for the government. The fact that banks are owned mainly by the government means that the ability to control who will get loans and development capital is available only to the government. Furthermore, since World War II there has been a high degree of control by civil servants and ministers, most of whom had been educated in the Grandes Ecoles system (Granick 1972).

With the creation of the five-year indicative planning system after World War II these ministers and civil servants, who had been educated and prepared to take control, gave a strong lead to the resurgence of the French economy. The results in terms of decisionmaking and planning at the organizational level are that French managers tend to opt out of decisionmaking on their own behalf and to merely confirm the plan as handed down to them by ministers and civil servants. Furthermore, in view of the fact that upper-level managers in French organizations have been similarly educated in the Grandes Ecoles system, they lack confidence in their middle managers, who have a different educational background (Bass and Burger 1979).

Furthermore, the communication dissonance is two-way. Not only do the senior managers and civil servants get recruited from the Grandes Ecoles, but their occupation of the senior positions acts as a blocking mechanism on all other people who were educated in other parts of the French system. Because of this, middle-level managers have very little incentive to display outstanding skills or capacities (Graves 1973). There is thus a double reinforcement of suboptimal performance at the middle-management levels in French organizations (Inzerilli and Laurent 1983). The final result of the two cultural and educational backgrounds outlined above is that the planning and decisionmaking system in France is highly centralized and very little delegation of power takes place.

One of the main platforms of the French indicative planning system has been that a lack of competition discourages firms from making the necessary R&D investment to develop and beat world competition. This type of planning has led civil servants to create a series of cartels in many industries. They have fairly ruthlessly forced some firms to go out of business in order to ensure that enough profit remains in any particular industry for the remaining firms to flourish. The medium-term result of these cartels is that the managers in these firms are no longer obliged to take high risks to make a satisfactory level of profit for their firms. This, in turn, leads to a low to average risk-taking profile on the part of French managers (Cummings, Harnett, and Stevens 1971).

Germany. The most important feature of the German management planning and decisionmaking system is the background work ethic in German society, which superordinates individual dignity and worth (Bass and Burger 1979). As a result, German organizations and managers are united in their focus on the concept of productivity and the high quality of the goods and services that they produce. Less emphasis is placed on interpersonal skills and the handling of subordinates, which might be necessary in more person-oriented societies such as Great Britain (Child and Kieser 1979) or France (Kanungo and Wright 1983).

A second important feature of the German planning system is that management education is highly technologically competent at all stages. The third feature is the codetermination system. This is a legally instituted system of codetermination by workers with their management with regard to decisions taken in the organization. This enables workers to feel that they have a say in the important features of their firm and, as such, feel less need to rebel or join strong unions or go on strike.

Because of these three important features of the German culture, management systems in Germany tend to be fairly centralized, autocratic, hierarchical. Managers do not have to worry too much about acceptance of their orders by their subordinates. Workers are happy about the participation guaranteed by codetermination, and all are united in their belief that quality control, productivity, and fine goods and service are the meaning and essence of the organization.

The Germans have a fairly low risk-taking profile (Cummings, Harnett, and Stevens 1971). This may be attributed to two factors. The first is their formal system and hierarchical domination, which does not allow much flexibility and does not call for a high level of risk taking in order to guarantee a manager's continued career ascendancy.

Second, and possibly more explicit, the German concentration on quality in their goods and services has created for them a specific market segmentation in the world markets in which they compete. In other words, in every market in which the Germans compete a segment buys a product or service not based on price but on quality. As this is an increasingly important feature of the affluent countries in which German goods and services sell, the market segments available to German goods, with their concentration on quality, has increased disproportionately during the years since World War II.

Scandinavia. Codetermination is also common in Scandinavia. Scandinavians are less organizationally oriented than the Germans, although less individualistic than the French or the Italians (Hofstede 1980).

Less emphasis is placed in Scandinavia on the organization and greater attention is given to individuals within the organization. However, the Scandinavians are as concerned with quality of goods and services as the Germans and consequently have achieved a high level of penetration in many of the European and U.S. markets.

Because of their greater emphasis on the individual in the organization, the decisionmaking structure is less hierarchical and more participative and decentralized. The job redesign system at Volvo is an example of the Scandinavian capacity for having less rigid structures in the organizations in order to enjoy the participating energy of lower-level managers (Gyllenhammer 1977). This has also enabled them to achieve high quality with greater delegation and less autocracy.

This open attitude toward organizational structure and decisionmaking process means that the planning systems in Scandinavian firms are long term. The planning process can look at the more distant-horizon industrial needs because, with their open attitudes toward structure and decisionmaking, Scandinavian managers can be confident that the organization will adjust itself to the short-term needs enabling the firm to achieve its long-term goals.

Italy. The Italian economic structure may be viewed in two parts. The first is dominated by very large government-controlled organizations in the major sectors such as the energy industries. On the other hand there is a rich structure of smaller family-dominated firms. Because of their smaller size these organizations are innovative in both design and technology, although it is known that family organizations tend to be centralized.

The Italians are highly individualistic and idiosyncratic (Bass and Burger 1979), which are characteristics that also increase their capacity for innovation. Against this background the government, as in France and Germany after World War II, has been strongly involved in the planning processes at the infrastructure and macroeconomic levels. Although the Italians, because of high levels of small-business penetration, have been less successful in their planning processes than France or Germany, the planning process has been conducive to their relative success in their economic growth over the last three decades.

Yugoslavia. Yugoslavia has interesting similarities with some West European systems while still being part of the communist block. Yugoslavia was dominated for many years by President Tito, who molded the country into his version of communist participative democracy. Economic organizations are meant to be an alliance of management and workers with only minimal pay differentials in order to reward higher levels of responsibility. The degree of participation by workers is, in theory, very high, and regular meetings are organized by the management at which all workers can have their say in both selecting the managers and guiding those managers in setting the objectives of the organization (Kavran 1972).

In practice, participatory democracy has been less than perfect. Putnam (1967) found that the level of participation by workers was low and that, in fact, managers had levels of autocratic decisionmaking power similar to their Western counterparts.

Yugoslavia is organized as a republic that comprises several states, which are in turn divided into communes. Power is concentrated at the level of the republic by the central government's capacity for giving loans through the republic's banking system. However, after this stage some decisionmaking power is delegated to the level of the state and then in turn to the communes. This leads to some level of autonomy in policy planning and decisionmaking and is common with some other communist block countries. For example, pricing is determined locally rather than centrally.

Within the enterprise managers are elected by the workers. However, a major criterion for the election of any manager is that he or she is competent to incorporate central state policy and ensure that the enterprise does not contravene regulations or the demands of the state. The power of the manager is vested in his or her level of skill in the particular interpretation process that is protecting the workers. It is also a condition of the managerial role that managers are not allowed to interfere in labor relations. This balances their power by assuring that control remains, to some extent, vested within the workforce.

Russia and the Satellites of the USSR. The Russian system is, in both theory and practice, centralized at the very highest level of the political infrastructure, the Politburo. This institution creates five-year plans that are interpreted by ministers. Subordinates subdivide the plan into required outputs in various parts of industry. This is organized within each state forming the republic. At the level of the state these orders are translated into specific demands for output from various factories and enterprises. At this stage the process becomes dialectic: The managers of enterprises propose counterplans that are versions of what they feel is feasible. This creates a form of balance and debate that should enable some compromise to be reached.

However, this is just the beginning of the complex system of management behavior and planning within a communist economy. A total centralized planning system combined with a population of 280 million spread over 8.65 million square miles (Shoemaker 1985) produces a high degree of suboptimization in the allocation and distribution of resources.

It is essential to remember that neither capital nor labor is an easily transferable resource. Practically, most personnel may not move from factory to factory without express permission of the communist party. Similarly, each factory has a system of stockpiling resources whenever it is possible to obtain them, for one is never sure when the next rationing or poor delivery or wrong delivery will take place. This, in turn, has led to the unofficial appointment by many factories of special operators (*Tolkachi*) who purchase and sell on behalf of the factory any slack resources (Rubin 1972). In this way factories stockpile resources that may fall into short supply and prevent them from achieving their allocated targets.

There is a high degree of risk taking involved in any communist state enterprise because the economic world is subjugated to the political world. This means that managers try to minimize decisions (Leites 1985). This in turn leads to a poor quality of products and to low levels of innovation, enterpreneurship, and resourcefulness (Ginsberg 1972).

Industrial Relations

The origins of trade unionism in Europe may be discovered within the origins of the industrial revolution itself. The effect of the industrial revolution was to concentrate capital in the hands of owners of enterprise and to create a disproportion between the wealth of those who owned capital and the workers who did not. Furthermore, as Marx pointed out, the workers who previously had worked in guilds and crafts and at least had owned their own tools of production had no tools of their own in the large factories.

Although the workers were agricultural employees and were woefully exploited, they were much better off than when working on the land. The increased average wealth also created a body of potential political power that political aspirants had identified. Socialist and communist movements sprang up throughout Europe during the nineteenth century. The links between the socialist, communist, and trade unions were very strong, and this unity was underscored by their advocacy of the interests of the working class and their belief that a universal solution would transcend national barriers.

The advent of World War I created a major schism between the international socialist and trade union movements because they all believed that the workers should not fight for national interests but cooperate internationally. Following the declaration of World War II the body of worker backing that had been so carefully molded disintegrated rapidly into national factions willing to fight for their various countries.

During the postwar period industrial relations have been a part of a successful economic system that enabled most West European countries to more than double their real income per capita, to ensure full employment, and to establish model welfare policies. This economic context has completely changed over the last fourteen years. Growth rates for the countries within the Organization for Economic Cooperation and Development (OECD) have come down from an average of 4.5 percent to between 2.5 and 3 percent (Tavitian 1985). This slowing down coincides with other changes: Japan and other Far East countries have emerged as international competitors to the European countries; international economic interdependence has created a global market that is difficult to regulate economically; information technologies and other sophisticated technologies (like robots) have evolved; more women and young people have entered in the labor market; and people's values about, attitudes toward, and expectations from their workplaces have changed as a result of more than two decades of prosperity.

All these segments of the European economy brought industrial relations in Europe to an era of changes. Traditionally there have been two main issues that differentiate national industrial relations in Europe. The first one is central versus pluralist unionism. Denmark, Norway, and Sweden are accustomed to strong central confederations with central collective bargaining. Most South European and Benelux countries have plural unions. Neither Germany nor Britain operates central bargaining, and in France it is very limited.

The second major source of difference is the degree of union participation in the management of social security. Scandinavia and Britain have a universal system of social security that is run by the state. Central and South European countries have shared the responsibility of social security management between the state and the boards of organizations in which unions have representation.

There have been two major aspects of unionism in Europe that unite unions across countries. First, the West European unions pursue a goal of solidarity that traditionally was associated with class solidarity but recently is viewed as social solidarity. This welfare state in the United Kingdom or Germany could be looked on as a consequence of this concept.

Second, most West European unions have an arbitration function. One of the major roles of this function is to choose between the varying and sometimes conflicting claims of their members. In this role unions all over Western Europe contribute to the cohesion of societies and to their evolution. To summarize, unions have been considered as representing the interests of their members both in the sharing of income and in the organization of work. They also represent members values and aspirations and have been used as countervailing power (Galbraith 1957) to balance, via the arbitration function, employers' needs and expectations and to balance the state's political powers and allow for social equilibrium.

However, this situation is changing. The capitalistic philosophy, so well anchored in the U.S. system (Lovell 1985), is strengthening and spreading to other countries. In many of these countries past emphasis on the responsibility of the state is losing ground in favor of an increasing reliance on economic organizations and enterprises (Tavitian 1985).

This situation challenges traditional industrial relations. The centralized collective bargaining systems appear unable to cope with the diversified approaches required for wages and for work organization. Thus, unions face less loyalty from their members and less acceptance by the public (Edwards, Garonna, and Todtling 1986).

In Western Europe unions are formed to protect the worker from the oppression of capital. But in the USSR, where the means of production are nationalized, it follows from the Soviet standpoint that antagonistic interests cannot occur between workers and state management.

The Central Council of Trade Unions has to be consulted by the Soviet government on matters concerning labor. The council issues rules and standards on occupational safety and health. In addition, the unions administer some of the schemes of social insurance, supervise the collection of premium, and determine the amount of benefits. The unions then act as advisory bodies on labor problems and also as government agencies (Lane 1978).

Although strikes are not specifically prohibited by law, there is no tradition of unions' organizing strikes to improve wages or conditions. Soviet industrial relations should not be regarded as the "bottling down" of legitimate workers' grievances by the trade unions as they are sometimes characterized in the West (Lane 1978: 314). Rather, unions are yet another governmental means of reducing stress in the factory and of stimulating the workers to increase production.

CONCLUSIONS

In this description of European management, we have tried to look at the macrovariables that will enable scholars and practitioners in Europe to understand the important parameters of our investigation into a firm within this context. At the beginning of the chapter we discussed Child's (1981) proposal that there may be three relevant schools of management thought: the contingency school, the culture school, and the school of capitalism. Child asked which school is most apt to predict a manager's behavior. The data and discussion within this chapter appear to indicate that a country's geography may not correspond with any single classification of the three theories.

The first question that may be asked about a European firm should be, "Is it in a Communist block country or a Western democratic state?" The answer to this question can provide more contextual data than any other question.

The second question that should be asked is, "Where in Europe are the firms located with which they are able to do business?" The description of European economics indicates that the level of business available is high in European Russia or within the areas bordered by London, Paris, Milan, and Hamburg. These centers are the outstanding places of trade and commerce. Following Dore's (1973) prediction, being involved with a highly industrialized country will also indicate its management style. Thus, Child's second school of thought, the contingency explanation, is also a powerful explanatory variable in both Western and Eastern Europe.

The third most important question that should be asked by an investigator in Europe is, "How is business done in a specific place?" Negandhi and Prasad (1971) claimed that business practices are influenced by education, sociology, legal, and political inputs and the general economy. Culture, as much as industrialization, can influence management philosophies and practices.

This analysis seems to indicate that the three different schools have a greater predictive power with regard to management philosophy and practice *within organizations* rather than *within countries*. Other organizational variables such as organization size, structure, and technology are then predictive. Consequently, a country's geographical boundaries are not the ideal framework to be used for forming generalized clusters. The contextual theoretical variables (capitalism versus communism, industrialization and culture) are better predictors of management philosophy and behavior.

The adoption of this view could help to answer the second question posed in this chapter. We pointed out that management philosophy has been defined as an independent variable when it might be an intervening variable. Using the three general variables as independent variables and eliminating the geographical cluster expose management philosophy as an intervening variable affected by the contextual variables. Although there may be some interactions it is not the firms' management philosophy in any particular country that might affect the economic system, industrialization, or culture but rather management philosophy in any particular firm that is affected by the contextual variables of the organization.

We have suggested a series of hypotheses related to the use of Hofstede's dimensions of culture throughout the communist system. This could be a rich source of a new understanding of economic and management systems under communist regimes as well as a possible validation of generalizations that emanate from Hofstede's theory.

Further, we have discussed the degree of involvement of senior managers in organizational operations in different countries. It was hypothesized that this related to education systems, as well as social class differentiation, in those countries. We believe that these hypotheses could be fruitfully investigated to yield important insights.

REFERENCES

Adams, W.J. 1981. "The Automobile Industry." In *The Structure of Europoean Industry*, edited by H.W. de Jong, pp. 187–208. The Hague: Martinus Nijhoff.

Adler, N.J., and M. Jelinek. 1986. "Is 'Organization Culture' Culture Bound?" *Human Resource Management* 25(1): 73–90.

Bass, B.M., and P.C. Burger. 1979. *Assessment of Managers: An International Comparison*. New York: Free Press.

Boisot, M. 1986. "Industrial Policy and Industrial Culture: The Case of European Petrochemical Industry." In *European Approaches to International Management*, edited by K. Macharzina and W.H. Staehle, pp. 163–84. Berlin: Walter de Gruyter.

Burmeister, I. 1977. *Co-Determination: Worker Participation in German Industry.* New York: German Information Center.

Carlsson, B. 1981. "Structure and Performance in the West European Steel Industry: A Historical Perspective." In *The Structure of European Industry*, edited by H.W. de Jong, pp. 125–58. The Hague: Martinus Nijhoff.

Child J. 1981. "Culture, Contingency and Capitalism in the Cross National Study of Organizations." In *Research in Organizational Behavior*, vol. 13, edited by L.L. Cummings and B.M. Staw, pp. 303–56. Greenwich, Conn.: JAI Press.

Child, J., and A. Kieser. 1979. "Organization and Managerial Roles in British and West German Companies: An Examination of the Culture-Free Thesis." In *Organization Alike and Unlike*, edited by C.J. Lammers and D.J. Hickson, ch. 13. London: Routledge & Kegan Paul.

Clawson, R.W., and L. Kaplan. 1982. *The Warsaw Pact: Political Purpose and Military Means*. Wilmington, Del.: Scholarly Resources.

Countries of the World. 1985. Detroit, Mich.: Gale Research.

Cummings, L.L., D.L. Harnett, and O.J. Stevens. 1971. "Risk, Fate Conciliation and Trust: An International Study of Attitudinal Differences Among Executives." *Academy of Management Journal* 14: 283–304.

Direction of Trade Statistics Yearbook. 1986. Washington, D.C.: International Monetary Fund.

Dore, Ronald P. 1973. *British Factory–Japanese Factory: The Origins of National Diversity in Industrial Relations*. Berkeley: University of California Press.

The Economist. 1986. Dec. 6: 62–64.

Edwards, R., A. Garonna, and F. Todtling, eds. 1986. *Unions in Crisis and Beyond: Prospectives from Six Countries*. Dover, Mass.: Auburn House.

Farmer, R.N., and B.M. Richman. 1965. *Comparative Management and Economic Progress*. Homewood, Ill.: Irwin.

Ferrarotti, F.E. 1959. "Management in Italy." In *Management in the Industrial World*, edited by F. Harbison and C.A. Myers, pp. 232–46. New York: McGraw-Hill.

Galbraith, J.K. 1957. *American Capitalism*. London: Hamish Hamilton.

Ginsberg, M.P. 1972. "Consumer Orientation: A New Dimension in Soviet Management." In *Managerial Styles of Foreign Businessmen*, edited by L. Stessin, Series 9, vol. 1, pp. 85–114. Hampstead, N.Y.: Hofstra University Yearbook of Business.

Gobbo, F. 1981. "The Pulp and Paper Industry Structure and Behavior." In *The Structure of European Industry*, edited by H.W. de Jong, pp. 57–91. The Hague: Martinus Nijhoff.

Granick, D. 1960. *The Red Executive*. Garden City, N.Y.: Doubleday.

———. 1972. *Managerial Comparisons of Four Developed Countries: France, Britain, United States and Russia*. Cambridge, Mass.: MIT Press.

Graves, D. 1973. "The Impact of Culture upon Managerial Attitudes, Beliefs and Behavior in England and France." In *Management Research: A Cross Cultural Perspective*, edited by D. Graves, pp. 282–304. San Francisco: Jossey Bass.

Gyllenhammer, P.G. 1977. *People at Work*. Reading, Mass.: Addison-Wesley.

Hartley, K. 1981. "The Aerospace Industry: Problems and Policies." In *The Structure of European Industry*, edited by H.W. de Jong, pp. 237–56. The Hague: Martinus Nijhoff.

———. 1983. *NATO Arms Cooperation: A Study in Economics and Politics*. London: George Allen and Unwin.

Hochmuth, M.S. 1986. "The European Aerospace Industry." In *European Approaches to International Management*, edited by K. Macharzina and W.H. Staehle, pp. 205–24. Berlin: Walter de Gruyter.

Hofstede, G. 1980. *Culture's Consequences: International Differences in Work-Related Values*. Beverly Hills, Calif.: Sage.

Hudson, R., D. Rhind, and H. Mounsey. 1984. *An Atlas of EEC Affairs*. London: Methuen.

Hunter, R., ed. 1984. *NATO: The Next Generation*. Boulder, Colo.: Westview Press.

Inzerilli, G., and A. Laurent. 1983. "Managerial Views of Organization Structure in France and USA." *International Studies of Management and Organization* 13: 97–118.

Kanungo, R.N., and R. Wright. 1983. "A Cross Cultural Comparative Study of Managerial Job Attitudes." *Journal of International Business Studies* (Fall): 115–129.

Kavran, D. 1972. "Management and Its Environment in Yugoslavia." In *Management in an International Context*, edited by J.L. Massie and J. Luytjes, pp. 154–78. New York: Harper & Row.

Kerr, A.J.C. 1977. *The Common Market and How It Works*. Oxford: Pergamon Press.

Kluckhohn, F.R., and F.L. Strodtbeck. 1961. *Variations in Value Orientations*. Westport, Conn.: Greenwood Press.

Kochan, L., and R. Abraham. 1983. *The Making of Modern Russia*, 2d ed. New York: St. Martin's Press.

Kogut, B. 1986. "Steel and the European Community." In *European Approaches to International Management*, edited by K. Macharzina and W.H. Staehle, pp. 183–204. Berlin: Walter de Gruyter.

Korman, A.K., and E.A. Locke. 1986. "Psychologists and the Denial of Evil: Dysfunctions of the Benign View of Man." Unpublished paper. City University of New York.

Lane, D. 1978. *Politics and Society in the USSR*, 2d ed. London: Martin Robertson.

Larrabee, F.S. 1984. "Soviet Crisis Management in Eastern Europe." In *The Warsaw Pact: Alliance in Transition*, edited by D. Holloway and J. Sharp, Ithaca, N.Y.: Cornell University Press.

Lawrence, P.R., and J.W. Lorsch. 1967. "Differentiation and Integration in Complex Organizations." *Administrative Science Quarterly* 12: 1–47.

Leites, N. 1985. *Soviet Style in Management*. New York: Crane Russak.

Lenel, H.O. 1981. "Hard Coal Mining in the EEC Countries, Especially in Germany." In *The Structure of European Industry*, edited by H.W. de Jong, pp. 159–86. The Hague: Martinus Nijhoff.

Linvill, J.G., et al. 1984. "The Competitive Status of the U.S. Electronics Industry." Washington, D.C.: National Academy Press.

Lovell, Jr., M.R. 1985. "Trade Union Trends in Western Europe: An American Perspective." In *Industrial Relations in Europe*, edited by B.C. Roberts, pp. 242–61. London: Croom Helm.

McHenry, W.K., and S.E. Goodman. 1986. "MIS in Soviet Industrial Enterprises: The Limits of Reform from Above." *Communications of the ACM* 29(11): 1034–43.

Minshull, G.M. 1985. *The New Europe: An Economic Geography of the EEC*. New York: Holmes and Meier.

Myers, K., ed. 1980. *NATO: The Next 30 Years.* Boulder, Colo.: Westview Press.

Negandhi, A.R., and S.B. Prasad. 1971. *Comparative Management.* New York: Appleton-Century Crofts.

Nove, A. 1977. *The Soviet Economic System.* London: George Allen and Unwin.

Nystrom, P.C., and W.H. Starbuck. 1984. "Managing Beliefs in Organizations." *The Journal of Applied Behavioral Science* 20(3): 277–87.

Prest, A.R., and D.J. Coppock, eds. 1982. *The UK Economy,* 9th ed. London: Weidenfeld and Nicolson.

Putnam, L. 1967. "Not Part of the Plan But Marketing Takes Root in Russia." *Industrial Marketing* (August): 63–65.

Renee, D., and J.B.C. Briley. 1985. *Major Legal Systems in the World Today,* 3d ed. London: Stephenson.

Rubin, I.L. 1972. "Entrepreneurial Behavior Patterns of Soviet Managers." In *Managerial Styles of Foreign Businessmen,* edited by L. Stessin, Series 9, vol. 1, pp. 13–43. Hampstead, N.Y.: Hofstra University Yearbook of Business.

Schein, E.H. 1984. "Coming to a New Awareness of Organizational Culture." *Sloan Management Review* (Winter): 3–16.

Shoemaker, M.W. 1985. *The Soviet Union and Eastern Europe 1985.* Washington, D.C.: Stryker-Post.

Sobell, V. 1984. *The Red Market: Industrial Cooperation and Specialization in Comecon.* Aldershot, Hants, England: Grower.

Suleiman, E.N. 1979. *Elites in French Society.* Princeton, N.J.: Princeton University Press.

Swann, D. 1985. *The Economics of the Common Market.* Harmondworth, England: Pergamon Press.

Tavitian, R. 1985. "Trade Union Trends in Western Europe: A European Perspective." In *Industrial Relations in Europe,* edited by B.C. Roberts, pp. 222–41. London: Croom Helm.

Van Meerhaeghe, M.A.G. 1980. *A Handbook of International Economic Institutions.* The Hague: Martinus Nijhoff.

Woodgate, R. 1979. "Participation in West Germany: Another Side of the Story." *Personnel Management* (February): 17–21.

The World Book Encyclopedia. 1983. Chicago: World Book Inc.

The World Factbook. 1986. Washington, D.C.: Central Intelligence Agency.

Young, S. 1986. "European Car Industry." In *European Approaches to International Management,* edited by K. Macharzina and W.H. Staehle, pp. 147–59. Berlin: Walter de Gruyter.

CHAPTER 5

People's Republic of China

Rosalie L. Tung

In order to analyze and understand management practices and organizational processes in a planned economy like that of the People's Republic of China (PRC), it is necessary to examine how broad societal-environment variables (such as the political, socioeconomic, and cultural systems) act as constraints on the operations of industrial enterprises. Even in free-market economies such as that of the United States, the role of such societal variables cannot be dismissed. Numerous studies (Thompson 1967; Lawrence and Lorsch 1967; Duncan 1972; Tung 1979) have shown the relationships between organizational environments and organizational process and performance.

Consistent with the conceptual framework set forward in this book, each of the six factors affecting the business and management systems in the PRC will be examined. The following points, however, should be borne in mind when reading the industrial practices discussed herein.

First, despite the fact that China is currently more willing than it has been in the past to provide information on the operations and performance of industrial enterprises to foreign researchers, particularly bilingual scholars, it is still very difficult to gather data using rigorous methodologies. Consequently, the researcher has to settle for empirical observations and personal interviews with Chinese managerial personnel and workers. This may prove disappointing from the viewpoint of the academician.

Second, China is a planned socialist economy. The state prescribes the overall policies and guidelines that industry should follow in the operation and management of its enterprises across different industries, both large and small. These policies ensure a certain degree of uniformity in the types of procedures used for organizing the productive forces within organizations.

Third, in striving toward the goals of the Four Modernizations, China is actively seeking to restructure its industrial enterprises and to learn modern management techniques from abroad to increase overall efficiency and effectiveness. The practices reported here represent the latest in vogue in the country, but they are subject to change. In industry, as well as in education, China introduces new techniques, practices, and procedures on an experimental basis among the leading factories and key schools. If these techniques prove effective, they will be implemented throughout the country. Thus, many of the practices presented here are innovations introduced on an experimental basis in the leading factories. Fourth, given space limitations here, the treatment of the various topics can be only superficial and does not purport to be comprehensive.

ECONOMIC SYSTEM

The year 1949 marked the end of the civil war in China and the establishment of the People's Republic. The same year also witnessed the beginning of the socialist reconstruction of the country—a colossal task that involved rebuilding it from the ruins of economic and technological stagnation, massive social disorientation, runaway inflation, and political chaos brought about by almost a century of imperialist exploitation, external wars, and internal strife.

The new government acted swiftly to embark on a series of national economic policies and plans that were known as the rehabilitation years (1949–52) and the first five-year plan (1953–57). Policies adopted during the rehabilitation years brought encouraging results. Within eighteen months of liberation, inflation was curbed. Prices of essential commodities, such as grain, salt, cooking oil, fuel, and cloth, were controlled. The first five-year plan marked the movement toward collectivization of both the urban and rural means of production. Control was established over private banking and businesses. By 1956 the nationalization of all private enterprises in the country was completed.

Central Planning

Because China is a planned socialist economy, all economic activities and undertakings are subject to a centrally developed and administered plan. Formerly, the state set production goals and targets for the enterprises, allocated resources and raw materials to them, laid down broad policies and guidelines to be followed in their operations and management, and distributed or marketed their output.

With 400,000 industrial enterprises operating in the economy and literally hundreds of thousands of products being manufactured, it has become virtually impossible for the state to devise a plan comprehensive enough to encompass all minute details and yet flexible enough to accommodate all contingencies. This practice has often led to the following problems: bottlenecks in operations; the production of certain commodities that had no immediate market; the production of desirable products in insufficient quantities; excessive delays in decisionmaking; and a spirit of unhealthy complacency among certain managers and workers in the industrial enterprises because state-owned enterprises were not treated as independent accounting units and hence not responsible for their own profit and loss. Until very recently, the concept of marketing was foreign to the Chinese industrial scene.

With the Four Modernizations effort, the government recognized the limitations inherent in the past economic structure and was determined to rectify the situation. Recent changes to the economic system include the following:

1. *Decentralization of authority to allow industrial enterprises greater autonomy with respect to decisionmaking, planning, and handling of financial matters.* A select group of enterprises were designated as experimental units. These were allowed the following rights: to retain a portion of the profit after the payment of taxes; to use their own funds to expand existing production facilities; to draw up subsidiary production plans after fulfilling the state plan; to market products manufactured by the factory that the state did not purchase; to export their products and to retain a portion of the foreign exchange thus earned. This foreign exchange could, in turn, be used for the import of foreign technology, equipment, and raw materials; to distribute bonuses at their own discretion, within the guidelines stipulated by the state; and to impose penalties on workers, factory directors, and party secretaries who through negligence incurred severe economic losses for the state. In Shanghai, the most advanced city in China, the stock market is making a comeback, albeit on a very limited scale.

2. *Simplification of the administrative organizations.* In the past, excessive administrative levels were necessary to some extent because

of the elaborate mechanisms by which the state assigned, allocated, and distributed all the means of production. With the granting of greater autonomy to the individual enterprise, many of these administrative organs could be eliminated and the number of cadres at all levels reduced.

3. *Use of economic means.* In the past, China relied primarily on administrative means to manage the country's economy. Since 1979, however, due emphasis was given to the law of value and the role of the market.

The law of value stipulates that commodities should be exchanged in proportion to their values. In the first thirty years of the PRC, because of Stalin's influence, the law of value was denounced as a capitalist principle and hence ignored. This meant that the principle of "gaining maximum economic results with a minimum expenditure of labor" was ignored. The present government, recognizing the limitations inherent in the former policy, stipulates that planning should be done in accordance with the law of value, which "requires an approximation of prices to values instead of a variance of the former from the latter" (Sun 1980: 157).

Closely allied with the law of value is the role of the market mechanism. Leading Chinese economists (Xue 1979; Sun 1980) whose opinions have influence in the new era of socialist modernization argue that the market mechanism is compatible with socialist planning, as exemplified by Yugoslavia. In this model, because the aim of production is to improve people's livelihoods, production targets are set according to consumer needs. The Yugoslav government permits limited competition, free trade between departments and enterprises, and floating of prices of nonessential commodities within a certain range.

Since 1979 "free" markets have been allowed to operate in the cities and villages. These are regulated and controlled by the government and are limited in scale. The government argues that the market mechanism will not replace central planning but will supplement the latter and play a subordinated role.

Besides the introduction of the law of value and the market mechanism, Xue Muqiao (1979) advocated the adoption of the following economic measures:

1. *Impose taxes to regulate the production of various categories of commodities.* Higher taxes could be levied in order to curb the production of certain less desirable commodities, whereas taxes could be waived on the production of desired commodities.

2. *Use price policy to regulate the production of certain categories of commodities.* Prices on desired commodities could be raised and prices on less desirable commodities lowered.
3. *Grant loans at reduced interest rates to those enterprises and industries that the government seeks to develop.*
4. *Give priority in the allocation of resources and raw materials to those industries and enterprises that the government seeks to develop.*

Besides these economic means, the state is actively promoting the use of the contract system between various sectors of the economy—for example, between suppliers and producers, between suppliers and distributors, among enterprises, and between the state and enterprises. Under the contract system, the terms and conditions of agreement are agreed on by both parties voluntarily. The use of such contracts allows each party to check on the performance of the other to ensure that the terms and conditions of the contract are being met and carried out.

Types of Ownership

Chinese industrial enterprises are of two main types: state-owned enterprises and collectively owned enterprises. State-owned enterprises represent "public ownership by the whole people . . . under which the state owns the means of production on behalf of the working people" (*Constitution of the PRC* 1978). State-owned enterprises constitute the backbone of the country's economy. Approximately 80 percent of the country's total industrial-output value comes from state-owned enterprises. Collectively owned enterprises represent "public-ownership under which the means of production are owned collectively by the working people in the enterprises and communes." Collectively owned enterprises supplement China's economy. Besides these two forms of ownership, the 1978 constitution authorized the development of the individual economy, provided that there is no exploitation of others and the activities engaged in are legal in nature. Since then individual operators have mushroomed throughout the country, primarily in the retail trade and service sectors.

In the past, state-owned enterprises were considered superior and hence were emphasized. The Chinese government now states that the superiority of an ownership system is not judged or measured by the extent of public ownership but in terms of economic results. The government contends that these three types of economy should be allowed to coexist because each plays a different role in the national economy and each supplements the others. For the development of large, modern industries, the establishment of state-owned enterprises may be most appropriate. In the countryside, however, collective ownership may be more appropriate. Also, collectively owned enterprises can be established with minimal capital investment and can provide an important source of employment for the huge Chinese population. In addition, because of their smaller size, such enterprises are usually more flexible. Consequently, they may be more adept at revamping their complete product lines within a relatively short period of time to meet changing market needs. Individual enterprises, on the other hand, can play an important role in the retail trade and service sectors, areas that were previously neglected in the national economy. All three forms of ownership are under the management of the industrial administration bureaus, which are part of the Ministry of Commerce.

The Four Modernizations

In August 1977 China embarked on the Four Modernizations program, which seeks development and progress in the fields of science and technology, industry, agriculture, and military defense. Through this effort, the country hopes to raise the per capita income of its people to $1,000 (U.S.) (from the 1977 level of $250) by the year 2000.

To attain the goals of the Four Modernizations, China's leaders are aware that it must enjoy relatively stable political conditions, both at home and abroad, and that the country must build its foreign exchange reserves through foreign trade and economic assistance from abroad in order to finance this mammoth program. To accomplish this goal, widespread reforms have been adopted in the political and economic arenas since 1978. Some of these changes have included resuming diplomatic relations with capitalist countries, permitting foreign firms to engage in joint-venture investments (including wholly owned subsidiaries in special cases) in China to develop the country's industries and natural resources, and engaging in technical and cultural exchanges with other countries. Many policies and practices that were denounced as capitalist and revisionist during the Cultural Revolution (1966–76) have now been reinstated, including the use of material incentives, such as bonuses, to spur production in both the agricultural and industrial sectors; encouragement of the establishment and development of collectively owned enterprises and of the individual economy as discussed previously; emphasis on technical expertise, innovation, and development through the reinstitution of entrance exams to universities and more rigorous curricula at both universities and technical colleges; and the use of expertness or technical competence as an important criterion for recruitment and promotion to managerial and technical positions.

Development of the Heavy Industrial, Light Industrial, and Agricultural Sectors

In establishing the base for China's heavy industrial sector, iron and steel were designated as key because they provide the raw materials for the development of other industries. Emphasis on the development of the iron and steel industries in the first twenty-nine years of the PRC's history accounts for the rapid growth of these industries. The output of steel expanded 218-fold and that of pig iron, 145-fold. This disproportionate allocation of resource resulted in an increase in the output value of the national economy, but there was no commensurate improvement in the people's standard of living. In 1978, the government recognized the fallacy of this policy and shifted emphasis to the development of textile and light industries and agriculture to correct past imbalances in the allocation of resources.

The reasons for this shift in emphasis to the textile and light industries are primarily threefold:

1. *To improve the overall standard of living of the people.* In the past, production was undertaken primarily for its own sake, largely ignoring consumer demand. There was an extreme shortage of consumer demands. This situation has changed. Since 1980 over 5,000 new commodities were added to the list of consumer goods, including washing machines, refrigerators, minibikes, and automatic calendar watches.
2. *To produce more goods for export in order to generate foreign exchange to purchase much needed equipment and technology and further the goals of the Four Modernizations.* Textile alone, for example, accounts for over 20 percent of the total value of China's exports.
3. *To invest in profitable industries.* Textile and light industries, although accounting for almost half of the total volume of retail trade, usually require less capital investment, yield higher profits, and are able to realize a quicker return on investments than other industries. Besides the textile and light industries, the emphasis has also been shifted to the development of the energy sector and improvement of the industrial infrastructure in the country, including port

development, construction of railways, and the building of the merchant-marine fleet to support the growth of the economy and to meet the demands of expanded foreign trade.

Because the emphasis here is on industrial society, reforms in the agricultural sector will be omitted. It should be noted, however, that approximately 80 percent of China's people still depend on agriculture as their principal means of livelihood and that there is a sevenfold difference in per capita income between the urban and rural populations, although the gap is narrowing because of the improvements made in the agricultural sector since the implementation of these reforms.

SOCIOPOLITICAL SYSTEM

In China, political considerations have a pervasive influence on all aspects of society. Political and economic considerations, for instance, are often inextricably intertwined. Consequently, in order to comprehend fully the complexities of Chinese industrial society, it is imperative to examine China's political system and the role played by the Chinese Communist Party (CCP) in influencing various aspects of Chinese society, including the operations and management of industrial enterprises.

The philosophy guiding the administration of China, as prescribed in the 1978 constitution, is primarily threefold: proletarian dictatorship, democratic centralism, and socialist democracy. Each of these principles is explained briefly.

Proletarian Dictatorship

Article 1 of the Constitution states: "The People's Republic of China is a socialist state of the dictatorship of the proletariat led by the working class and based on the alliance of workers and peasants." Dictatorship of the proletariat means that the working class will exercise leadership over the state through the CCP, the leading political party in the country. The National Congress, the highest organ in the party, is convened once every five years. When the Congress is not in session, the Central Committee serves as the highest authority in the party. Below the national level, the party congresses at the various levels are the leading political organs. Party branches and party committees are set up in factories, schools, neighborhoods, and detachments of the People's Liberation Army.

The leading organs in most enterprises consist of a Party Committee and a Working Committee. Each Party Committee is headed by a party secretary. The Working Committee is headed by the factory director and is made up of deputy directors and responsible technical and administrative cadres. In the past, the Working Committee was under the leadership of the Party Committee. Changes are now underway to separate the Party Committee from the administrative organization in an enterprise. It has been proposed that the Party Committee should engage in political and ideological work and should no longer assume administrative duties, whereas the Working Committee under the leadership of the factory director should be responsible for the operations and management of the enterprise. However, the party committee will continue to play a supervisory role to ensure that party policies and state laws are adhered to and that production targets set forth in the state plan are fulfilled.

Democratic Centralism

Article 3 of the Constitution states: "The National People's Congress, the local people's congresses at various levels and all other organs of state practice democratic centralism." Although encouraging democracy, China must ensure unity and enforce discipline among its 1 billion people. This dual policy of allowing democracy on the one hand, and centralizing authority, on the other, is referred to as the principle of democratic centralism. The party has prescribed the authority relationships that should prevail among the various elements of society: "the individual is subordinate to the organization; the minority is subordinate to the majority; the lower level is subordinate to the higher level; and the entire Party is subordinate to the Central Committee" (*Eleventh National Congress* 1977: 104).

Socialist Democracy

Article 17 stipulates: "The State adheres to the principle of socialist democracy, and ensures the people the right to participate in the management of state affairs and of all economic and cultural undertakings, and the right to supervise the organs of state and their personnel." All citizens other than those who have committed crimes against the state (such as murder, rape, other serious criminal offenses, or counterrevolutionary activities) are guaranteed certain fundamental rights.

In 1977 the country's leaders declared that the primary mission for the party, and for the country as a whole, for the last quarter of the twentieth century is no longer that of class struggle but rather socialist modernization. The country's leaders emphasize that although it is important to build a strong material base for economic development and progress, success in this area does not necessarily result in a spiritual civilization, which is also fundamental to human existence. China's leaders emphasize that the pursuit of a "socialist spiritual civilization" complements and will facilitate the early attainment of the goal of material civilization — the Four Modernizations. Building a spiritual civilization involves the communist ideal of subordinating one's self-interest to that of the state and the common good. This spirit is conducive to economic progress and development because the people will identify closely with state goals and thus will work wholeheartedly toward the attainment of the Four Modernizations. The key to building a spiritual civilization depends on ideological and political work. In early 1981 the Propaganda Department of the Central Committee, in conjunction with three ministries under the State Council, issued a decree calling on all the people in the country to support the movement of the "Five Stresses and the Four Points of Beauty." The five stresses call on the people to pay attention to socialist decorum, manners, hygiene, discipline, and morals. As of fall 1981 children of all primary schools must take a course in ideology and socialist decorum. The four points of beauty call for beautification of the mind, language, behavior, and the environment. Beautification of the mind means developing a strong moral character and upholding socialism and the party's leadership. Beautification of behavior means engaging in productive activities and assisting others. Beautification of the language means using decorous language and improving literary styles. Beautification of the environment refers to personal hygiene and protection of the physical environment.

THE LEGAL SYSTEM

Although China has shared with most other Southeast Asian countries a traditional distaste for law and legal concepts, the Chinese realize that law constitutes an important part of any modern society. The government has enacted laws governing various aspects of societal functioning, including criminal law, joint ventures with Chinese and foreign investment, wholly owned subsidiary law, patent law, individual income tax law, regulations on labor management in joint ventures, nationality law, marriage law, and so on. Laws pertaining to other aspects of operations of foreign corporations are being drafted.

Although it is impossible to go into all aspects of these different laws here, the following points should be kept in mind when examining the legal environment in China: (1) Chinese culture and tradition emphasizes mediation and reconciliation over litigation. This is exhibited in all aspects of societal functioning, whether it pertains to the resolution of disputes over business contracts or marital relationships. (2) China attempts to provide an environment conducive to foreign investment, which is essential to the success of the Four Modernizations effort. Although complaints among foreign investors remain, a short decade ago China would not even entertain the idea of foreign investment. The country's legal framework pertaining to the operations of foreign enterprise is yet in its infancy. (3) China espouses the principle of revolutionary humanitarism—that is, combining punishment of criminal offenders with leniency. Essentially, this means that the imposition of penalties is designed not to inflict punishment on the offender but to reform the individual through a combination of "punishment and public surveillance and ideological remoulding, and combining productive labor with political education" (Beijing Review 1980: 18). The government seeks to rehabilitate prisoners through ideological education. Every day each prisoner engages in two hours of study. Ideological education is conducted by the prison staff and may take the form of "patient talks," a method commonly used in China to help an individual reform. This literally means that a staff member sits down and talks to the individual for hours in a friendly manner, trying to help the person understand why he went wrong and how to make amends.

THE TECHNOLOGICAL SYSTEM

Because China is a technologically backward country, it is difficult to analyze its technological system in the same way that an advanced, industrialized nation would be analyzed. Rather, the discussion here will center on the Chinese attitude toward achievement and innovation and the country's educational policy. This will facilitate projection of the shape that China's technological system will take in the years ahead.

Attitude toward Achievement

In The Achieving Society McClelland (1961) hypothesized that there is a fairly high correlation between the achievement drive of different peoples and their respective countries' rate of growth. McClelland applied this hypothesis to several Southeast Asian countries, including the PRC, Taiwan, and India. From an analysis of Chinese children's readers, McClelland (1963) concluded that the need for achievement (nAch) in the PRC between 1950 and 1959 was significantly higher than that for pre-1949 China and for Taiwan between 1950 and 1959. The nAch score for China in the late 1920s was substantially below the world average, whereas the score in the 1950s had surpassed it. The nAch score for Taiwan in the 1950s was higher than that for the 1920s, although it was still below the world average.

Although it may be true that the communists are more concerned with raising the achievement level of the population, the low nAch score for China in the 1920s should not be interpreted to mean that the Chinese then were little concerned about achievement. The Chinese have always stressed achievement, as witnessed by the existence of the Civil Service Examination System in ancient China and the considerable success that Chinese who left the country before the 1920s achieved in other parts of the world. The reasons for China's low nAch score in the 1920s can be attributed in part to two factors: (1) In ancient China, those persons who had a high nAch drive were typically more concerned with political power than with economic growth and development. This is understandable because the merchant class occupied a low social status in ancient China. (2) There are methodological problems associated with the nAch score. Researchers (Atkinson and Feather 1966; Clarke 1973; Cofer and Appley 1965) have pointed to the problems inherent in the nAch score and in projective techniques in general.

Because the achievement motive is not alien to the Chinese mentality, what the communists had to do when they came to power was to harness the energy of the population toward economic activities by emphasizing that economic and technological development is essential to China's survival in the industrial world. In China's current drive to attain the goals of the Four Modernizations, one of which is development in the area of science and technology, the achievement drive is emphasized more than ever. The following are some of the policies the government has instituted to advance this goal:

1. The reinstitution of entrance examinations to college and universities, so that only the best and the brightest will be admitted;
2. The use of exams to determine a candidate's suitability for a job opening and for promotion to the level of engineer or technician;

3. The use of mass-scale education programs on the television and the institution of spare-time and factory-run colleges to provide alternative means of education to those who are not fortunate enough to gain admission to the universities;
4. The nomination of advanced workers, units, and factories to serve as models for emulation by the less productive ones;
5. The practice of awarding bonuses and certificates of merit to those who fulfill and overfulfill their production quotas;
6. The inclusion of the need to "study diligently" as one of the ten-point rules for primary- and middle-school students.

Attitude toward Innovation

Like their counterparts in the United States, Chinese workers are encouraged to innovate. A common slogan in the factories is "go all out for technical innovations and technical revolution." In fact, Article 12 of the 1978 Constitution stipulates: "The State devotes major efforts to developing science, expands scientific research, promotes technical innovation and technical revolution and adopts advanced techniques wherever possible in all departments of the national economy."

To further encourage innovation among the people, the government adopted the following two policies: (1) the granting of awards (including monetary rewards of 1,000, 2,000, and 5,000 and 10,000 yuan) for inventions and technical innovations, which become the property of the state and hence are provided to enterprises throughout the country; and (2) the encouragement of scientific and technical research projects in the research institutes associated with the enterprises, the Chinese Academy of Sciences, and the universities.

Educational Policy

China recognizes the need to upgrade its educational standards in order to attain the goals of the Four Modernizations. In fact, senior-ranking officials readily concede that education should be considered the fifth modernization.

Although much of the population is literate (70 percent of the rural population and a higher percentage for urban areas), the educational levels in the country are still low. Approximately 70 percent of the industrial workers are employed at the grade three level and below. Chinese industrial workers are classified into eight categories, with grade one being the least skilled. Only 3 percent of the industrial workers are qualified as skilled technicians or engineers. The government seeks to promote higher education in the country. However, given limited facilities, less than 4 percent of applicants to universities can gain admission. To rectify this situation, the government has introduced the following reforms:

1. *Enrollment of day students.* In the past all students lived in university dormitories. The enrollment of day students can reduce costs and living space requirements, thus permitting the admission of more students.
2. *Introduction of diverse methods of education.* The television university, correspondence schools, and night colleges have been established.
3. *Encouragement of private study.* In major cities, such as Beijing, any person, regardless of age and official educational level, will be granted a diploma and considered a college graduate if he or she passes the required examinations.
4. *Promotion of scholarly and scientific exchanges with foreign countries.*
5. *Upgrading of the technical and educational skills of cadres, workers, and staff members.* To attain this goal, all enterprises must establish a training program.

THE INFORMATION SYSTEM

In China, the information system is almost synonymous with the role of the press. There are some 382 newspapers in the country with a total circulation of 70 million copies. The most important newspaper and the one with the largest circulation is the *Renmin Ribao (People's Daily)*, which is published under the auspices of the Central Committee of the CCP. To ensure that the masses are knowledgeable about the content of the paper, it is posted on bulletin boards in public places throughout the country. In addition, editorial highlights are broadcast over the radio and television stations. With its large circulation, the *Renmin Ribao* serves as an important mechanism for keeping the masses informed of official party views on practically all aspects of societal functioning—political affairs, education, culture, art, and literature. For most of the population, this is the only source of information about domestic and international events.

As noted previously, the industrial infrastructure in the country is presently very underdeveloped. The government has assigned priority to the development and upgrading of the country's roads, railways, port facilities, and telecommunication networks.

THE CULTURAL MILIEU

It is impossible to describe all the rich cultural traditions that have shaped China over the millenia. Instead, the focus here is on analyzing China along the four cultural dimensions hypothesized by Hofstede. In analyzing each of these dimensions, it is important to bear in mind the following two points.

First, one can question the validity of Hofstede's findings among the Hong Kong and Taiwan samples of HERMES corporation. The questionnaire was administered in English in these two samples. Although the respondents were presumably fluent in English, research has shown that native and nonnative speakers of English can interpret the same message differently. Even among samples of native speakers of English, for example, Americans and British, similar words may carry quite different conotations between the two groups.

Second, the cultural milieu shaping the mentality and behavior of the mainland Chinese is a unique blend of socialism mixed with Confucianism. As an illustration of this, consider the brand of Marxism-Leninism espoused in China. When Mao Zedong and his party tried to convert China into a socialist state, they recognized that the political, economic, social, and cultural conditions in China were very different from those of the Soviet Union. Mao was acutely aware of such differences and of the futility of attempting to transplant Marxism-Leninism to China without first modifying and adapting it to suit the objective conditions. Although Mao wanted the Chinese to become modern people as quickly as possible, he did not want them to feel emotionally indebted to foreign sources of knowledge. In 1938 Mao asserted, "We must not cut off our whole historical past. We must make a summing up from Confucius to Sun Yat-sen and enter into this precious heritage" (Creel 1953: 18). In a society like that of China, which places heavy emphasis on tradition, the communist leaders were much too wary and intelligent to attempt to abandon Chinese cultural traditions altogether. A number of the principles espoused by Confucius seemed to blend in well with Marxist-Leninist orthodoxy. The long tradition of rule by a Confucian elite, for instance, undoubtedly makes it easier for the Chinese to accept as perfectly normal the continued dominance of the Communist elite. The teachings of Confucius—such as "hear more and see more," "learn a lot and ask questions," "review what you have learned in order to learn something new," and "study must go hand in hand with thinking"—appear to fit in well with China's current emphasis on the idea that "practice is the sole criterion for truth" and on the need to absorb positive experiences from different countries. Mao's major contribution to the development of Marxist theory lies in the fact that he combined the theory and practice of Marxism with concepts and patterns of behavior drawn from the Chinese past in such a fashion as to render it comprehensible and acceptable to the Chinese people. This "sinicization" of Marxism-Leninism to Chinese reality is generally referred to as Mao Zedong Thought, which China's present leaders explicitly stated is not the product of a single person. Rather, the term *Mao Zedong Thought* refers to the application and development of Marxism-Leninism in China to fit the country's objective conditions, in order to bring about socialist revolution and reconstruction in China.

The vast majority of Chinese on the mainland have been raised under this blend of Marxism-Leninism-Mao Zedong Thought. The average age in China is twenty-six, with approximately 65 percent of the population under thirty years of age. Given the very different socioeconomic and political systems of the PRC, Hong Kong, and Taiwan, it would be erroneous to generalize from the findings of Hong Kong and Taiwan to that of the PRC. Because no empirical study has been done on the PRC using Hofstede's conceptual framework, I can only hypothesize along these four dimensions.

Power Distance

Hofstede found that Hong Kong and Taiwan scored higher on the power distance index as compared to the United States. In the PRC, I would expect it to be substantially lower for several reasons: (1) China is deemed to be a classless society; (2) there is less disparity in income distribution among the masses (there is a mere tenfold difference in income between the highest and the lowest paid persons in the country); (3) the country encourages worker participation in management and management participation in physical labor (this is elaborated on subsequently); (4) in recent years, the CCP has criticized the special privileges enjoyed by some of its cadres, and reforms have been implemented to do away with such abuses of power.

Uncertainty Avoidance

Hofstede found that Hong Kong Chinese exhibited a low uncertainty avoidance, whereas Taiwan Chinese scored high along this dimension.

In the PRC, I would expect a low uncertainty avoidance for several reasons. First, political upheavals have plagued the country since its establishment in 1949. As such, the people have acquired a certain tolerance for such vicissitudes in life. Second, like many of its Asian counterparts, the Chinese possess a very long-term orientation toward planning. When projecting ten, twenty or even fifty years into the future, it is inevitable that ambiguities and uncertainties will abound. Third, since China is a centrally planned economy, its people know that the state will provide. Once hired, there is virtually no layoff of workers. This is referred to as the policy of the "iron rice bowl." The state pays a generous retirement benefit including funeral costs. Thus, much of the uncertainty about the future is eliminated.

Individualism

Both the Hong Kong and Taiwan samples scored low on Hofstede's individualism dimension. In China, I would expect a similar situation because of the following reasons. First, the tenets of socialism call for communal sharing. As noted earlier, the CCP preaches that the interests of the individual should be subjugated to that of the State. Second, Chinese culture emphasizes that one's identity is derived from the family or the village to which one belongs. Under communism, the concept of family was broadened to that of the nation state. Thus, individualism as stressed in the United States is alien to the Chinese mentality.

Masculinity

Both the Hong Kong and Taiwan samples scored high on Hofstede's masculinity dimension. In China, I see a mixed picture because it scores high on some of the masculinity norms and low on others. For example, people orientation is strong in the PRC. Until very recently, material possessions were frowned on. Furthermore, male domination is deemphasized in the PRC. Men and women enjoy the same pay for the same work. Women are elected or appointed to high-level positions in factories and ministries, although the number of women in senior administrative positions is fewer than that of men. This latter situation stems from the fact that prior to 1949 higher education for women was discouraged. Consequently, among the older generation, the sample from which most senior administrators are drawn from, there are comparatively fewer qualified women. Perhaps the most outstanding demonstration of this equality between the sexes is the fact that women now retain their maiden name after marriage and children (particulary the second born in the family) can adopt the mother's surname. The PRC scores low on these masculinity norms but high on others, such as the emphasis on work and achievement. Article 10 of the 1978 Constitution dictates that "he who does not work, neither shall he eat" and that "work is an honorable duty for every citizen able to work." All able-bodied persons in China have to work in order to earn their means of livelihood. As noted earlier, the achievement motive is emphasized in China.

THE BUSINESS AND MANAGEMENT SYSTEM

The structure of industry, the government/enterprise interface, and organizational structure within enterprises have been discussed in the previous sections. This section will focus on business and management practices unique to China.

Recruitment of Workers

Since 1956 China has adopted a system whereby the state labor department in the various towns and cities assume responsibility for the recruitment and placement of all workers and staff members in state-owned enterprises. This practice applies to the joint-venture concerns with foreign entities as well. Under this system, workers have the right to refuse a job assignment. However, this would mean that their names would once again be placed into the common pool of people applying for jobs, and it might be quite some time before another suitable opening came along. This, coupled with the fact that those "waiting for employment" (interpreted by many as a euphemism for unemployment) amounts to approximately 25 percent of the industrial workforce, means that, in practice, most people accept the jobs assigned to them by the state.

In 1979 the state introduced, on a trial basis, the method of recruiting workers in the various trades and professions through examination. Applicants were examined in general and specialized subjects to determine their suitability for the particular trade or industry for which they were applying. This ensured a better fit between the requirements of industry, on the one hand, and the interests and aspirations of the applicants, on the other. This policy is conducive to industrial growth because it ensures that workers employed in a particular enterprise would possess the minimal qualifications for performing the job satisfactorily.

Collectively owned enterprises and private operators are free to recruit their workers from neighboring communities and elsewhere.

Promotion to Managerial Level

In the past, managerial personnel were appointed or selected from among those workers who were considered both "red" (that is, politically sound) and "expert" (that is, technically competent). This was done through recommendation and discussion by fellow workers, Party Committee members, and managerial personnel in the enterprises concerned.

With the current emphasis on technical competence and leadership abilities as two important qualifications for managerial positions, reforms in the cadre system are conducted on an experimental basis throughout the country. Some of the reforms already introduced include the recruitment of managerial personnel through examinations, the election of cadres by secret ballots, the holding of opinion polls once every six months to check and appraise the performance of elected cadres, the demotion of cadres who are technically incompetent, and the provision of continuing education to cadres.

Training programs for cadres generally emphasize the development of business and management skills, which are recognized as weak links in the nation's economic work. Most of the advanced factories now sponsor lectures on special subjects, such as the role of the factory director, the duties of chief engineers and chief accountants, and computer technology. In addition, the China Enterprise Management Association (CEMA) was established in 1979 to further the goal of developing enterprise management. CEMA sponsors workshops, seminars, and vocational training for management personnel. In addition, exchange programs are established with foreign countries, such as the Euro–China Association of Management Development and Japan–China Association on Economy and Trade.

Role of Factory Director

The current attempts by the government to separate the Party Committee from the Working Committee were discussed earlier. The discussion here will focus on the relationships between the leader and the led. Although leadership abilities are now emphasized more than ever before, factory directors and cadres are reminded constantly that they should not alienate themselves from their subordinates. In many respects, the Chinese workers appear to be more powerful vis-à-vis their superiors as compared with their counterparts in the West. The workers are encouraged to be outspoken or critical of any situation in which they feel improvement ought to be made. The ideal management/labor relationship in a Chinese enterprise is one of peaceful cooperation. The aim is not for one party or group to dominate the other but for both parties to learn from each other and carry out the responsibilities and duties assigned to each.

Worker Participation in Management

The degree of worker participation in management affairs has oscillated with periods of thought reform. In the post-Mao era, the principal vehicle through which workers take part in management is the congress of workers and staff. All the advanced factories have established their own congresses of workers and staff, which are convened annually. At each congress, the factory's leading members give a report on their work over the past year, listen to criticisms and suggestions from the representatives, and adopt resolutions on various matters. At each congress, an inspection group is elected to check one implementation of the resolutions adopted once every three months. Representatives to the congress are elected directly by the workers and staff. All workers and staff have the right to vote and stand for election, provided they meet the following qualifications: (1) are politically and ideologically sound; (2) do well in production, fulfill assignments, and abide by rules and regulations; (3) have close ties with the workers; and (4) are good at collecting the workers' opinions and relaying fully the spirit of the resolutions adopted. The representation to the congress of workers and staff at one of the advanced factories was as follows: 66 percent of the representatives were workers; 26 percent were cadres; and 8 percent technicians. This representation appears to be characteristic of most enterprises that have established a congress of workers and staff. When the congress is not in session, the representatives are divided into several groups on the basis of workshops, sections, or offices. Each group elects one member to the inspection group of the congress. This group checks on the implementation of the resolutions adopted by the congress every quarter; reports to the Party Committee, the cadres, or the workers and staff respectively on problems it has discovered; criticizes those who have not met their quotas; and recommends ways and means of solving outstanding problems. The trade union attached to each enterprise is a working body of the congress and directs the work of the inspection group.

In addition to the congress of workers and staff members, the party requires that Party Committee members, the factory director, and the deputy directors go among the workers as frequently as possible to keep themselves abreast of actual conditions on the shop floor. Meetings between leading cadres and workers are scheduled regularly, so that any problem encountered in production can be brought up for discussion before the Party Committee and the Working Committee. When important matters need to be decided on, the workers' opinions are solicited so that their views can be heard and their concerns taken into consideration. In all workshops, work shifts, and work groups, there are workers in charge of equipment, safety devices, sanitation, materials, recording attendance, checking and testing products. In addition, workers sit on other administrative and technical committees of the enterprise.

Trade Unions

The All-China Federation of Trade Unions, which is the leading body of trade unions across the country, was established in May 1952. Except for the years 1967 to 1978, when they were forced to suspend their activities, the trade unions have played an important role in Chinese society.

Chinese trade unions are mass organizations of the working class, formed on a voluntary basis under the leadership of the CCP. Trade unions are organized according to trade and geographical locations. Each and every factory, school, and hospital has a union.

Although the Constitution provides for the right to strike, strikes and walkouts are very rare because enterprises are either state owned or collectively owned. In the trade unions the spirit of cooperation between workers and management is emphasized. This notion is rather foreign to the Western world, where the trade union is basically looked on by the workers as a citadel from which they can bargain with management from a position of strength.

The activities performed by the trade unions in China are primarily fourfold:

1. They serve as a link between the Party and the worker. On the one hand, the trade unions frequently transmit the workers' opinions and needs to the party to provide a basis for the latter to formulate or readjust its principles and policies. On the other hand, the trade unions educate the workers to understand and properly implement the party's policies.

2. They serve as a communist school. The trade unions conduct ideological, cultural, and technical education programs among the workers. They run spare-time schools, cultural palaces, and recreational halls, launch socialist emulation campaigns, and draw workers into enterprise management.
3. They serve as the pillar of state power. Trade unions organize workers to fulfill the state production plans, educate them to observe the Constitution, laws, and policies of the state, and recommend outstanding workers to leading posts at various levels of the party.
4. They promote the welfare of the workers. In addition to organizing schools and recreational halls, trade unions also run workers' sanatoriums and help workers to solve problems—for example, by building houses with funds provided by factories and by rehabilitating workers that have committed mistakes in the past.

In short, the function of the trade union is primarily to promote cooperation between labor and management, foster enthusiasm for work, and boost morale among the workers.

Motivational Devices

Katz and Kahn (1978) in *The Social Psychology of Organizations* identify three basic types of motivational pattern: (1) rule enforcement, wherein organization members accept role prescriptions and organizational directives because of their legitimacy; (2) external rewards, wherein incentives tied to desired behaviors/outcomes are instrumental in achieving specific rewards; and (3) internalized motivation, wherein organizational goals are internalized and become part of the individual's own value system.

The motivational devices used in Chinese industrial enterprises can be analyzed according to these three basic motivational patterns. Each of them is discussed briefly below.

Rule Enforcement. As compared to their Western counterparts, Chinese industrial personnel (both managers and workers) are given very exact and detailed prescriptions of what is expected of them as members of a factory, workshop, or work unit. China is a planned socialist economy. Besides setting production targets, allocating raw materials, marketing, and purchasing for the enterprises, the state also prescribes the overall policies and guidelines that industries should follow in its enterprises.

The principles, policies, and guidelines adhered to in the current operation of Chinese industrial enterprises include the thirty-point Decision on Industry and the Plan on Readjustment, Restructuring, Consolidation, and Improvement of China's economy.

1. The main policy guidelines under the thirty-point Decision include the system of division of labor and the undertaking of responsibility by the factory directors under the supervision of the Party Committee; the reorganization of industry in accordance with the principles of specialization and coordination; the application of the principle of "from each according to his ability, to each according to his work"; the improvement of workers' and staff members' welfare; and the enforcement of strict discipline.

2. Under the plan for readjustment, conscientious efforts are made to bring about relatively good coordination in the development of agriculture and light and heavy industries and to maintain a proper ratio between consumption and accumulation.

3. Under restructuring, the earnings of an enterprise and the income of its workers will be commensurate with their contributions to the state. Absolute egalitarianism should be eliminated because it tends to breed complacency among workers. In addition, overlapping and inefficient administrative organs will be eliminated, and greater powers will be granted to the local authorities in planning, capital construction, finance, materials, and foreign trade.

4. The principle of consolidation calls for the establishment of a system of clearly defined responsibility for everyone in the enterprise; the establishment of a system of specialization of labor and coordination of economic activities across different enterprises to achieve greater economies of scale in production; consolidation of badly managed enterprises through reorganization and mergers; and establishment of rules and regulations to govern all aspects of factory operations and to ensure the strict implementation of these rules and regulations. In all the factories and enterprises that I visited, rules and regulations to be followed in the operation of machinery and equipment, and in the process of production, were displayed on large charts in very prominent places throughout the factory so that there was little question in the worker's mind as to how things ought to be done.

5. The principle of improvement calls for upgrading the existing levels of production, technology, and management. Practices recommended in this regard include the organization of socialist labor

emulation drives, which are discussed subsequently; the raising of vocational skills of cadres and workers through education; the learning of science, technology, and management techniques from foreign countries; and the development of foreign trade to generate sufficient funds for importing foreign technology and equipment.

External Rewards. The Constitution prescribes two types of incentives to motivate workers to heighten their performance. The state "applies the policy of combining moral encouragement with material reward, with the stress on the former." China's leaders, both past and present, have emphasized the superiority of nonmaterial incentives. However, they realize that man's desire for material gains and the promotion of self-interest could not be eliminated at once.

The principal forms of material incentives used are wages, subsidies, and bonuses. China's wage policy is governed by two basic principles: It is opposed to wide wage spread, but it also is opposed to absolute egalitarianism. In state-owned enterprises, the wages of workers are governed by the eight-grade wage system, differentiated according to variations in skill. Wages are fairly uniform across enterprises in different types of industry and across different parts of the country.

The current system dictates that bonuses should not exceed two months of the workers' annual wage and that they should be tied to individual performance. In addition to wages and bonuses, the workers are provided generous benefits for sickness, injury, disability, maternity, retirement, and death.

Internalized Motivation. In China, internalized motivation is almost synonymous with moral encouragement. Moral encouragement involves the principle of "fight self" — that is, the individual must seek to emulate the ideal communist man, one who is prepared to sacrifice his own self-interest for the general welfare and progress of all others and of the state. It also involves the application of the principle of "from each according to his ability," whereby every worker should do his or her very best, regardless of wage. The principal means of moral encouragement used are socialist labor emulation drives, commendations as pace-setters, and political indoctrination.

1. *Socialist emulation drive.* In China, certain factories, work units, and individuals periodically are designated as advanced factories, units, or workers. These serve as models that other factories, work units, and workers should seek to emulate, learn from, and catch

up with. Socialist emulation drives are designed to serve two major purposes: (a) to develop friendly competition between factories, workshops, and individuals so that they will surpass past performance records and set new highs; and (b) to help the less advanced units and workers to catch up with the work of the more advanced. The latter notion is foreign to U.S. enterprises. In China, the most productive unit or person is not supposed to develop an "I am better than thou" attitude and remain aloof from less productive units and workers. Rather, the aim of such campaigns in China is to develop a spirit of cooperation to enable the more advanced units and individuals to help the less productive ones improve on their past performance. In enterprises throughout the country, one comes across colorful charts drawn on blackboards or huge posters, complete with statistics, indicating the targets set for and the results attained in the emulation campaigns between workshops, groups, or individuals. Little red flags, cut out of paper, are pinned next to the winner's name. The practice of publicizing the productivity rates of each worker generates a lot of peer pressure among the less productive workers to improve performance.

2. *Commendations as pace-setters at national meetings.* The outstanding achievements of certain advanced workers and work units are publicized nationally via radio, television, and newspapers so that workers and units from other parts of the country can seek to emulate, learn from, and catch up with these advanced units and individuals. In addition, there are national conventions where the most illustrious workers are praised and commended by leading party officials as pace-setters.

3. *Political indoctrination.* China's leaders recognize that material incentives and moral encouragement by themselves may not work unless they are accompanied by effective political indoctrination. At each factory, the Party Committee and the trade union organize weekly political discussion sessions for the workers. At present, workers at most factories are discussing and studying how they can make their own contributions toward realizing the goals of the Four Modernizations. As noted previously, the emphasis is not only on material progress but also on building a "socialist spiritual civilization." Constant political work enhances the workers' consciousness of their historical mission, heightens their sense of responsibility as masters of the country, and fosters within them the spirit of working selflessly.

The material incentives in vogue in Chinese enterprises are essentially similar to those in capitalist economies—that is, in return for their contribution to the organization's goals, the employees earn the means of livelihood. The nonmaterial incentives used in China are somewhat foreign to the Western mentality. Because many observers of the Chinese industrial scene are amazed to see how nonmaterial incentives can serve as a motivating device, I would like to postulate some reasons or factors that contribute to the relative success of moral encouragement in Chinese industrial society. First, in accordance with Maslow's theory of the hierarchy of human needs, once the basic physiological needs of the worker have been satisfied, he or she seeks to satisfy higher needs. In China, the basic physiological needs of all workers are taken care of by the state—social insurance benefits for workers cover sickness, retirement, disability, death, and so forth. Consequently, the workers aspire to fulfill their higher-level needs. Of course, it can be argued that the living standard of the Chinese worker is still far below that of his or her Western counterpart. Nevertheless, the second and third reasons for success, outlined below, coupled with the fact that the workers' lot has improved substantially (as compared to pre-1949 China) should be taken into consideration in evaluating the needs of a Chinese worker.

Second, although the amount of consumer goods available to the Chinese has increased over the past two years, they are still very limited compared to Western standards. Even though the Chinese are currently willing to spend more on clothing and other so-called luxury items, they are still very cautious about such purchases lest they be criticized by their colleagues. In China, if an individual flaunts his wealth, he can easily fall victim to the following situations: "red-eye disease" (that is, jealousy by one's neighbors) or "white-eye disease" (that is, ostracization by one's neighbors). In China, criticism by one's peers, subordinates, and superiors exerts considerable pressure on an individual to conform.

Third, the CCP carries out very effective indoctrination and mass education campaigns to ensure that the people will conform to the party's policies and guidelines.

Reprimands

Chinese enterprises use two primary means for dealing with individuals who have deviated from the work and performance standards prescribed by the state and the enterprise. One is through patient talks, criticisms, and political indoctrination. The other involves more drastic measures, such as economic sanctions, demotion, or dismissal from the job altogether. Each of them is discussed briefly below.

1. *Patient talks, criticisms, political indoctrination.* At the quarterly meetings of the congress of workers and staff, the representatives report on the implementation of resolutions passed at the congress and on the work performed by the cadres and workers. Those who have performed well are commended, and those who have erred are criticized. The purpose of such criticism is not to tarnish a person's reputation or to breed ill-feelings among fellow workers but merely to help those who have erred to see what is wrong, what needs to be done, and how they can change for the better. This technique of criticism is similar to the T-group sessions in the West. Criticism is often combined with patient talks and political indoctrination.

2. *Demotion, dismissal, and imposition of economic sanctions.* Cadres who do not perform up to standard are demoted. Economic sanctions are imposed on those who fail to fulfill their quotas. Dismissal is seldom used at present because most enterprises still adhere to the "iron rice bowl" practice or system of lifetime employment. The government is trying to eliminate this deeply engrained system because it tends to breed complacency among some workers.

CONCLUSION AND DISCUSSION

This chapter has provided a brief overview of Chinese business and management practices and how these are influenced by the broad societal-environment variables. As noted earlier, the Chinese are anxious to learn new management techniques from abroad in order to improve the overall efficiency of their enterprises. Consequently, in the years ahead, new practices and procedures will be adopted. However, it would be erroneous to assume that China will transplant Western management techniques in their entirety and apply them indiscriminately to Chinese factories. Even in espousing the socialist principles of Marxism-Leninism, the Chinese did a sort of preliminary screening and "sinicized" Marxism-Leninism somewhat in its eastward movement before its principles were implemented. China's leaders are aware of the tremendous differences, both cultural and economic, that exist between socialist China and the Western capitalistic nations. They have emphasized that China should adopt only those practices and procedures that are suited to the peculiar conditions of the country.

Throughout the course of history, the Chinese have proven themselves to be a very pragmatic people with an uncanny instinct for survival, who are ready and willing to change and follow the times. This attribute, above all else, may account for the fact that the country has been able to survive for thousands of years despite all the civil wars that took place within the country between the changing imperial dynasties; foreign domination by the Monguls during the Yuan dynasty and during the Ching dynasty by the alien Manchus; and a semicolonial status for almost a century-and-a-half under the Western imperialist powers. The Chinese have proved that they were able to "rise from the ashes" and rebuild the country. After the latest debacle of the Cultural Revolution (1966–76), which brought the country to the verge of political, economic, and social collapse—a plight that ended a little less than a decade ago—the country has recovered sufficiently to display rising productivity in various sectors of the economy. It is this Chinese ability to survive in the face of tremendous adversity and, more remarkable yet, to recover from these havocs and disasters, that has intrigued and fascinated Western observers for so long. Many of these fine qualities and attributes are kept alive today in the organization and running of Chinese industrial enterprises. They make for interesting study on the part of researchers who are interested in the principles of organizational theory and behavior. When the Chinese indicate a desire to learn advanced management techniques from the West, they are chiefly interested in things like cost accounting, quality control, cost/benefit analytic techniques, forecasting, how to accommodate the role of market factors in the drafting of production and purchasing plans, and how to raise worker productivity. It does not mean an abandonment of the principles and practices that have served the country well over the past decades.

Although many of the principles and techniques currently in vogue in China may not be applicable to the United States, given the tremendous cultural, political, and economic differences between them, nevertheless it would benefit both practitioners and academicians to be aware of the differences and similarities. Such information would be particularly useful to practitioners who have business dealings with the Chinese and who are engaged or will be engaging in joint ventures with the Chinese for manufacturing and processing in the country. It is imperative for these practitioners to be aware of the country's organizational practices and principles if they expect to reap the full benefits of such business relationships.

Knowledge of the similarities and differences in various aspects of organizational functioning and processes, such as leader–member relations and motivational practices in the two countries, could help theorists and researchers in comparative management, organizational theory, and organizational behavior to understand better how broad environmental variables, such as ideology and socioeconomic variables, can influence the functioning of organizations and their effectiveness. Comparisons of similarities and differences would enable researchers to have a better comprehension of the antecedents and outcomes of certain organizational practices or variables, and the dynamics of the relationships between various organizational variables. Such knowledge could prove invaluable in the development of principles of organizational theory and organizational behavior and could contribute to the development of better frameworks or models of comparative management, which is very important to the advancement of theory and knowledge in international business.

REFERENCES

Atkinson, F.W., and N.T. Feather, eds. 1966. *A Theory of Achievement Motivation*. New York: Wiley.

Beijing Review. 1980. June 9, p. 18.

Clarke, D.E. 1973. "Measures of Achievement and Affiliation Motivation." *Review of Educational Research* 43: 41–52.

Cofer, C.N., and M.N. Appley. 1965. *Motivation: Theory and Research*. New York: Wiley.

Constitution of the People's Republic of China. 1978. Beijing: Foreign Languages Press.

Creel, H.G. 1953. *Chinese Thought*. New York: Mentor.

Duncan, R.B. 1972. "Characteristics of Organizational Environments and Perceived Environmental Uncertainty." *Administrative Science Quarterly* 17: 313–27.

Eleventh National Congress of the CCP (Documents). 1977. Beijing: Foreign Languages Press.

Katz, D., and R.L. Kahn. 1978. *The Social Psychology of Organizations*. 2d ed. New York: Wiley.

Lawrence, P.R., and J.W. Lorsch. 1967. *Organization and Environment: Managing Differentiation and Integration*. Homewood, Ill.: Irwin.

McClelland, D.C. 1961. *The Achieving Society*. Princeton, N.J.: Van Nostrand.

———. 1963. "Motivational Patterns in Southeast Asia with Special Reference to the Chinese Case." *Journal of Social Issues* 19: 6–19.

Sun, Y. 1980. "What Is the Origin of the Law of Value?" *Social Sciences in China* 3: 155–71.

Thompson, J.D. 1967. *Organizations in Action*. New York: McGraw-Hill.

Tung, R.L. 1979. "Dimensions of Organizational Environments: An Exploratory Study of Their Impact on Organizational Structure." *Academy of Management Journal* 22: 672–93.

Xue, M. 1979. *A Study on the Problems of China's Socialist Economy.* Beijing: People's Press.

CHAPTER 6

Africa

Moses N. Kiggundu

This chapter is about management in Africa and the context within which it takes place. It uses the open systems framework (discussed in Chapter 1), which views organizations as open systems continually interacting with the environment and exchanging inputs and outputs with that environment in a process of mutual adjustment.

Throughout history, very little of Africa was known to the outside world. To the Greeks, it was the land of the unknown. The Arabs and the different waves of Europeans who came to Africa were interested only in its conquest and the development of an asymmetrical dependent and extractive relationship whose effects still characterize most of Africa. Even today, Africa remains the "dark continent" to most outsiders as well as some living on the continent. To the outsiders, Africa either conjures romantic images as depicted in films like *Out of Africa* or depressing thoughts of starvation, hunger, violence, and death. Both of these are gross simplifications of the African reality.

In Africa, as elsewhere in developing countries, society and the environment pervade organization and management (Faucheux, Amado, and Laurent, 1982). Therefore, it is necessary to understand Africa, its geography, peoples, and relationships between itself and the rest of the world in order to understand the unique character of this vast land and its diverse people, and the management challenges and prospects that it poses.

It should be noted at the outset that Africa is not a unified region but is characterized by diversity, contrast, and contradiction. It is a large continent almost three and a half times the size of the United States. To the north lies the sandy, hot, and hostile Sahara Desert, which throughout the ages helped to isolate the rest of Africa from the early centers of civilization in Europe and Asia. The western and central parts are covered with thick tropical forests, hard to penetrate, and teeming with tropical disease carriers. To the east and south one finds mountain ranges and rift valleys that make surface transportation difficult and expensive. Between the desert and forests are the vast savanna areas or grasslands, not unlike the prairies of the Midwest but still home to millions of wild animals instead of mechanized farms. The continent has some of the biggest lakes and rivers in the world, which are not easily navigable due to falls and rapids, but offer a tremendous potential for hydroelectric power generation.

The people of Africa are of diverse and differing cultures both among themselves and with outsiders. There are significant differences in the basic defining elements of culture including language, religion, values and attitudes, laws, education, politics, technology and material culture, and social organization (Gladwin and Terpstra 1978; Ronen 1986). One would expect to find differences across Africa in how the people understand the world around them, define their purpose for being, make moral judgments of right or wrong, communicate with one another, and are willing to integrate foreign ideas and cultural practices with traditional practices. For example, in Cameroon, French, English, and twenty-four African languages are spoken. Nigeria has about 250 African languages and dialects, and, in addition, the population is divided among the Moslems, Catholics, protestants, and animists.

It is necessary to keep this introductory background information in mind for several reasons. First, it provides the context within which the management process in Africa takes place. No serious study or organizational intervention can be undertaken without regard to this context. Although separate studies of the geography, history, cultural anthropology, sociology, and political science of Africa can be found, however, very few of these are directly related to problems of organization and management. Second, caution must be exercised in making generalizations about Africa. Empirical findings or prescriptive statements developed for one setting do not necessarily generalize to others on the same continent. Third, Africa is still made up of traditional societies intimately connected to nature and the land. Consequently, the social, economic, and political organizations must be managed in accordance with the dictates of tradition and the relationships between the people and the laws of nature.

THE AFRICAN CULTURAL MILIEU

The African continent is so rich in its cultural practices and diversity that even today, despite several hundred years of continuing powerful outside cultural influences, the African cultural milieu remains distinctive. Space does not allow for a discussion of the continent's cultural richness and diversity—values, beliefs, languages, religions, gods, art, music, dance, customs—and their likely effect on the context and process of organization and management in Africa. Instead, consistent with other chapters, we will use Hofstede's (1980) model of cultural dimensions to discuss the African cultural milieu and its consequences at the workplace.

In the 1970s Hofstede studied workers and managers of a large U.S. multinational corporation, collecting data first from forty countries and later increasing this to sixty countries. When he analyzed the results of his work, he found that certain countries clustered along specific cultural dimensions and that these dimensions could not be explained by other factors (such as job level, country's level of economic development, and so forth), except for the cultural attributes. Hofstede came up with four cultural dimensions, which are discussed below.

Individualism/Collectivism

This is the extent to which members of a cultural group define themselves either as individuals or as members of a collectivity. Those who score high on individualism would subscribe to the notion of a nuclear family, as the British or Americans tend to do. Those who score high on collectivism, however, would define themselves as being part of an ingroup or an outgroup, and they would expect (and be expected to) give support, favors, assistance, or help to other members of the ingroup and to receive help from others as well.

One would expect most African cultural groups to score high on collectivism because of the prevalence of the extended family social fabric that characterizes most societies in Africa. A number of factors, however, would moderate these scores. The rural/urban dichotomy, so distinctive in Africa, could lead to differences such that rural dwellers score higher on collectivism than their urban brothers and sisters. Likewise, one could find differences between lower-level employees and higher officials who would normally be more educated and more exposed to alien Western ideas of self. These intracountry and intraorganizational differences could well complicate the management process in Africa.

Power Distance

This is the extent to which less powerful members of society accept the unequal distribution of power and subscribe to the view that the "boss knows best." High power distance means acceptance of unequal distribution of power, and Hofstede found the Philippines, Mexico, and India to score high on this dimension. Once again, one would expect most African cultural groups to score high on power distance, suggesting a big social distance between superior and subordinates. Hofstede also suggests that societies with a large power distance believe that "the way to change a social system is to dethrone those in power" (1980: 46). This may explain the high frequency of violent changes in leadership in form of coup d'états, which today characterize Africa more than any other continent. It also may explain why senior managers are reluctant to delegate downward or engage in participative forms of management and why efforts at decentralization or devolution of power have been largely unsuccessful (Kiggundu, in press).

Uncertainty Avoidance

This is the extent to which people in a society feel threatened by unclear, ambiguous situations and the tendency for them to avoid such situations. Within the organizational context this is displayed when individuals seek greater career stability, and formal rules and avoid taking risks. Hofstede found Japan, Portugal, and Greece to score high on uncertainty avoidance. Likewise, one would expect most African cultural groups to score high on this dimension, suggesting the need to seek absolute truth, higher levels of aggressiveness, and a strong inner urge to work hard.

Masculinity/Femininity

This is the extent to which the dominant values in society emphasize assertiveness and the acquisition of material wealth. Femininity, on the other hand, would emphasize relationships among people, concern for others, and overall quality of life. Japan and Austria score high on masculinity, according to Hofstede (1980), and Denmark and Sweden score high on femininity. I suspect that most African countries would score closer to Sweden and Denmark than to Japan or Austria.

In summary, we hypothesize that most African countries would be associated with high collectivism, high power distance, high uncertainty avoidance, and high femininity. These speculative results seem to be consistent with Hofstede's findings that there is a tendency for large power distance to be associated with collectivism and that collectivism is associated with poor countries in terms of wealth.

It should be pointed out that Hofstede's sample did not include any African country except South Africa. There is, therefore, no empirical evidence to suggest that those four dimensions are relevant or comprehensive enough to capture the essence of the African cultural milieu. Research is needed to address this and other findings by Hofstede. Until then, the above discussion must be understood as being only speculative.

THE SOCIOPOLITICAL CONTEXT

This section discusses various aspects of the sociopolitical context of management in Africa. These are discussed under the following six categories: (1) the legal framework; (2) the trends in social developments; (3) business/government relations; (4) interorganizational relations; (5) political/economic groups; and (6) the role of trade unions. Each of these contributes to the enactment of the general and specific task environment that African managers, both in the public and private sectors, must deal with in the performance of their operational and strategic tasks.

The African Legal Framework

In sub-Saharan Africa, European legal institutions and concepts have been superimposed on the native, traditional, indigenous legal structures. This has resulted in dualistic and at times multiplistic legal systems dominated by the European codified or written laws on the one hand, and the indigenous or customary laws on the other. Although customary law has suffered from the effect of Europeanization, it is still very strong because the courts are required "to observe and enforce every applicable Customary Law which is neither repugnant to natural justice, equity and good conscience nor incompatible either directly or by implication with any law for the time in force" (Elias 1972: 27–28). Therefore, both customary law and European legal concepts define the context and drive the process of modern management in Africa.

It should be pointed out that like European law, customary law is not a unitary concept but a collectivity of many customary legal systems that vary across social structures such as the family, clan, and tribe. Confronted with the pressures for modernization and social change, customary law is continually adapting to changing circumstances, is becoming more and more contemporary and organic, and although "oral" by origin, is becoming increasingly written and codified as precedents are established in modern courts of law. Because African national borders cut across indigenous social institutions, certain customary laws cut across national borders.

In most African states, European law forms the most dominant source of the modern legal framework because it is written and because it provides consistency with other modern institutions. Most Africans, however, look to customary law to organize their private and public affairs, especially because European laws are written in European languages that only a small minority among the Africans can read and understand. Since independence African states have, to the extent possible, revised the European laws to reflect the African reality. For example, shortly after independence the Nigerian military government passed the Companies Decree of 1968, which repealed the English Companies Act of 1922. Other states have followed suit, and although the changes are not fundamental, they reflect the desire, if not the reality, to develop a truly African legal framework.

How does a dualistic "half-caste" legal system affect the context and process of management? Three illustrations show how such a legal system affects business transactions and management. In the area of land ownership, there is a dual system of land tenure that makes it difficult for peasant farmers who occupy (possession) but do not necessarily own the land to use it as collateral for bank loans. At the same time, the land owners cannot sell the land without regard to the interests of the occupants. This complicates the assessment of land as a commercial asset.

In the area of contract law, both customary and European law are relevant. Customary law tends to be rather vague in certain aspects of the execution of contracts. Therefore, European law tends to dominate in matters of contract law with only minor local modifications. Practical problems, however, arise when one of the parties to the contract makes assumptions about the implied aspects of the contract based on customary law, while the other, often a foreigner, makes the opposite assumptions based on European tradition and legal concepts. Under these circumstances, it can be demonstrated that there was "no meeting of the minds" of the two contracting parties and therefore no binding contract. This can cause delays, frustration, mistrust, and financial loss in the execution or discharge of commercial or business contracts.

A third and final illustration is in the area of foreign ownership. Most African states have explicit laws and administrative procedures governing the terms and conditions under which foreigners—both individuals and corporations—can own property and conduct business. The problem is that there are several sources of legal authority and therefore these laws can change almost overnight without warning. This has been done in many African countries including Tanzania where in 1967 under the Arusha Declaration foreign ownership was abolished, in Uganda where in May 1970 the Nakivubo Pronouncements nationalized eighty of the leading foreign firms, and in Zambia where as Amoo (1984) has shown expropriation laws have significantly affected private ownership of land.

This brief description of the African legal framework illustrates several points of importance to the context and process of organization and management. First, the African legal system is characterized by a multiplicity of different and at times conflicting sources of law. Second, the two dominant legal sources of influence, customary laws, and European laws are both in a state of flux because both are being modified to suit the every changing African reality. Under these circumstances, the African manager must constantly watch for new legal developments and determine the extent to which they have the potential to affect the context and process of management of a particular organization.

Trends in Social Developments

Although most of Africa has made remarkable improvements in the relatively short period of twenty-five years since independence, it still lags behind other developing regions. Table 6–1 gives trends of various social development indicators for selected sub-Saharan African (SSA) countries. It also gives comparable figures for the weighted averages for the low-income and middle-income economies including those outside Africa. Figures for Canada and the United States are also provided for comparison with two high-income countries.

As Table 6–1 shows, life expectancy in Africa is still low. For sub-Saharan African low- and middle-income countries, the average life expectancy is eleven years lower than the respective averages for the same

Table 6–1. Africa: Indicators of Social Development.

	Life Expectancy at Birth (years) 1983	Average Annual Growth of Population (%)		Percentage of Married Women of Childbearing Age Using Contraceptives 1982	Percentage of Labor Force in:					
					Agriculture		Industry		Service	
		1973–83	1980–2000e		1965	1981	1965	1981	1965	1981
Low Income Economies	59	2.0W	1.8W	—	77W	73W	9W	13W	14W	15W
SSA	48	2.8W	3.0W	—	84W	78W	7W	10W	9W	13W
Ethiopia	43	2.7	2.6	2	86	80	6	7	8	13
Mali	45	2.5	2.5	1	93	73	4	12	3	15
Zaire	51	2.5	3.1	3	81	75	10	13	9	12
Malawi	44	3.0	3.1	1	91	86	4	5	5	9
Uganda	49	2.8	3.3	1	88	83	5	6	7	11
Burundi	47	2.2	2.9	1	89	84	4	5	7	11
Niger	45	3.0	3.2	1	94	91	1	3	5	6
Tanzania	51	3.3	3.4	1	88	83	4	6	8	11
Somalia	45	2.8	3.0	1	87	82	5	8	8	10
Rwanda	47	3.4	3.4	1	94	91	1	2	5	7
Central African Republic	48	2.3	2.7	—	93	88	3	4	4	8
Togo	49	2.6	3.2	—	81	67	10	15	9	18
Benin	48	2.8	3.1	18	52	46	10	16	38	38
Guinea	37	2.0	2.1	1	87	82	7	11	6	7
Ghana	59	3.1	3.5	10	61	53	16	20	23	27

Madagascar	49	2.6	3.1	—	92	87	3	4	5	9
Sierra Leone	38	2.1	2.3	4	75	65	14	19	11	16
Kenya	57	4.0	3.9	8	84	78	6	10	10	12
Sudan	48	3.2	2.8	5	84	78	7	10	9	12
Chad	43	2.1	2.4	1	93	85	3	7	4	8
Mozambique	46	2.6	2.9	1	77	66	10	18	13	16
Middle Income Economies	61	2.4W	2.2W	—	57W	44W	16W	22W	27W	35W
SSA	50	2.9W	2.1W	—	70W	60W	11W	16W	19W	24W
Senegal	46	2.8	2.9	4	82	77	6	10	12	13
Lesotho	53	2.5	2.6	5	92	60	3	15	5	25
Liberia	49	3.3	3.1	—	78	70	11	14	11	16
Mauritania	46	2.2	2.6	1	90	69	4	8	6	23
Zambia	51	3.2	3.3	1	76	67	8	11	16	22
Ivory Coast	52	4.6	3.6	3	87	79	3	4	10	17
Zimbabwe	56	3.2	3.6	22	67	60	12	15	21	25
Nigeria	49	2.7	3.3	6	67	54	12	19	21	27
Cameroon	54	3.1	3.2	11	86	83	6	7	8	10
Canada	76	1.2	0.9	—	11	5	33	29	56	66
United States	75	1.0	0.7	76	5	2	36	32	59	66

Table 6-1 continued.

	Urban Population as Percentage of Total Population		Population Per Physician		Number enrolled in Higher Education as Percentage of Population 20–24	
	1965	1983	1965	1980	1965	1986
Low Income Economies	17W	22W	12,419W	5,556W	3W	4W
SSA	11W	20W	38,268W	27,922W	(.)W	1W
Ethiopia	8	15	70,190W	69,390	(.)	1
Mali	13	19	49,010	22,130	(.)	(.)
Zaire	19	38	39,050	13,940	(.)	1
Malawi	5	11	46,900	41,460	(.)	(.)
Uganda	6	7	11,080	26,810	(.)	1
Burundi	2	7	54,930	45,020	(.)	1
Niger	7	14	71,440	38,790	–	(.)
Tanzania	6	14	21,840	17,740	(.)	(.)
Somalia	20	33	35,060	15,630	(.)	1
Rwanda	3	5	74,170	31,340	(.)	(.)
Central African Republic	27	44	44,490	26,750	–	1
Togo	11	22	24,980	18,100	(.)	2
Benin	11	16	28,790	16,980	(.)	2
Guinea	12	26	54,610	17,110	(.)	3
Ghana	26	38	12,040	7,160	1	1

Madagascar	12	20	9,900	10,220	1	3
Sierra Leone	15	23	18,400	17,520	(.)	1
Kenya	9	17	12,840	7,890	(.)	1
Sudan	13	20	23,500	8,930	1	2
Chad	9	20	73,040	47,640	–	(.)
Mozambique	5	17	18,700	39,140	(.)	(.)
Middle Income Economies	36W	48W	11,388W	5,995W	4W	12W
SSA	16W	27W	35,517W	11,929W	(.)	3W
Senegal	27	34	21,130	13,780	1	3
Lesotho	2	13	22,930	18,640	(.)	2
Liberia	23	38	12,450	8,550	1	2
Mauritania	7	25	36,580	14,500	–	–
Zambia	24	47	11,390	7,670	–	2
Ivory Coast	23	44	20,690	–	(.)	3
Zimbabwe	14	24	5,190	5,900	(.)	1
Nigeria	15	22	44,990	12,550	(.)	3
Cameroon	16	39	29,720	13,990	(.)	2
Canada	73	75	770	550	26	39
United States	72	74	670	520	40	58

Note: Figures beside low and middle income economies and SSA are summary measures. W = weighted average; (.) = less than half the unit shown; – = not available; e = estimate; SSA = Sub-Sahara Africa. All growth rates are in real terms.

Source: World Bank (1985b: 174–229).

income levels. The table also shows that even within SSA, there are variations in life expectancy ranging from a low of thirty-seven years for Guinea, to a high of fifty-nine years for Ghana. What the table does not show is that these trends have been improving so that for a country like Tanzania life expectancy has improved by almost ten years since independence. Both the levels and trends in life expectancy have implications for human resource management, especially in the areas of compensation and retirement benefits.

Population growth rates in SSA are among the highest in the world. Moreover, as Table 6-1 shows, the *rate* of growth is expected to increase for the remainder of this century because family planning and population control programs are not expected to have any significant effects before then. For countries like Kenya and the Ivory Coast with growth rates of over 4 percent, the population is expected to double in twenty-five years' time. Moreover, the median age distribution of the population is such that about 40 percent of the population is fifteen years or younger. As these people become adults, they will create tremendous pressures on economic and social institutions as they demand jobs, housing, land, health services, and education. If these pressures are not effectively managed, the potential for social unrest would be high, especially in the urban areas.

The population implications for management are far-reaching. For example, the supply of cheap labor will increase, and, left to market forces, real wages for unskilled and semiskilled labor will fall. Because SSA economics are not growing at the same rate as the population, employment and real incomes are expected to fall leading to higher levels of unemployment. However, the increased number of people would lead to increases in the demand for certain goods and services—especially for basic needs and low-income consumer goods (such as food, water, clothing, and housing). It is also expected that the pressure on urban and municipal services will increase as more people move into cities and towns—a trend that started back in the 1960s due to the relative neglect of the development of rural social and economic services.

Business/Government Relations

In Africa government is the most important factor in the management of organization/environment relationships. It is so pervasive in regulating, controlling, owning, or managing business organizations that it is believed to be detrimental to the development of local entrepreneurship and competitive market conditions (Berg 1981; Jorgensen, Hafsi, and Kiggundu 1984). During the colonial period, African economies were developed in order to serve their respective European colonial masters. These economies were developed as suppliers of raw materials for foreign markets. Consequently, the emphasis was on extractive industries like mining and agriculture. Any physical, social, or institutional infrastructure developed during this period was to serve these colonial economic and political interests (Tangri 1985). There were strong transcontinental links with Europe but very little interdependence among the African countries.

After independence the African governments wanted to reverse this trend and have more control of the development and management of economic institutions. Because there were no developed indigenous private sectors, the government took on the role of economic managers by creating parastatal or state-owned enterprises, nationalizing subsidiaries of foreign multinational corporations, forcing foreign investors into joint ventures, controlling marketing by the creation of marketing boards, state trading companies, and cooperatives, and passing laws and regulations that effectively make it impossible to establish businesses of any size without government involvement. Strong sentiments of economic nationalism fueled government policies of Africanization of economic institutions.

There are two modes of achieving greater indigenous ownership. The first—and most representative of the majority of African countries like Kenya, Nigeria, Ivory Coast, and Zaire—was to create economic development through private capital by using indigenous entrepreneurs. The second approach—exemplified by Tanzania, Angola, Mozambique, and Zambia—was through state capitalism, whereby the government plays the leading role in economic activities and private indigenous entrepreneurship is actively discouraged.

These two approaches have had different implications for management. For example, where foreign investment has been encouraged, more private capital has come into the country introducing new technology and, more important, assisted in the development of managers and technical personnel. Some of these managers have then gone on their own to form the core of the indigenous cadre of entrepreneurs. Business acumen and risk taking have become normal in these countries, more so than in countries where the government was more pervasive.

Market distortions, overregulation, and political interference in the regular conduct of business are generally more prevalent in countries like Tanzania than in Nigeria or Kenya. Productivity in the agricultural sector, in industry, and in service organizations has declined as a result of inappropriate government pricing policies and incentives. It is also generally believed that governments have been overburdened as they tried to do too much in the management of both the government bureaucracies and business organizations. Consequently, countries that adopted the later approach have experienced more inefficiency, misuse of organizational resources for personal gain, and promotion of political interests over economic or business missions of these organizations.

These countries, however, have avoided the more extreme uneven distribution of income, wealth, and opportunity that characterize the more capitalist-oriented countries like Nigeria. For example, a recent Canadian International Development Agency internal study (CIDA 1986) estimates that in Kenya the highest 10 percent of households earn 48.5 percent of total national household income, whereas the lowest 20 percent earn only 2.5 percent. Land, an important economic and traditional symbol of wealth, is also unevenly distributed. Education, one of the most important determinants of future earning power and of the propensity to respond positively to development initiatives including population control, is not available to everyone. Only 1 percent of Kenyans in the appropriate age group attend universities, and women constitute only one-tenth of this group. Almost half of the rural population live below the poverty line. Because up to 90 percent of the population live in rural areas, it is imperative that management research, practice, and expertise be directed to these areas.

Interorganizational Relations

Using the open systems framework, the literature on organization theory routinely discusses the relationships between the organization and significant others in the environment (Emery and Trist 1965; Miles 1980; Pfeffer 1982). In Africa, like in other developing countries, the management of the external or contextual interdependencies takes on added significance because of the asymmetrical relationship between the organization and its relevant environment (Facheux et al. 1982; Kiggundu, Jorgensen, and Hafsi 1983; Kiggundu 1985; Kiggundu 1986a).

In this section, we present a model for the analysis and management of these interorganizational relations using a hypothetical rural development agency (RDA). A rural development agency is a semi-autonomous organization created for the development of a defined rural area focusing

Figure 6–1. Interorganizational Relations of an African Rural Development Agency.

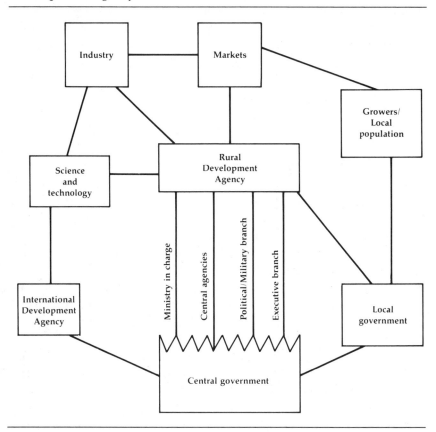

Note: Zigzag line shows the many facets of government.

on one or several sectors. For example, the Kenya Tea Development Authority (KTDA), created to promote and develop tea growing by Africans in specified Kenyan rural areas (Paul 1982; Kiereini 1985; Steeves 1975, 1978), can be regarded as an RDA.

Figure 6–1 maps out the more important and most common organizations likely to constitute the organizational network or contextual interdependencies for a typical African RDA. In the simplest form, there are two types of interdependencies: (1) the direct and relatively simpler interdependencies and (2) the indirect or higher level interdependencies that tend to be more complex to detect, manage and make the RDA more vulnerable.

The direct interdependencies, characterized by direct transactions between the RDA and the environment, include the markets for the RDA's inputs and outputs, the industry within which its primary mission is located (such as tea growing), the science and technology behind the industry, the local populations from whom the clients are defined, the different levels of government, and the local and international financing agencies. The central government interdependencies are shown with a zigzag line in Figure 6-1 to show the many facets of government and the complexities of managing the associated interdependencies.

These concepts can be illustrated using the KTDA as an example. The KTDA's relations with the government of Kenya are very complex. The agency reports to the government through the minister of agriculture, but it also deals with the treasury for funding, the public service commission for staffing, and the president's office for more nationally sensitive issues like land utilization. Because most of the tea is exported, KTDA's market interdependencies concentrate on the international marketing of tea and management watches development in the leading tea-producing countries (such as India, Sri Lanka, and China) and importers (such as the European Common Market and the United States) with keen interest. It also watches the large tea-marketing organizations like Brooke Bond of London to ensure that their conduct does not go against Kenya's interests.

Domestically, the agency must manage its relations with the local governments as well as the local growers who supply the bulk of the tea. It must operate as a responsible corporate citizen by providing economic and social opportunities for growth and development, without violating local norms and practices. For example, it must not promote excessive inequalities (Steeves 1978).

The higher-level interdependencies have no direct linkages with the RDA but could be of vital importance to its survival. For example, what the industry does or fails to do in relation to the market or technology may affect the RDA's ability to dispose of its products and acquire necessary raw materials, as well as the type and conditions of acquiring new technology or scientific knowledge for its internal use. If the International Development Agency (IDA) is contracted to provide both the finance and technology, the nature of its association with science and technology would affect the type of technology and transformation processes that the RDA ends up with.

On the more political level, the two levels of government can get together to negotiate deals harmful to the interests of the RDA without its being consulted or informed. The rivalry and competition among the various government agencies and ministries may also prove dysfunctional to the RDA. The central government often monopolizes the contacts with the IDA especially during the project design and planning stages so that by the time the RDA is invited to participate it is too late to make any significant changes.

Where the RDA is a rural community, the local population and their local leaders (both formal and informal) may get together and decide on their own without consulting with the agency as to how they will respond to its initiatives. For example, a family-planning clinic in an African village is most likely to receive this kind of treatment so that no matter how good the RDA and its organization is, the intended users and beneficiaries may have already colluded and conspired to make it fail.

Drawing from the KTDA once again, these more complex interdependencies can be illustrated. Suppose KTDA wants to undertake a major capital expansion project requiring funds beyond its internal resources. It would approach the government of Kenya, which would in turn approach an international development agency like the United States International Development Agency (USAID) for funding and technical assistance. The USAID and the government of Kenya would engage in negotiations that would affect KTDA without its direct involvement in those negotiations. Likewise, the USAID would deal with organizations producing and marketing tea-growing science and technology (such as universities and equipment manufacturers) as well as industry major players (such as General Foods) to negotiate a deal with the government of Kenya that is in the best U.S. interests. Once again KTDA would not be involved in these processes, and yet the attitude and behavior of these organizations, individually or collectively, would have significant effects on its success as an organization.

In summary, it must be emphasized that these contextual interdependencies must be managed over and above the internal management processes required of all organizations. In Africa the tendency has been to pay more attention to internal management processes—getting the work out—and less on the effective management of the environment. In some cases, the government has taken on the task of managing the environment on behalf of the state-owned enterprises with devastating results. In general, the more effective the RDA is, the more respect it earns from the government and the more freedom it acquires for managing its task environment.

It should be noted that some contextual interdependencies are more critical for the survival and growth of the organization than others. In Africa interdependencies involving scarce resources like finance, technology, markets, and central government political support are more critical than others. Failure by the RDA or any other organization to manage these interdependencies could lead to institutional decay (Kiggundu 1985), decline, or complete demise (McHenry 1985). McHenry found that the Agricultural Development Corporation, a state-owned enterprise of the Cross River State of Negeria, was dissolved by the politicians in part because it failed to (1) create jobs for politically sensitive groups, (2) provide services to small palm oil producers (such as roads, houses, and agricultural training), and (3) generate growth or expand production to meet the needs of the local political leaders.

Political/Economic Groups

In the previous section, discussion was focused on the relationship between the organization and the environment, and the management of the resulting contextual interdependencies. We now turn to a discussion of political/economic groups or powerful stakeholders both inside and outside the organization whose individual or collective behavior or attitude toward the organization significantly affects its management.

Within the organization, a distinction can be made between engineers and commissors. Following Escobar (1982) and Hafsi, Kiggundu, and Jorgensen (1985), *commissors* are defined as those employees who identify with one or more outside interests like a political interest group, the military, civil servants, or any other external coalition. The commissors' role, career paths, and rewards are bound to their ability to understand and represent the interests of the external interest group within the organization. To them, the organization is a resource or means, and they are expected to respond to the needs of their "client" group in the external environment by using the organization's resources. These extra-organizational demands, common in Africa, are often in conflict with the *raison d'être* of the organization.

Engineers, by contrast, identify with the organization, its conventional economic and technical functions, as well as its long-term survival and growth. Their expertise, career paths, motivation, and rewards are linked to the technical/economic performance of the firm. Although previous discussions (Hafsi, Kiggundu, and Jorgensen 1985) have limited the use of commissors and engineers to discussions of the strategic apex of state-owned enterprises, we extend these concepts to apply to other types of organizations.

In a typical African organizational setting, the commissors and engineers would be expected to be in conflict over the mission, the objectives and strategies of the organization, and the proper allocation and utilization of its resources. They would also disagree on the utilization of its resources as well as the appropriate performance criteria for the organization. Commissors would tend to use extraorganizational indicators of effectiveness reflecting the needs of their external interest groups, whereas engineers would prefer to use traditional economic and technical measures. Commissors would, for example, want to know how many people from a certain interest group are employed by the organization, whereas engineers would be more interested in return on investment, profitability, market penetration, and so forth.

It is important to distinguish between the organization's technical core and its environment. For example, in reviewing the utilization of administrative theory and practice in developing countries, Kiggundu, Jorgensen, and Hafsi (1983) found that organizations used Western-based management theories and techniques with little or no major adjustments when applied to the organization's technical core. If, however, these theories or techniques were applied to the organization's relationship with the environment, serious difficulties were experienced necessitating major adjustments to these theories and techniques. One explanation for this is that management tended to protect the technical core from the commissors and their respective external interest groups, which worked through their commissors to ensure that their interests were not at risk due to the introduction of any new management theory or technique. The need to satisfy these external competing interests inevitably necessitates major compromises or adjustments to the original theory or techniques.

Western political scientists tend to analyze the political/economic groups in terms of Marxist class conflicts (Jorgensen 1981; Tangri 1985). It should be noted, however, that these groupings are based on different dimensions and that they are not fixed or permanent but dynamic and fluid subject to change with changing circumstances. Some of the more powerful groups or stakeholders include tribal chiefs, farmers and their cooperative unions, the military, students, manufacturers' associations, civil servants, other professionals, merchants and shopkeepers, women, and political parties. Although the tendency is for each of these groups to pursue only its own interests, recent military coups in Ghana and Uganda have sought to bring about fundamental social, political, and economic structural changes as opposed to manifesting power struggles within existing systems.

Three examples are given below to illustrate how outside stakeholders affect the management and development of organizations in Africa. The Masai Range Management and Livestock Improvement Project operated in northern Tanzania for ten years (1970–80) funded by the United States Agency for International Development (USAID). In spite of the realization that improvements in traditional pastoralism required a lot of time, money, and effort, and in spite of the best U.S. range management technology applied to it, the project was deemed a failure and was terminated by the USAID (Moris 1981). There were many environmental reasons for the project's failure, including the following: (1) The government of Tanzania, the local authorities, and the Masai themselves were not adequately equipped to fulfill their project requirements; (2) the project was perceived by the Masai as a threat to their traditional pastoral way of life; (3) developments in other rural subsystems (such as land use, disease control, water and food supply, physical infrastructure, and marketing) did not take hold; and (4) even the relatively minor fall-back project objectives like the development of a self-sustaining logistical and human capital base were not successful enough to get the Masai interested.

In the early 1970s the government of Tanzania wanted to decentralize its administration to give more power to the local authorities. The president of Tanzania engaged the services of the McKenzie management consulting firm, based in New York, and asked it to work out the design and implementation process of the program. In July 1972 the program was officially launched with far-reaching structural and personnel changes. During its implementation, the program failed because it was not supported by the civil servants or party officials who were expected to promote it and explain it to the rest of the population. These powerful stakeholders did not support the program partly because they were not consulted or involved by the consulting firm in developing the program and partly because it was not in their interest to give up power to the villages.

The third example comes from Uganda, where a U.S. scholar was engaged to analyze the performance and institutional arrangements of the country's Coffee Marketing Board (CMB). The scholar assumed that the most important requirements for the CMB was to be efficient and cost effective while fulfilling its mandate of marketing coffee overseas. Based on these assumptions recommendations were made for the management of CMB that were rejected not because they were technically incorrect but because they ignored the interests of powerful outside stakeholders.

At that time the CMB's relevant environment was so highly divided that the conflicting rival stakeholders could not sacrifice their interests for the sake of the rational international performance of the CMB. After this frustrating experience, it was recommended that "those who seek to study and reform institutions . . . must not only comprehend the incentives which are created by their internal dynamics, but also those which are generated by their relationship with significant interests in their political environment" (Bates 1985: 19).

The Role of Trade Unions

The trade union movement in Africa dates from colonial times and takes on the character of the former colonial power with modifications reflecting the realities of each country's economic, political, and industrial relations system since independence. As Damachi, Seibel, and Trachtman (1979) have indicated, trade unions were encouraged to grow in the colonial period in order to control the flow and conduct of native labor. During the struggle for independence, trade unions became most active and emerged as one of the most powerful national institutions.

Since independence, trade unions have not done well partly because of their own internal organizational and management problems but most important because of severe restrictive laws, regulations, and institutions like industrial courts (such as Kenya), which have been instituted by government. In French Africa, governments act as wage pace-setters and view unions as instruments for government policy. Even in English Africa where unions enjoy relatively more autonomy in the collective bargaining process, the institutional restrictions are so serious as to almost eliminate the possibility of strong political or industrial action against the government or employers.

Drawing from Ananaba's (1979) comprehensive analysis of the trade union movement in Africa, Blunt (1984) concluded that the record of trade unions as an instrument of workers' need satisfaction is poor. Some of the reasons for this include (1) severe legal and political restraints placed on their operations; (2) low membership and participation rates partly because of large proportion of the agricultural labor force, which is hard to unionize (see Table 6-1), and partly because of low member satisfaction; (3) ineffective, corrupt union leadership operating with low budgets; (4) conflicts between trade unionists, new elites, the peasant farmers, and the politicians; (5) restricted contacts with and assistance from international unions; and (6) deteriorating labor, economic, and political conditions.

After analyzing the Nigerian industrial relations systems, Ubeku (1983) observed that in order to have a stable industrial relations system with a changing environment, Nigeria has designed its system such that both the trade unions and the employers are organized along industrial lines. The government regulates the system with income policies, compulsory arbitration, and approval of collective agreements.

In summary, it would appear that for most organizations in Africa, organized labor is not a major environmental concern. The government has taken on the job of managing the trade unions with severe restrictions. One obvious consequence of this arrangement is that most organizations' personnel and human resource management functions are likely to be relatively undeveloped (Henley 1977). Personalized styles of human resource management often lead to incidents of favoritism, nepotism, patronizing, and employee abuse and harassment, especially where management and the workers are differentiated along racial lines (Blunt 1984). The African union movement, restricted as it is, cannot be blamed for the continent's economic difficulties (such as high inflation rates) or lack of rapid industrial development experienced in other parts of the developed world.

THE ECONOMIC SYSTEM

This section discusses the economic system of SSA, which provides the income, wealth, and other resources for the creation, survival, growth, and developent of organizations. It is highly interdependent with the type of quality of organization and management of institutions.

The World Bank Report and the Lagos Plan of Action

A lot has been said about the causes and solutions of the African economic crisis (Hull 1980; Adedeji and Shaw 1985). One of the best presentations of these arguments is found in the 1981 World Bank, recently revised by Berg (1984), and the Lagos Plan of Action (Browne and Cummings 1985; Hull 1980; Adedeji and Shaw 1985). The first document is produced by the leading international development financial institution heavily influenced by conservative supply economics thinking, and the Lagos Plan of Action is produced by African nationalist leaders with extensive practical experiences of the limitations under which they must manage their respective economies.

Drawing from the major economic indicators of SSA for the last twenty years (see Table 6-2), it is obvious, and both reports agree, that

1. The economic crisis is severe, general, and worsening (Berg 1984).
2. It is a crisis of stagnant or declining production. For example, as Table 6-2 shows, between 1965-83, the average annual GNP growth rate ranged from a low of -4.4 for Uganda (negative growth) to a high of 6.3 for Lesotho, with most countries recording a growth rate of less than 2 percent.
3. It is a crisis in internal and external balances—budget squeeze, current account deficits, higher debt service obligations, and shrinking domestic resources and foreign capital (see Table 6-2).
4. It is an agricultural crisis with falling per capita production, declining share in world trade, and increasing food dependency on foreign sources (see Table 6-2).
5. It is an institutional crisis with weak and ineffective government decisionmaking and implementing capability, poor investment and resource utilization decisions, weak industrial sector, and inefficient and often compromised parastatal sector (Berg 1984).
6. It is an external crisis caused by factors outside SSA's control, such as the oil shocks of 1973 and 1979, the world recession of 1982, food price shocks, declining terms of trade, and the vagaries of nature, especially drought, pests, and desertification.

The World Bank report recognizes the diversity of SSA and recommends individual country-by-country program solutions. However, based on the firm belief that domestic policy inadequacies are primarily to blame for the crisis, the report recommends the following:

1. Financial restraint and fiscal responsibility by way of budget cuts especially on social programs or subsidies, currency devaluation, and competitive pricing policies.
2. Export stimulation of agricultural and industrial sectors.
3. Reduced role of the public sector, including parastatals and encouragement of the private sector and foreign private investment.
4. More efficient use of scarce resources by way of incentives (such as to progressive farmers), user fees for government services, reduced urban wages, and more effective population control.
5. Doubling of foreign aid to provide the external financial and technical assistance required to support these action programs.

Critics have dismissed this report as no more than a deliberate attempt at Africanization of supply-side economics.

Table 6-2. Africa: Economic Development Indicators.

	GNP per capita Average annual rate (%)	Average Annual Rate of Inflation (%)		Growth of (Average Annual Agriculture	
	1965–83	1965–73	1973–83	1965–73	1973–83
Low Income Economies	2.7W	1.4W	5.4W	2.6W	2.9W
SSA	−0.2W	3.9W	17.5W	3.1W	1.2W
Ethiopia	0.5	1.8	4.4	2.1	1.2
Mali	1.2	7.6	10.3	0.9	5.0
Zaire	−1.3	18.7	48.2	−	1.4
Malawi	2.2	4.5	9.8	−	4.1
Uganda	−4.4	5.6	62.7	3.6	−1.6
Burundi	2.1	2.9	12.4	4.7	2.3
Niger	−1.2	4.0	11.8	−2.9	1.6
Tanzania	0.9	3.2	11.5	3.1	2.6
Somalia	−0.8	3.8	20.1	−	3.5
Rwanda	2.3	7.7	11.2	−	−
Central African Republic	0.1	3.0	14.4	2.1	2.4
Togo	1.1	3.1	8.3	2.6	1.1
Benin	1.0	3.6	10.8	−	2.7
Guinea	1.1	3.0	4.0	−	2.4
Ghana	−2.1	8.1	51.6	4.5	−
Madagascar	−1.2	4.1	13.9	−	−0.2
Sierra Leone	1.1	1.9	14.7	1.5	2.2
Kenya	2.3	2.3	10.8	6.2	3.4
Sudan	1.3	7.2	18.0	0.3	3.5
Chad	−	4.5	8.3	−	−
Mozambique	−	−	−	−	−
Middle Income Economies	3.4W	5.2W	29.3W	3.3W	2.5W
SSA	1.9W	4.8W	12.4W	2.4W	−1.3W
Senegal	−0.5	3.0	8.9	0.2	0.3
Lesotho	6.3	4.4	11.9	−	−
Liberia	0.8	1.5	7.2	6.5	2.0
Mauritania	0.3	3.9	7.8	−2.1	2.6
Zambia	−1.3	5.2	10.3	−	1.4
Ivory Coast	1.0	4.1	11.9	3.7	4.0
Zimbabwe	1.5	3.0	9.7	−	1.2
Nigeria	3.2	10.3	13.3	2.8	−1.9
Cameroon	2.7	5.8	12.6	4.7	1.8

Production Growth Rate %)		Average Annual Growth Rate (%) Gross Domestic Investment		Merchandise Trade ($ Million)	
Industry				Exports	Imports
1965–83	1973–83	1965–73	1973–83	1983	1983
7.2W	7.1W	6.4W	5.7W	45,991t	57,333t
6.9W	0.6W	6.3W	2.2W	7,827t	11,501t
6.1	2.6	1.5	2.6	422	875
5.2	0.6	1.0	4.2	106	344
–	–2.0	10.2	4.9	1,459	953
–	4.2	16.0	–	220	312
3.0	–10.1	2.1	–5.2	354	340
10.4	8.3	–1.4	15.7	76	194
13.2	10.9	4.6	3.5	301	443
6.9	0.2	9.6	4.4	480	1,134
–	1.1	–	–8.2	163	422
–	–	6.3	–	80	279
7.1	1.0	2.3	–6.7	106	132
6.2	2.6	3.3	–0.2	242	284
–	6.9	3.9	10.3	85	523
–	6.7	–	–0.7	390	279
4.3	–7.0	–3.5	–8.1	895	719
–	–1.8	3.9	–1.0	329	439
1.9	–2.9	–1.4	1.1	202	171
12.4	5.3	15.9	3.4	876	1,274
1.0	6.7	0.2	5.6	624	1,354
–	–	4.5	–	58	109
–	–	–	–	260	635
9.1W	4.9W	8.8W	4.2W	333,532t	350,734t
17.7W	1.0W	12.3W	3.2W	27,201t	25,961t
3.5	6.1	8.1	–0.7	585	984
–	–	11.0	–	–	–
6.2	–1.5	5.6	1.5	841	415
3.5	–	12.5	7.0	246	227
–	–0.3	6.2	–12.5	866	690
8.8	7.4	10.2	6.0	2,068	1,814
–	–	9.2	1.9	1,273	1,432
19.7	0.3	15.2	3.5	17,509	17,600
4.7	13.7	8.6	10.6	1,067	1,226

Table 6–2 continued.

	Exports		Imports		Average Annual Growth Manufacturing	
	1965–73	1973–83	1965–73	1973–83	1965–73	1973–83
Low Income						
Economies	1.5W	0.9W	−2.0W	1.4W	−	−
SSA	2.4W	−4.0W	2.3W	−2.2W	−	−
Ethiopia	3.0	1.4	−0.2	2.7	8.8	3.5
Mali	13.1	5.1	8.5	3.9	−	−
Zaire	6.5	−8.7	9.6	−13.7	−	−
Malawi	3.8	2.8	6.4	−0.6	−	−
Uganda	0.2	−8.0	−2.5	1.9	−	−
Burundi	−	−	−	−	−	−
Niger	6.1	19.0	4.4	11.5	−	−
Tanzania	0.9	−4.6	7.1	−2.7	−	−
Somalia	6.7	7.3	1.4	0.0	−	−
Rwanda	6.3	2.6	4.6	12.9	−	−
Central African						
Republic	−0.4	3.8	−0.5	2.5	−	−
Togo	4.4	3.5	6.6	7.4	−	−
Benin	12.4	−1.4	13.2	4.5	−	−
Guinea	−	−	−	−	−	−
Ghana	3.5	−6.4	−3.3	−8.0	6.5	−6.2
Madagascar	5.4	−4.3	1.5	−2.5	−	−
Sierra Leone	2.2	−5.3	0.9	−5.0	3.3	2.5
Kenya	3.8	−4.8	5.9	−4.6	12.4	6.3
Sudan	3.8	−1.5	4.9	1.3	−	−
Chad	−3.5	−3.1	18.7	−8.6	−	−
Mozambique	−7.9	−8.3	−8.9	−4.2	−	−
Middle Income						
Economies	5.9W	−0.4W	8.3W	4.1W	9.3W	4.9W
SSA	6.9W	−5.8W	6.5W	8.2W	−	−
Senegal	−1.3	−0.9	5.4	−1.2	−	−
Lesotho	−	−	−	−	−	−
Liberia	8.9	−2.3	3.6	−4.3	13.2	0.5
Mauritania	9.7	0.5	15.4	−0.8	−	−
Zambia	−0.3	−0.8	3.0	−7.3	−	−
Ivory Coast	7.1	−1.4	7.8	0.1	8.9	4.5
Zimbabwe	−	−	−	−	−	−
Nigeria	8.9	−6.2	8.9	13.6	15.0	10.7
Cameroon	4.2	3.9	6.3	5.1	7.5	9.9

Rate (%)		Average Annual Growth Rate (%)		Average Annual Growth Rate (%)	
Services		Public Consumption		Private Consumption	
1965–73	1973–83	1965–73	1973–83	1965–73	1973–83
4.2W	5.0W	5.9W	6.8W	3.5W	4.5W
4.6W	2.9W	4.7W	2.7W	2.8W	0.9W
6.7	3.6	3.7	7.1	4.2	2.6
4.7	4.5	–	7.5	3.9	2.8
–	–1.1	5.8	2.2	2.2	–7.7
–	4.2	3.0	–	4.0	–
3.8	–1.0	–	–	3.8	–6.4
3.0	5.3	12.3	5.4	4.7	2.8
–1.5	5.9	2.1	2.3	–3.3	6.6
6.2	5.4	–	–	5.0	3.0
–	2.6	–	1.5	–	7.9
–	–	2.8	–	7.7	–
1.6	–0.7	1.7	–1.5	3.6	3.2
7.3	3.0	7.9	8.4	6.0	3.3
–	6.0	3.6	3.7	1.1	3.1
–	1.9	–	6.4	–	2.0
1.1	–0.3	1.1	4.8	2.3	–1.3
–	1.2	3.3	3.9	4.0	–0.5
7.1	4.1	5.3	–2.1	3.8	3.2
7.8	5.3	13.1	6.3	5.8	3.6
0.5	8.6	1.4	4.5	–1.7	7.6
–	–	6.0	–	0.7	–
–	–	–	–	–	–
7.5W	5.3W	7.0W	4.9W	6.8W	4.8W
7.1W	3.5W	12.0W	4.3W	4.3W	2.8W
1.5	2.2	–1.2	6.6	0.1	3.3
–	–	5.4	–	5.9	–
3.8	0.8	4.5	4.1	0.3	–0.1
8.7	3.9	6.1	1.4	2.7	3.0
–	0.6	10.4	–0.8	–1.2	3.9
8.5	4.1	15.2	9.6	5.1	3.7
–	3.3	6.9	10.8	7.3	2.9
8.8	4.1	16.1	3.3	4.9	2.5
3.6	7.3	4.6	5.9	3.4	5.4

Table 6–2 continued.

	Current Account Balance ($ million)		Gross Inter- national Reserves ($ million)	
	1970	1983	1970	1983
Low Income				
Economies	–	–	–	–
SSA	–	–	–	–
Ethopia	–31	–171	72	206
Mali	–2	–103	1	23
Zaire	–64	–559	189	269
Malawi	–35	–72	29	29
Uganda	20	–256	57	–
Burundi	–	–	15	34
Niger	–	–	19	57
Tanzania	–36	–	65	19
Somalia	–6	–150	21	16
Rwanda	7	–49	8	111
Central African				
Republic	–12	–28	1	51
Togo	3	–32	35	178
Benin	–1	–	16	8
Guinea	–	–	–	–
Ghana	–68	–218	58	291
Madagascar	10	–369	37	29
Sierra Leone	–16	–33	39	16
Kenya	–49	–174	220	406
Sudan	–42	–213	22	17
Chad	2	38	2	32
Mozambique	–	–	–	–
Middle Income				
Economies	–	–	–	–
SSA	–	–	–	–
Senegal	–16	–	22	23
Lesotho	–	–14	–	67
Liberia	–	–135	–	20
Mauritania	–5	–196	3	110
Zambia	108	–252	515	137
Ivory Coast	–38	–743	119	37
Zimbabwe	–	–459	59	300
Nigeria	–368	–4752	223	1252
Cameroon	–30	–289	81	170

Total Government Expenditure (% of GNP)		Total Government Current Revenue (% of GNP)	
1972	1982	1972	1982
20.8W	16.3W	16.4W	13.2W
21.7W	18.0W	17.1W	11.2W
13.8	–	10.5	–
–	33.7	–	15.5
38.6	35.6	27.9	21.6
22.1	27.0	16.0	17.4
21.8	5.0	13.7	3.1
–	23.9	–	13.4
–	–	–	–
19.7	32.2	15.8	19.6
13.5	–	13.7	–
–	–	–	–
–	21.9	–	16.4
–	32.8	–	29.1
–	–	–	–
–	–	–	–
19.5	10.8	15.1	5.4
20.8	–	18.8	13.6
–	22.7	–	11.6
21.0	29.7	18.0	22.8
19.2	16.9	18.0	11.8
18.1	–	13.1	–
–	–	–	–
19.8W	25.8W	17.8W	22.2W
13.3W	33.1W	13.3W	24.3W
17.4	30.9	16.8	20.1
16.6	–	11.7	–
–	39.4	–	25.2
–	–	–	–
35.4	41.9	24.2	24.9
–	–	–	–
–	39.0	–	31.3
10.2	–	11.6	–
–	21.9	–	18.5

Starting with the same diagnosis, the Lagos Plan of Action, based on progressive left-wing Pan-African views, advocates individual and collective state self-reliance by

1. Reducing SSA's dependence on international resources (capital, technology, markets, and so forth);
2. Securing adequate food supplies and the achievement of self-sufficiency;
3. Selectively promoting exports based on key sectors producing intermediate or capital goods rather than raw materials;
4. Reducing dependence on expert foreign agencies.

The two documents are not as different as they may appear. They both acknowledge the existence of the economic crisis and the need to do something about it. They both recognize that more effective management of scarce resources is essential for improving the economic condition and social well being of the majority of the people. Because the economic situation in Africa has tended to worsen since the World Bank report was published (Berg 1984), the World Bank solution, supported by the International Monetary Fund (IMF), has become more widely enforced as more and more SSA countries must accept IMF conditions in exchange for the foreign exchange credit facilities that they so badly need. These conditions are so severe and associated with many social, economic, and political risks that many African governments (such as Tanzania) have been very reluctant to accept them (Mohiddin 1985).

The Role of Agriculture

In sub-Saharan Africa, agriculture still remains the most important sector of the economy either by employment (see Table 6–1), by contribution to gross national product, or as a source of household income or government revenue. It is estimated that agriculture accounts for more than 35 percent of GNP and over 60 percent of export revenue (Hull 1980). Consequently, when agricultural productions or prices are depressed, other economic activities are equally affected.

Notes to Table 6–2 (pp. 192–197)

The figures beside low and middle income economies and SSA are summary measures. W indicates that it is a weighted average; t indicates that it is a total. All growth rates are in real terms.

Source: World Bank (1985b: 174–229).

African agriculture serves two primary purposes. It provides for domestic household and industrial consumption by way of food, income, and basic raw materials for food and agriculture-based processing industries and services like textiles, food processing plants, transportation, finance, and so forth. Second, it provides for export crops like coffee, cotton, tobacco, sugar, pyrethrum, and cocoa, which are grown almost exclusively for international markets. Agriculture, as the primary "engine of growth" of these economies, directly or indirectly supports organizations and institutions. Consequently, as African agriculture has declined to crisis proportions by the 1980s, the performance and management of other African organizations has also suffered.

African agriculture is still largely organized along traditional subsistence methods. It is estimated that about 60 percent of the continent's arable land and 75 percent of its labor force in 1970 were still engaged in subsistence production involving peasant farmers working small scattered plots of land either individually or as an extended family unit. They use little or none of the modern methods or techniques of farming and are vulnerable to unpredictable changes in soils, climate, and government policy. This mode of production has proved to be extremely resistent to change; numerous attempts to modernize peasant agriculture have been unsuccessful (Moris 1981).

The estate or plantation agriculture—originally introduced by European settlers and promoted by the more market-oriented countries like Malawi (World Bank 1981) and, to a limited extent, Kenya (World Bank 1983)—is more productive but very limited in scope. Population pressures and government policies have tended to discourage large-scale plantation farming leading to Africanization and balkanization of the farms. This has often led to decline in managerial efficiency and productivity.

African agriculture has been on the decline since the 1950s partly because of unfortunate natural causes like drought but mostly because of mismanagement, ill-advised government policies, inappropriate pricing, incentives, and marketing strategies, poor storage and distribution channels, and fluctuating but declining external terms of trade. Investment in agriculture has been minimal in most of SSA.

Part of the significance of the poor performance of the agricultural sector for management is its effect on the behavior of the workers. It is estimated that most urban workers do not get a high enough caloric intake, especially because most of the local staples are protein deficient. Accordingly, workers are susceptible to ill health and disease. They cannot put in a full day's work, although they expect a full day's pay. Food shortages in urban areas mean that workers take off time to line up for food in the market and then ask for overtime work in order to pay for their food bills because most food is imported and therefore quite expensive relative to local wages.

A sociotechnical systems study of a locomotive maintenance workshop of the Sudan Railway Corporation (Kidwell, El Jack, and Ketchum 1981: 17) illustrates this problem. The study found that workers were frequently absent from work for up to four hours a day in order to "fetch scarce consumer goods." Scheduled work would not be done on time, and therefore workers expected to be asked to put in overtime work. Similar experiences have been reported in Ghana, Uganda, and Tanzania leading to productivity and morale problems both for the workers and their managers.

Agriculture, Africa's most important economic sector, is in need of urgent and fundamental changes if the consequences of its declining output are to be avoided. A 1981 World Bank report on Africa suggested four policy initiatives for the improvement of agriculture: (1) correcting distorted prices and pricing mechanisms; (2) reducing the monopoly power of parastatals in marketing and supplying inputs; (3) reducing the extraction of resources from the agricultural sector; and (4) devaluing inflated currencies. These prescriptions are based on the erroneous assumption of the existence of effectively managed organizations for their implementation.

The Private Sector and Public/Private Transitions

Among the most hotly debated issues in sub-Saharan Africa today are the appropriate relative size of the private and public sectors and the role that each sector should play as an agent of change for economic development, resource distribution, and social justice. In a typical African country, the indigenous private sector is very small and consists of mostly small traders, truckers, artisans, and a few small simple processing manufacturers. This group is overshadowed by the foreign-owned private-sector organizations, most of whom are subsidiaries of large multinational corporations and state-owned commercial enterprises. The modern mining and industrial sector organizations are owned, managed, and controlled by foreigners. Although the indigenous private sector has remained relatively small and insignificant, the size and role of the public

Table 6–3. Economic Indicators of the Importance of State-Owned Enterprises in Selected African Countries (percentage).

	State Owned Enterprises' Share of:			
	(1) Gross Domestic Product (%)	(2) Gross Fixed Capital Formation (%)	(3) Nonagricultural Employment (%)	(4) Public Employment (%)
Algeria	66.0	67.6	–	–
Benin	7.6	–	37.1	42.7
Botswana	7.3	7.7	–	–
Egypt	31.4	47.8	10.3	26.0
Guinea	25.0	–	–	–
Ivory Coast	10.5	39.5	–	–
Kenya	8.7	17.3	8.4	21.5
Mali	9.4	7.6	–	–
Senegal	19.9	17.9	12.9	28.2
Sierra Leone	7.6	19.6	–	–
Tanzania	12.3	16.3	31.9	40.8
Togo	11.8	–	–	–
Tunisia	25.4	35.8	–	–
Zambia	37.8	61.2	36.5	45.0

Source: Shirley (1983: 95–97). Figures for individual countries are for different years from 1974 to 1981.

enterprises has been extensively expanded (Berg 1985; Nellis 1985; Morrison 1986).

Africa as a whole possesses a large number of public enterprises, which dominate the national economies. For example, during 1980–81 public enterprises were responsible for 76 percent of modern sector employment in Guinea, 58 percent in Niger, and 40 percent in Burundi (Nellis 1985). Table 6–3 shows the size of the contributions of state-owned enterprises to the national economy by way of gross domestic product at factor cost, gross fixed capital formation, nonagricultural employment, and total public employment. All figures are in percentages. The table shows variations among countries as to the relative importance of state-owned enterprises' contributions to their respective economies. For example, although Algeria's state-owned enterprises contribute 66 percent of gross domestic product and about the same percentage for gross fixed capital formation, Mali's comparable figures are 9.4 percent and 7.6 percent, respectively. In general, state-owned enterprises are large, pervasive, capital intensive, bureaucratic, overstaffed, and inefficient and borrow heavily from domestic and international markets (Nellis 1985).

State-owned enterprises were established in Africa for a variety of economic, social, and political motives. According to Ghai (1985) the main reason for the creation of these enterprises was the deficiencies and consequences of African imperfect markets, which were unable on their own to provide the required momentum for development. These enterprises were expected to bring about more equitable distribution of income, wealth, and opportunity to all the people and counterbalance the concentration of benefits to a few elites or foreign capital. According to Ghai (1985: 16), "The private sector in Africa, with its monopolies and protections, and linkages abroad, was hardly likely to be the engine either of domestic accumulation or of the efficient utilization of economic resources."

State-owned enterprises in Africa, as elsewhere in the world, are being criticized for their monopolistic market positions, poor return on investment, failure to bring about more equitable distribution of income and employment, ineffective utilization of local resources, poor record of technology transfer, being highly politicized, and being unable to contain corrupt practices of senior officers. Still, it is hard to determine whether African state-owned enterprises perform significantly worse than those from other regions "because authorities frequently lack fundamental data as regards the operations of state-owned enterprises" (Morrison 1986). According to Shirley (1983), however, a study of twenty-six countries shows that when normal depreciation is included and subsidies excluded, these enterprises showed a loss that by private-sector standards would lead to their closure.

In response to these pressures, a complex and long-term process is underway in which the role of the state in development is under systematic review, in which a new emphasis is placed on the private sector, and in which economic functions and resources are increasingly transferred from the public to the private sector (Morrison 1986). The debate for and against privatization in Africa is epitomized by Berg (1985) and Ghai (1985), respectively. Although recognizing the political, social, and institutional problems of privatization and the need to proceed slowly on a case-by-case basis, Berg argues that Africa has plenty of unexploited private-sector and entrepreneural potential for development. Acknowledging that this potential is too small to take on the big multinational corporations or to buy up the state-owned enterprises, he nevertheless identifies several areas where the indigenous private sector can be more fully developed. Marketing, transportation, social services, and construction are some of the areas that, according to Berg (1985), are suitable for indigenous private sector growth. For example, it is costly and inefficient to undertake agricultural marketing using large-scale bureaucratic organizations. Agricultural marketing in Africa involves many small transactions taking place over large physical areas and is therefore best performed by local, small, decentralized organizations or individuals. Berg (1985) recommends getting rid of state trading corporations and gradually transferring the trading functions to small traders. Small transport companies operate more efficiently than large state-owned transport companies, and this sector also can be privatized to small operators. Likewise, servicers like private education, construction and engineering, and other service areas requiring small-scale or dispersed transactions can be privatized. However, none of these sectors is big enough to act as a spur to growth.

Ghai (1985), on the other hand, does not agree with Berg or the World Bank. He argues that the World Bank's drive for privatization is based on misleading conceptions of the performance of the public and private sectors in the economy. The bank's analysis, based on simple calculations of profits and return on investment, obscure the diversity of purposes underlying public enterprises and are inappropriate in highly uncompetitive markets. He implies that it is unrealistic and premature for Africa to talk about the development of a private sector built on competitive forces when there are no competitive markets. He therefore advocates reforming and improving management of state-owned enterprises rather than selling them off to hypothetical private buyers.

The positions represented by Berg (1985) and Ghai (1985) are not fundamentally different. Although they both make different prescriptions, they agree on current levels of unsatisfactory performance and the need to allocate and utilize the country's scarce resources in the most effective way over the long run. For most African countries, a mixed economy is the most likely scenario. It is therefore possible to draw on both the Berg (1985) and Ghai (1985) strategies by privatizing those sectors promising the best results and minimal political, social, and institutional losses or costs. In the short run, those sectors where immediate privatization is not possible, either because of market imperfections (Jorgensen, Hafsi, and Kiggundu 1986a; Frohlich 1982), political realities, or lack of adequate information for quality strategic decisions, reforms should be directed at improving the management capabilities of the state-owned enterprises. In addition, government policies can be initiated to facilitate the growth and development of the indigenous private-sector organizations. International development agencies can play an important facilitating role by creating business opportunities and technical assistance to private-sector organizations. For example, the USAID is currently working on a project for the nine SADCC countries and seeking indigenous private-sector organizations from each country to form a consortium and a joint venture with a U.S. company with which they would contract for the project.

Tony Killick (1983: 87), director of the Overseas Development Institute, summarizes the view of most Western economists in his advice to African governments: "To an African Government contemplating the creation of a substantial public sector as a means of promoting industrialization, the advice of this writer would have to be: don't do it; there are better ways of stimulating industrial growth."

TRADE, MONEY, BANKING, FINANCE, AND THE PUBLIC DEBT

Despite the present economic crisis, trade between Africa and the rest of the world has been steadily growing. Figures show that the average rate of growth was 5 percent in the 1950s, almost doubled to 9 percent in the 1960s, and was about 17 percent in the 1970s. The volume of trade and investment from the United States has also grown very fast as African countries, helped by Japan's aggressive marketing strategies and the formation of the European Economic Community in 1957, have attempted to diversify their trade links away from their respective former colonial masters.

Trade within the continent, however, has not grown as fast. Political, ideological and economic considerations have limited free movement of people, goods, money, and ideas across national or regional boundaries. The results of regional organizations have been rather mixed. For example, the East African Community, made up of Kenya, Uganda, and Tanzania, collapsed in 1977 as a model of regional cooperation in spite of the history and binding institutional arrangements established during colonial times in favor of such regional cooperations (Hull 1980, Jorgensen 1985).

On a more positive note, two attempts made at regional cooperation have met with some success. The Economic Community of West African States (ECOWAS) was founded in 1975 by fifteen member states with the aim of establishing by 1990 a customs union similar to the European Economic Community. Second, the Southern African Development Coordinating Conference (SADCC) was founded in 1980 by the nine front-line states bordering on South Africa (Angola, Botswana, Lesotho, Malawi, Mosambique, Swaziland, Tanzania, Zambia, and Zimbabwe). These two regional organizations have not made significant changes in the structure or direction of African trade, but their existence provides hope that most of the countries are moving in the right direction. In both cases there are internal and external forces working against strong regional associations. In West Africa France is concerned that such a strong association would weaken its hold on Francophone Africa. For SADCC South Africa and its European allies work for regional disunity as a way of preserving the status quo in South Africa.

For the manager, the implications are quite clear. First, the African market for select goods should not be ignored by U.S. export managers. It is a small but growing market. For some countries like Nigeria, the demand for consumer goods remains largely unsatisfied. For the African manager the limitations on the freedom of goods and services is a source of frustration especially because individual country domestic markets are too small for efficient operations. For example, Kenya's industrial organizations were originally designed on the assumption that they would be serving the entire market in eastern Africa. When the East African common market broke down, the border with Tanzania was closed and chaotic conditions in Uganda made it difficult to transport goods to Eastern Zaire, Southern Sudan, Burundi, and Rwanda, Kenya's plants were no longer able to enjoy economies of scale. Likewise, as Jorgensen (1985) has shown, the transport corporations created by each of the three East African countries after the break up of the East African Community in 1977 are too small to operate efficiently. One of the limitations of management and organization research is that it makes very little contribution to the management of small organizations.

Currencies and Monetary Systems

The former British colonies moved very quickly after independence. Each created its own central bank with a reserve system allowing it to issue its own currency and make its own clearing arrangements. The former French colonies, on the other hand, have remained in the franc zone and held on to a system based on a precise monetary relationship with France. Most West African Francophone states (Ivory Coast, Niger, Benin,

Togo) participate in the West African Monetary Union (UMOA) and share a common central bank. The equatorial states – Cameroon, Chad, Congo, Gabon – also have their own central bank called the Banque des Etats de l'Afrique Centrale. Both institutions maintain most of their foreign exchange reserves at the French Treasury in Paris, and the currencies of member states have parity with the French franc. Compared to the former English colonies, Francophone African states' currencies are relatively stronger and more stable. This has tended to encourage smuggling of goods from countries of weaker currencies to those with stronger ones. For example, in the early 1970s Ghana's cocoa crop was smuggled into the Ivory Coast and Togo where it could be exchanged for a more valuable currency. It is estimated that during the 1974-75 coffee boom, about one-third of Uganda's crop was lost to neighboring Kenya through smuggling.

As the African monetary system has become more independent and as the economies have declined, the fixed exchange rates have tended to be higher than market rates. Unrealistic exchange rates have the effects of making the country's exports rather uncompetitive. It is for this reason that one of the International Monetary Funds' (IMF) conditions for its assistance is that of currency devaluation and free-floating exchange rates determined by market forces of supply and demand.

Development Banks have been established in SSA to facilitate the financing of vital development projects. These banks operate at three different levels. First, the national development banks are limited to financing projects within the national economy. Most African countries have such a national development bank. Second, there are regional development banks owned and managed by a group of countries with the desire for joint financing and coordination of their development programs. The East African Development Bank is an example of a regional development bank. Originally started as one of the institutions of the East African Community, the bank still operates on a regional basis. It was specifically charged with the responsibility of financing development in such a way as to reduce the imbalances between the three member states. Accordingly, it was to spend more funds for projects in Tanzania and Uganda than in Kenya, which had a more developed industrial base than the other two partner states. Africa's belief in the importance of development banks is illustrated by the fact that the East African Development Bank is still operational almost ten years after the break up of the East African Community.

Third, the African Development Bank operates more or less like the other continental development banks – the Asian Development Bank, the Caribbean Development Bank, and the Arab Development Bank. The African Development Bank was created in 1963 and until 1982 admitted only independent African states as members. Non-African countries like the United States could participate only in the Bank's African Development Fund, which handles the grants to member states. In May 1982 the bank passed a resolution admitting non-African countries as members. This action was designed to increase the bank's share of capital and widen its money market experience and status as an international financing institution. The biggest outside shareholders in order of contributions are the United States, Japan, West Germany, France, and Canada.

As of December 1982 the bank's volume of cumulative loans since the start of operations stood at $2,061,790,000 (U.S.) with disbursements of over $800 million. In 1982 the bank approved thirty-three loans totaling $327.9 million. The coming in of new non-African members is expected to increase this considerably, thus generating more economic activities and business opportunities for all the member states (African and non-African members).

Table 6–4 gives a breakdown of the sectorial and regional cumulative loans that the bank made from 1967 to 1982, as well as the performance record for 1982. The figures show that on a sectorial basis public services get the single largest share of approved loans (30.7 percent in 1982). Agriculture has increased its share to 25.5 percent in 1982 from only 17.8 percent during the 1967–82 period. East Africa continues to get the single largest share of approved loans, and this increased from 33.8 percent to 39.6 percent in 1982. West Africa's share, on the other hand, has declined from 24.8 to only 16.5 percent in 1982. This is due to the relatively better performance of the West African economies as compared to East Africa over the same period (CIDA 1986).

The commercial banking industry is still dominated by branch banks of British banks like Barclay's and the Standard Bank. They are, however, increasingly facing competition from newly created indigenous banks as well as U.S. and European financial institutions. U.S. banks like Chase Manhattan are not involved in retail personal banking but tend to concentrate on financing large U.S.-financed development or military transactions. With the help of the IMF, the World Bank, and other U.S. institutions, these banks have helped to maintain a capitalist monetary system that uses the U.S. dollar as the currency for foreign trade transactions. African small businesses continue to experience difficulties securing loans from these banks for lack of acceptable collateral or business experience.

Table 6-4. The African Development Bank: Sectoral and Regional Breakdown of Loans, 1967–82 (percentage).

	Cumulative 1967–82 (%)	Approved Loans 1982 (%)
Sectoral breakdown:		
Public service	32.2	30.7
Industrial and banks	24.5	21.1
Transport	22.5	16.9
Agriculture	17.8	25.5
Education and health	2.8	5.8
Total	100.0	100.0
Regional breakdown:		
East Africa	33.8	39.6
Central Africa	20.9	29.9
North Africa	20.6	18.9
West Africa	24.8	16.6
Total	100.0	100.0

Source: Canadian International Development Agency (1984: 10).

The tax base for generating government revenue is small in Africa. The industrial and commerical sectors are quite small, and therefore most government revenue is generated by indirect taxation like import/export duties, excise taxes, and royalties on minerals. Since the mid-1970s extended government expenditures resulting from increased costs of government operations, declining sources of revenue, worsening terms of trade, the oil and agricultural crises, corruption and wasteful utilization of public goods have resulted in perpetual budget deficits. Foreign exchange reserves have dwindled to dangerous levels. For example, in the last five years Kenya's foreign exchange reserves have fluctuated between 1.1 to 2.6 months of imports. Other African countries experience similar or worse situations in terms of foreign exchange reserves in months of imports.

Faced with limited internal sources of funds, African countries have borrowed extensively from outside sources. Africa's total external debt stands at about $80 billion ($U.S.), of which about 75 percent is bilateral. Unable to borrow from the open international money market, many African countries had no choice but to arrange for bilateral loans with the industrial countries. The relatively small percentage of the public debt owed to international commercial banks makes Africa's debt problems rather less onerous than is the case for countries like Mexico, Brazil, or Argentina.

Table 6–5 shows the escalating debt burden from 1970–72 to the 1980–82 period. The three columns show the movements in the debt as a percentage of GNP, exports, and debt servicing, respectively. For example, during 1970–72, Zaire's debt as a percentage of GNP was about 25 percent. By 1980–82 it had gone up to 78 percent. During the same period, Table 6–5 shows that for the Sudan, the public debt as a percentage of total exports rose from about 90 percent to 437 percent. For Niger debt service as a percentage of exports rose from less than 5 percent during 1970–72 (before the first oil shock) to over 30 percent by 1980–82. In fact, it is not unusual for a non–oil producing sub-Saharan African country to spend up to 35 percent of its current expenditure on debt servicing. These fiscal, monetary, and budgetary conditions constitute immediate constraints within which public-sector managers must operate and the contextual or environmental challenges that private-sector managers must meet.

TRANSPORTATION, COMMUNICATIONS, AND INFORMATION FLOWS

The physical and administrative infrastructure for transportation, communication, and information flows remains relatively underdeveloped. Yet these systems play a key role in the process of economic, commercial, social, and political integration as well as administrative efficiency. These systems provide the best opportunity for the development of linkages among the rural communities, between the rural and urban areas, and among the major urban centers within and across national borders.

Africa's transport system is made up of roadways of varying conditions, railways, airways, and to a limited extent waterways. The original railway lines were built about 100 years ago in order to serve European strategic and commercial interests. Most of the lines originate either from a mining town or a major industrial city to the sea port. Most railway lines are unprofitable, except those geared to mining. Railway integration has been difficult because there are almost ten different rail gauges reflecting original differences in European railway systems.

Railways are expensive to build and maintain especially in mineral-poor large countries like Tanzania and the Sudan. Jorgensen's (1985)

Table 6-5. Sub-Saharan Africa: The Public Debt Ladder (percent).

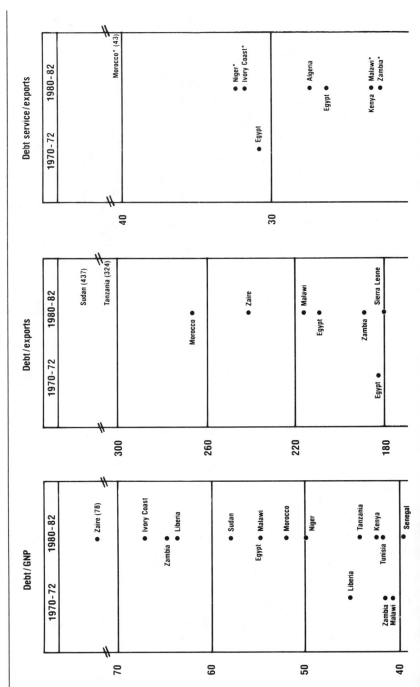

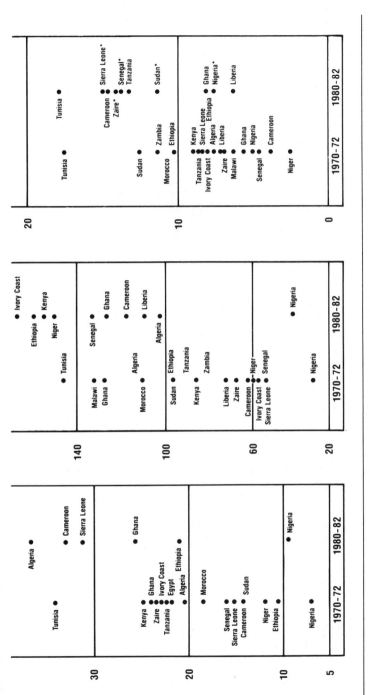

Note: Debt is defined as medium- and long-term public and publicly guaranteed plus private nonguaranteed debt outstanding and disbursed. Short-term debt is not included. For the major borrowers, the inclusion of short-term debt would raise the external debt registered during 1980–82 by about 30 percent. The debt service figures used are those for actual (not contractual) debt service paid during the period. Exports cover goods and total services. An asterisk indicates that the country rescheduled its debt between 1975 and 1984.
Source: World Bank (1985b: 44).

recent study of the railway corporations of the former member states of the East African community found problems with management, maintenance, repairs, replacement of cars and trucks, employee motivation, and small-scale operations.

Some of the more recent railway construction projects have been motivated by regional geopolitics. For example, the government of Tanzania invited the Chinese to build the Tanzam railway line of 1,162 miles linking Zambia to the Tanzanian port of Dar es Salaam (Hull 1980). The project had been rejected by Western investors on grounds of economic considerations, but landlocked Zambia, then the most active and most vulnerable front-line state, badly needed an alternative route to the sea. This would lessen its dependence on hostile South Africa, Rhodesia (now Zimbabwe), Mozambique, and Angola. (Kasuka S. Mutukwa 1979, a Zambian nationalist, provides an interesting discussion and background to the politics and international intrigue behind the Tanzania–Zambia railway project.) Likewise, the Botzam railway line joining Botswana's railway to Zambia was designed to reduce the latter's dependence on hostile South Africa. One railway line that has been built more for economic reasons is the one across Gabon designed to haul manganese, iron, and other minerals from the interior to the port. Similarly, Malawi's recent additions to its railway systems financed in part by the Canadian International Development Agency had no obvious geopolitical considerations.

Railways are facing increasing competition from road transportation and often need government protection to remain operational. In East Africa, for example, the government of Kenya had to prohibit the movement of certain commercial goods by road in order to ensure the railways a reasonable volume of business.

Roads are a much more attractive alternative for transportation in Africa. They are cheaper to build and maintain, more flexible, and are more likely to develop into a real transport network than the railway lines that radiate from one point to the sea with little or no feeder lines. For this reason African states decided to build a trans-African highway designed to link Kenya's Mombasa port on the Indian Ocean to the Port of Lagos in Nigeria. This 4,000-mile highway would go through six different countries and connect to a West African highway joining Algiers in Algeria to Lagos. Eventually another highway would be built to join Harare in Zimbabwe (later Cape Town) to Cairo in Egypt. When these connections are completed, and if interstate transport restrictions can be eased, the continent's movement of goods and services, people, and ideas will be greatly enhanced.

Before independence all shipping lines serving Africa were foreign owned. Today several states, including Ghana and Nigeria, own and operate their own shipping lines. The shipping business, however, is still dominated by Japanese, European, U.S., and even Soviet large companies. These form monopolistic shipping conferences that regulate tariffs and control the market. For example, in West Africa Hull (1980) identified the U.K./West Africa Lines (UKWAL) and the France/West Africa and the Continental West Africa merger (COWAC) as two of the dominant shipping conferences in West Africa.

African ports and harbors are congested. It takes weeks and months to clear goods from the busiest ports like Lagos, where up to 400 vessels at a time may be waiting to enter the port (Hull 1980). This adds to the cost and administrative inconvenience of doing business in Africa and creates opportunities for corruption. In Nigeria, it is not unusual for industrial goods to be brought in from Europe by air in order to avoid Lagos.

Port facilities are often inadequate to handle extra volume. For example, Ethiopian ports were found unequipped to handle the extra volume of food aid that was coming in during the 1984–85 national famine. Dar es Salaam in Tanzania could double its volume of business from neighboring states if it had the proven capacity to handle the extra volume. One of the problems with the Tanzam railway is that the port of Dar es Salaam could not handle Zambia's copper exports and imports. Since the introduction of container shipping in the 1960s, African ports have had to make large capital investments to develop their port facilities to be able to attract international shipping business.

Air travel in Africa is limited to connections with Europe, Asia, and the Middle East. Internal air transport is underdeveloped, is available only for major urban centers, and is too expensive for most of the local population. Most African countries have their own carriers, which are small, uneconomical, and losing money. Jorgensen (1985) found that landlocked countries justify owning their own airlines on account of national security. About one-third of all the African states are landlocked.

Attempts to run regional airlines have not been successful. The East African Airways Corporation was dissolved in 1977 when its parent organization, the East African Community, was broken up by its member states. Air Afrique, started in the early 1960s by a group of Francophone states, became unoperational when member states pulled out to form independent national airlines. It is now able to operate scheduled flights only because of an association with Air France. Other African airlines have been able to improve their operations only by developing associations with large European or U.S. airlines. The best known example is

Ethiopian Airlines, which, in spite of Ethiopia's domestic political, economic, and security problems, is one of the most successful African airlines. This is because the airline has had a long standing working relationship with Trans-World Airlines. Zambia Airways and Air Zaire have also developed similar relationships with Alitalia and Pan-American, respectively (Hull 1980).

Postal, telegraph, and telephone comunications are not fully developed either. Africa is now working toward a continental telecommunications network that will link with individual national networks. This network will be connected by microwave, telephone, telegraph, telex, and data transmission, making it unnecessary to depend on European centers for connections across Africa. Space satellites are also being slowly introduced to provide enhanced communication capabilities. The larger and more prosperous countries like Nigeria, Zaire, and Algeria have made use of satellite technology more than the small or impoverished ones. Currently, Bell Canada International, a subsidiary of Bell Canada Enterprises of Montreal, is actively involved in the development, maintenance, and management of an integrated communications network linking together many African countries, especially among the West African Francophone countries.

Radio and television stations are owned and operated by the government. Nigeria has one of the most advanced broadcasting systems on the continent. High linguistic differentiations within each of the states make programming and broadcasting difficult for most of the African countries. Consequently, most of the entertainment programs are brought from Europe and the United States. Radio and, to a limited extent, television have much potential as a means of communication especially with the rural population where illiteracy is still high. Although governments have been unable to use these media effectively to reach and influence the peasant farmers, guerilla movements and freedom fighters in countries like Angola, Mozambique, Rhodesia, and Uganda have used the radio quite effectively in reaching potential recruits and supporters.

Newspapers, magazines, and periodicals are found only in the urban areas. Although some of these are privately owned, African governments have worked hard to assume a considerable degree of ownership and control of the print media. Consequently, the more authoritative and critical African magazines are not published on the continent. The collection of international news is still dominated by the international news organizations, especially the Associated Press and United Press International.

Timely and accurate information is key to effective decisionmaking, yet national, sectorial, and organizational statistics are hard to come by. They are often dated, incomplete, unreliable, or of unknown quality. National bureaus of statistics operate on small budgets and lack experienced personnel and effective administrative and technical support to provide all the required statistical databases. Efforts have been made to improve economic statistics, especially by the international organizations like the World Bank, which need the data for aid and technical assistance. Population statistics are steadily improving in quality, especially because population growth has been identified as a serious problem for a number of African countries. Social statistics on the other hand, are not as good.

At the organizational level, there are serious problems of obtaining information, especially relating to the performance of African organizations. This is particularly true for government departments and agencies as well as state-owned enterprises. For example, it is not uncommon for a state-owned enterprise to have no statements of final accounts for a period of three years. In some cases, this may be due to lack of professional accountants, but in others, top management may not be keen to make such information public for fear that it would reflect badly on their management capabilities.

The small private-sector organizations simply do not keep systematic records. Even those used for income tax purposes are often suspect. Subsidiaries of multinational corporations collect and keep systematic records but do not publish them separately from their parent operations. At the microlevels, individual managers or employees often do not know how well or badly they are doing their jobs. The internal management information system is simply not developed well enough. Computers, wherever they have been introduced in Africa (Ingle and Smith 1984; Taylor and Obudho 1977), have tended to be used only for routine administrative and accounting tasks like billing, payroll, and recordkeeping.

Consequently, the movement of goods, services, and people and the flow of ideas, data, and information in Africa remain circumscribed. National, sectorial, institutional, and individual operational and strategic decisions are made with very incomplete information.

THE STATE OF TECHNOLOGY

Although the state of technology in Africa varies by country and sector, it is generally less advanced than most other developing countries. Within agriculture, one finds two distinct types of technology. Peasant farming, carried out by the majority of the farming population, uses the simplest agricultural tools and implements and has been the most resilient to technological change. Large-scale farming, on the other hand, uses fairly modern agricultural equipment from the world's largest suppliers (such as International Harvester). These, however, often experience service and maintenance problems and are not regularly updated. Production costs are higher on these firms, but the technology is necessary for the required increases in agricultural output to feed the increasing population and attempt to counteract falling commodity world prices.

In mining, modern equipment is used to keep within the international competitive cost structure, but because of the large sums of money involved, these are not often kept regularly upgraded. Some countries are also putting relatively less emphasis on mining (especially in the face of widely fluctuating base metal prices) and are giving agriculture more emphasis. This means less money for modernizing the mining industry.

Africa's contribution to the world's manufacturing sector has remained almost constant since the 1960s at about 0.6 percent. Attempts have been made to bring in modern technology, but these are hampered by at least two problems. First, the average size of the African manufacturing plant is quite small, largely because of the small size of the domestic or regional market. Consequently, large-scale mass production manufacturing technology is not common in Africa. Second, attempts, though unsuccessful, have been made to import labor-intensive types of technology. Because most of the modern technology on the world markets is designed to save on labor, Africa's public policy has tended to discourage its importation.

In other industries like energy, construction, transportation and communication, and the service industry in general, the state of technology is modern but not in the leading edge. Computer technology has not made a significant impact on Africa except in a few limited areas—especially in the area of office automation. In general, Africa lags ten to twenty years behind the industrialized countries in technological advancement, and in some sectors, the gap is widening.

TECHNOLOGY AND TECHNOLOGY TRANSFER

From the preceding discussions it should be clear that sub-Saharan Africa is lagging behind in the importation and effective utilization and management of foreign technology. This holds true in all regions and sectors of Africa. The promise of the availability of technology has not solved problems of underdevelopment and its consequences. For example, modern farming methods and techniques have not persuaded the peasant farmers to give up their traditional farming or pastoral practices in Tanzania (Moris 1981), the Sudan (Gallais and Sidikou 1978; Pelissier and Diarra 1978), or elsewhere in Africa. Factories continue to operate well below capacity. Modern family planning techniques have not brought about any significant changes in birth rates.

Africa is not a technology developer because almost no research and development takes place on the continent. It is also a poor copier of technology. There is a tendency to view new technology as static, fixed, and monumental and not to take a functional perspective of such technology as a dynamic process that is constantly changing and evolving to higher levels of performance. While the rest of the world is grappling with the problems of living with and managing advanced information technology based on sophisticated high technology, Africa is still preoccupied with problems of perfecting mechanical systems (such as the railway steam engines) that have been used elsewhere for at least 100 years. Although robotics are not likely to be widely used in Africa for a long time to come, automation especially in the industrial, commercial, and service sectors is highly likely. This is because in the past, industrial organizations have tended to favor capital- rather than labor-intensive technology (Chambua 1985; Babatunde 1986; Williams 1984). Efforts to rekindle old African technologies based on local technical and social support systems are under way but are of limited scope (Asiegbu 1985).

There are numerous studies of the process, problems, and prospects of technology transfer in Africa (such as Gallais and Sidikou 1978; Ingle and Smith 1984; Taylor and Obudha 1977; Wallender 1979). These studies cover a wide range of issues, and their conclusions will not be repeated here. Instead, we present a process model of international transfer of technology that explains the origin, evolution, and processes of technology transfer across national borders, over time, and at different levels of analysis.

Figure 6–2 gives the basic elements of the model. It covers two distinct time periods: the period immediately after World War II and the period following independence for the African or developing country in question. The figure also shows that the model is transactional and identifies the major actors for each time period and their respective roles either as recipients or providers of technology. The arrows indicate the direction of the flow of the technology.

Five different levels of technology transfer are identified in the model.

Figure 6–2. A Process Model of International Transfer of Technology.

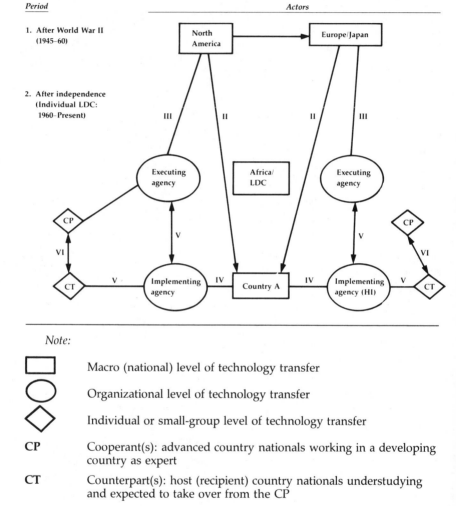

Note:

▭	Macro (national) level of technology transfer
◯	Organizational level of technology transfer
◇	Individual or small-group level of technology transfer
CP	Cooperant(s): advanced country nationals working in a developing country as expert
CT	Counterpart(s): host (recipient) country nationals understudying and expected to take over from the CP
LDC	Developing countries
⟶	Direction of technology transfer
I–VI	Different levels/types of technology transfer

Level I involves technology transfer among developed countries. The best known example of this type of transaction is the Marshall Plan (OEDC 1978), which shows the United States exporting massive forms of technology (such as capital goods and financial assistance) to European countries whose economies and industrial physical infrastructure had been destroyed by the war. Even today there is a lot of ongoing technology transfer among the industrialized countries, particularly Japan, the United States, France, West Germany, and the United Kingdom. Here, but also in other levels of technology transfer, it is not implied that the actor or actors receiving the technology play only a passive role. For example, speaking of the Marshall Plan, Gordon pointed out that although the initiative came from the United States, "its development into operational form and its subsequent implementation were joint products of trans-Atlantic political, intellectual, and administrative collaboration" (Organization for Economic Cooperation and Development 1978: 16–17). The Marshall Plan is important for Africa and other developing countries because it provides the basis, rationale, and mechanics for subsequent levels of technology transfer.

Level II technology transfer directly involves both the industrialized and developing countries as provider (donor) and recipient, respectively. This is the level most commonly discussed in international development, aid, and technical assistance. It often starts on a large scale only after a developing country has achieved political independence and is therefore free to seek development assistance from a variety of countries. The most recent example is Zimbabwe, which gained independence in 1980 after a period of destructive internal strife and economic sanctions imposed on the illegal (Rhodesian) regime. Today, most industrialized countries are involved in a mini-Marshall Plan providing technology and other forms of technical assistance to the new Zimbabwe. Level II technology transfer can also involve countries that have been independent for a long time, like Egypt, Ethiopia, and Liberia, each of which has at one time or another received massive assistance from the United States and other industrialized nations.

Technology transfer at Levels I and II are at a macro-, country-to-country level of transaction and analysis. Subsequent levels, however, deal with more microlevels of the actors involved in the process down to the individual counterpart or cooperator (technical advisor). Discussions of the first two levels tend to be concerned with matters of international relations and are global, political, bilateral, ideological, and often lacking in operational details of implementation.

Level III identifies the actors as the technology-exporting country and the agency or organization that it uses to undertake the actual transfer. The executing agency may be a subsidiary of a multinational corporation operating in the recipient African country, or, as is often the case in international development, it may be a nongovernment organization (NGO) like a university, which is contracted by the technology-donating nation to undertake the actual implementation of the transfer. For example, when the USAID wanted to transfer management know-how to the SADCC countries of southern Africa, it contracted the work out to the University of Maryland and to the National Association of Schools of Public Affairs and Administration (NASPAA). These two organizations would be called the *executing agencies*. Level III transactions tend to receive little or no attention because African governments often fail to make the important distinction between the funding agency (such as USAID) and the executing agency that plays the most critical role in the whole transfer process.

Level IV specifies the relationship between the technology-receiving country and the agency or organization in which the technology is to be introduced. This is called the *implementing agency*. It may be a government department, a state-owned enterprise, a service organization like a hospital, or in rare cases, a privately owned business organization. Earlier, we discussed the Kenya Tea Development Authority (KTDA). If the United States wanted to give technical assistance to Kenya in modern methods of processing, packaging, and exporting tea, the KTDA might be used as the implementing agency. Once again it is important to distinguish between the government of Kenya, representing the receiving country, and KTDA as the focus of the intended organizational change and development.

Levels V and VI are more micro and relate to the operational and interpersonal relationships between the individuals directly involved in the implementation of the technology transfer process. Level V focuses on the relationship between the implementing agency and the counterpart(s). Counterparts are the receiving (host) country nationals who are charged with the responsibility of learning all about the new technology to be able to use it on a continuing basis in solving work problems. The counterpart may be a single individual, a work group, or in case of new projects, the staff of the entire organization. The counterparts must be able and willing (motivation) to learn the knowledge and skills associated with the effective utilization of the new technology. They must also have the motivation to use such expertise on a continuing basis in solving work problems.

Level VI deals with the relationship between the executing agency and the cooperant. The cooperant is an agent of the executing agency charged with the responsibility of passing on the knowledge, skills, expertise, professional values, attitudes, and conduct to the counterpart(s).

Although often employed by the executing agency, the cooperants work within the implementing agency, which may require them to report to two masters. Both the counterparts and the cooperants are considered change agents and should, among other things, have the knowledge and practical experience in the management of change and organization development (Kiggundu 1986a).

Several points should be noted about this model. First, it provides an analytical framework for technology transfer at different national and organizational levels of analysis. It is expected that in the determination of effective technology transfer, different factors are operative at different levels of transactions. Second, the model is based on the existence of the counterpart system. Literal replications of the Marshall Plan in Africa and other developing countries were not successful because, unlike Europe and other industrialized recipient countries, Africa lacks the necessary physical, technical, intellectual, institutional, and social infrastructures. The counterpart system deals with these limitations by providing counterparts with on-the-job training to acquire the necessary expertise and build the required infrastructure. Yet on-the-job training as a method of transferring knowledge and work experience can be ineffective (Goldstein 1974).

What is the relevance of this model for understanding and managing technology transfer in Africa? It specifies the process, identifies the major actors, the direction of technology flow, and the different levels of transactions. Any proposed technology transfer project can be analyzed using this model to assess its likelihood of success. Previous technology transfer projects (such as Moris 1981; Wallender 1979; Paul 1982) can be analyzed to explain past failures or successes. Comparisons can also be made among technology transfer projects across time, sectors, or countries.

It is generally believed that the most serious problems or bottlenecks to effective technology transfer to Africa are at the microlevels of the individuals or organizations directly involved in the transfer process (Figure 6-2, Levels III to VI). Future research and intervention should therefore be aimed at improving our understanding of the determinants of effective or ineffective technology transfer at these levels.

INDUSTRIAL ORGANIZATION

Africa's industrial organization can be described as small, beautiful, and vulnerable. There are a few monopolistic large firms in each of the leading sectors, very few medium-size firms, and a large number of very small entrepreneurial firms. The large firms are either subsidiaries of large multinational corporations, state-owned, or international joint ventures between the state and the MNC. The medium-size firms tend to be locally owned either by the rising African entrepreneurial class, by Africans of Asian or Middle East origin (such as in Kenya and Ivory Coast), or by a combination of domestic and foreign private interests. The small firms are usually family owned, and their growth is limited by capital, managerial skills, or hostile government policies.

There is a very active informal sector both in the African urban centers and in the rural areas where the large MNC subsidiaries and state-owned enterprises are not active. This sector, usually made up of firms with a few operations, is very active especially in services, construction, carpentry, transport, metal works, and mechanical repairs and services. These firms provide the greatest opportunity for permanent employment, but they suffer from competition from the larger firms and government policies that range from neglect to outright hostility. Rural technical institutes, like the Kenya institutes of technology, are designed in part to provide technical and managerial skills in the rural areas to support the budding informal sector.

Recent attention in Africa has been paid to the importance of small-scale enterprises (SSE) as agents of industrialization. For example, a recent World Bank report by John Page and William Steel (1984) observed that SSE play an important role in the development of entrepreneurship in Africa as they do in other low-income regions. It further argues that SSE are particularly advantageous to Africa because they (1) are labor intensive; (2) provide for higher total factor productivity; (3) concentrate among lower-income population and contribute to more even distribution of income; (4) facilitate greater share of ownership by nationals; (5) depend largely on domestic sources of capital and savings; (6) conserve scarce managerial abilities and technical skills; (7) use technology more appropriate to local conditions; (8) do not compete directly with large-scale firms; and (9) do not need sophisticated infrastructures. Small-scale industries employing no more than fifty employees are particularly common in clothing, manufacturing and repair, furniture and woodworking, metalworking, food products, shoemaking and repair, transport, pottery, and other agribusinesses. In countries like Botswana and Dumndi, SSEs constitute more than half of industrial output.

There are a few private international firms (of which Bata Shoe Company of Toronto is the most active) in most countries in Africa. Bata Shoe is now being challenged by the local indigenous shoemakers, thus creating a more competitive climate in the footwear industry. In a situation of high concentration of a few large, often foreign organizations, there is an urgent need to develop an active and fairly sizable indigenous private sector. In the long run, this may be the best strategy toward eventual privatization of the industrial and commercial sectors.

ORGANIZATION AND MANAGEMENT SYSTEMS

In this section, emphasis is on the internal management systems of individual organizations. Previous sections have discussed the general and environmental context within which African organizations are managed. These contextual factors must be kept in mind as the discussion shifts to the internal systems and processes. The six internal management systems discussed below are (1) management philosophy and organization process, (2) organization structure, (3) leadership and management, (4) motivation, (5) marketing, and (6) human resource management.

Management Philosophy and Organization Process

This section is concerned with two related aspects of management in Africa. It discusses the basic elements of the prevailing management philosophy in African organizations today and describes the inside of such organizations.

The dominant management philosophy, although not necessarily the practice, is similar to the principles of classical management. There are sharp distinctions and status differences between management and workers. Management has the power, the controls, the authority, and the rewards and punishments. The workers are expected to do their work and obey management's instructions and directives. The resulting organizations are hierarchical, tall, highly bureaucratic, and mechanistic, and communication is mainly one way, from top to bottom. Fear seems to be the greatest driving force for everyone in the organization including management. In these organizations, one detects various sources of fear including fear of punishment, fear of losing one's job, fear of victimization, and fear of fear. There is a generalized sense of helplessness—of not being in control of one's destiny.

The work ethics and corresponding work habits are different from what are found in the United States and Europe. Loyalty and commitment to the organization is nebulous and elusive. People do not stay in a job or work for the organization out of a sense of organizational commitment, but personal, social, or family needs and circumstances. Individual rather than organizational goals seem to drive employee behavior as organizational goals remain unknown or ignored in the majority of cases. The idea of a fair day's work for a fair day's pay is not operative. Instead, there is a generalized attitude of entitlement, such that members of the organization believe that they are entitled to receive and enjoy the benefits and pecuniary advantages from the organization regardless of their individual contribution to the organization's goals. In some African countries, there is no fair pay compared to the cost of living.

Management's concept of rewards and incentives tends to be narrowly defined and limited to monetary and extrinsic rewards. Performance tends to be measured in terms of ideals (plans) and symbols. Psychic income is important. Performance-based reward systems and incentives are rare except in the private sector. There is a socialist belief in some African organizations that private business is exploitative, that profits are dirty, and that government should own, manage, and control means of production in order to protect the workers from capitalists' exploitations. It is hard to determine the extent to which this ideological position pervades organizations in Africa. It is clear, however, that it is a popular theme among young intellectuals, politicians, journalists, and some labor leaders. It does not seem to be strong among the workers, farmers, and managers—even those who manage state-owned and state-controlled enterprises.

Innovation, entrepreneurship, risk taking, and individualism are not valued or rewarded. Instead they are discouraged, and as a result, African organizations are short of "change masters." There is little support for change even when the status quo in these organizations is unsatisfactory. Long-range planning is not taken seriously, and even when plans and budgets are made, they have little effect on the day-to-day management of the organization. Very few African organizations have explicit mission statements.

What does the inside of an African organization look like? It would be characteristically overcrowded and improvising in a number of areas. Jobs would be narrowly designed, and all important decisions would be made by senior management and communicated down through the chain of command. Facilities, equipment, machinery, and buildings would look overutilized and in need of repair and maintenance.

The composition of the members of the organization would be heterogenous with subgroups clustered based on race, religion, education, or ethnic background. These subgroups would be internally homogenous but distinct from one another. Some members of the organization would identify with these subgroups more than with the organization. Formal communication would be in English, French, or another European language, but informally people would communicate in various African local languages.

There would be an atmosphere of management by crisis as events would seem to take everybody by surprise. Conflicts would tend to be avoided, smoothed over rather than directly confronted. Direct confrontation is not a common method of conflict resolution. Although there would be a lot of activities in these organizations, very few people would be able to assess how well or badly they or the organization as a whole was performing.

Organization Structure

African organization structures can be differentiated by type, size, and ownership of the organization. Government bureaucracies and public enterprises are often large, hierarchical, and mechanistic, with highly centralized and formal systems of administration. Small indigenous organizations are often informal, nonhierarchical, flat, and lacking in formalization but have centralized or individual decisionmaking practices. Subsidiaries of foreign multinational corporations are truncated both at the strategic apex (top) and operating core (Mintzberg 1979).

A recent evaluation of a government educational institution in Kenya describes a typical structure of a government agency. In their evaluation report, Nicholson, Ostrom, Bowles, and Long (1985) describe the bureaucracy as too large, mismanaged, and costing more money than it is worth. They also found that the overstaffed bureaucracy was seriously underemployed in the lower ranks, understaffed in the middle technical and professional ranks, and overworked at the senior and executive levels. Accordingly, such a bureaucracy cannot fulfill its responsibilities because it tends to be weak, vacillating, with a poor sense of direction and a debilitating unwillingness to take independent action.

The management philosophy is authoritarian, politicized with highly personalized leadership. According to Nicholson et al. (1985) this leads to the emergency of a strong executive, a weak bureaucracy, and a highly centralized allocation of resources.

Lower-level employees are neither encouraged nor rewarded for taking initiative. In a recent study of Canadian business executives who had returned from a business development tour of Kenya, it was found that lack of management was reported as one of the problems of doing business in Kenya (Dasah and Kiggundu 1985). Expressing concern about lack of middle-management talents, one of the executives put it, "Black top level officials have a pathological reluctance to delegate and they tend to cut off winners for fear of exposing their own weaknesses" (Dasah and Kiggundu 1985: 5).

Attempts at decentralization or devolution of power to lower levels of the organization have been largely unsuccessful in Africa (Blunt 1984). The African social organizations have demonstrated tremendous resistance to different forms of bureaucratic reorientation and reform. Writing about bureaucratic orientation for participatory rural development, Korten and Uphoff (1981) observed that although these reforms inevitably involve changing individual attitudes and values, the most important part involves changes in job definitions, performance criteria, career incentives, bureaucratic procedures, and organizational responsibilities. They also observed that these structural changes need, but are unlikely to get, continuing support and commitment from top bureaucratic and political echelons. Given the highly complex, dualistic and divided environment in which African organizations operate (Kiggundu 1985), it would appear that centralized, hierarchical structures would be highly dysfunctional. To date, however, no effective strategies of organization development leading to more decentralized or participatory forms have been found.

Leadership and Management

There is an acute shortage of quality leadership and management in Africa. Management is perhaps the most critical, but often neglected, link between plans, hopes, expectations, opportunities, and aspirations of the vast majority of the Africans, and the harsh realities of scarcity, deprivation, despair, and powerlessness that have come to characterize the continent. Various studies have documented the shortages of managerial skills and experience and their individual and cumulative negative impact on development (Blunt 1983; Haddow 1982; Honadle 1986; White 1986). Yet prevailing management styles whereby the formal leader remains the unquestioned authority on all matters of importance is not conducive for management development and the emergence of new leadership. Entrepreneurial, creative, and development talents are suppressed in favor of bureaucratic risk-averse administration based on absolute obedience.

Leadership and management require two basic but rather different tasks: (1) the effective management of the organization/environment relations to continue to exchange critical resources including political support and (2) effective utilization and management of these resources to enable the organization to meet its goals and objectives. The first requires the articulation of the organization's long-term strategies, goals, and objectives based on a dynamic understanding of the organization's mission and the opportunities and constraints of the environment within which the organization operates. The second set of tasks requires good understanding and applications of modern management techniques. In Africa, most organizations are weak in the management of both types of tasks.

The importance of these tasks for effective management was recently demonstrated in an evaluation study of six agricultural projects in six different African countries (Kenya, Lesotho, Liberia, Niger, Senegal, and Zaire). In this study, Honadle (1986) found that effective management of these projects requires

1. The management of the interactions between the project and other organizations,
2. The effective use of informal communication and decisionmaking processes, and
3. The development of teamwork and compensation, which creates conditions for shared responsibilities among the various stakeholders.

Projects in which these tasks were well managed were also more effective than the others. This requires management expertise not readily available in African organizations, especially in government departments, agencies, and enterprises. It was with this experience in mind that a recent study of postgraduate training and utilization of professionals concluded that "to the extent that a trade-off exists between training more analysts and technical professionals and training Governmental managers, the Government should give priority to the training of managers" (Haddow 1982: 133).

Although it is widely acknowledged that the management capabilities of African organizations need to be more fully developed, there is little agreement as to the details of what needs to be done. A recent study of the management critical incidents collected from senior government department heads and their deputies of the nine SADCC countries provides some indication of the management problems facing African organizations. The purpose of this study was to identify the management training and development required for these countries. The study (NASPAA 1985) found the following areas where African managers were particularly weak and required support and assistance:

1. Accounting and financial management skills and practices,
2. Special management skills for senior management,
3. Clear understanding of government rules and regulation, especially at the middle level,
4. Entrepreneurial skills and behavior both in the public and private sectors,
5. The management and utilization of expatriate staffs,
6. Development of negotiation skills,
7. The development and training of junior and middle-level managers for high positions,
8. Improvements in the management of the training function, and
9. The development and utilization of organization development consultants.

These recommendations, together with Kiggundu's (In press) suggestions that emphasis should be given to the development of change agents, may provide the basis for addressing the serious problem of managerial shortages in Africa. Again, the focus must be on the individual manager as well as his or her organizational context in which the organization's most important tasks are performed.

Motivation

The following dialogue (Oshagbemi 1983: 23) between a Nigerian civil servant and his wife illustrates the operational needs, motives, expectations, and fears of the African worker:

Wife: Babi Bisi, you need to change your car soon.
Ojo: What type of car do you recommend that I buy?
Wife: You know that I am not choosy. Any new car that is air-conditioned will do. How about a Volvo? The type that Baba Jide bought last month.
Ojo: Baba Jide is a company director. I am a civil servant. Where do I get the money?
Wife: Why do you stay in that useless job? Everybody else is now a contractor and living fine. Ours is a case of living from hand to mouth. And I am fed up living in this house. It is too choked up.
Ojo: Then I too will go into business.
Wife: That is better. Then we can spend our holidays in Paris and London.

This dialogue is quite suggestive. First, it clearly shows that the urban educated African worker is driven by conspicuous consumption dictated by foreign tastes and fueled by unreasonable family and social pressures. Second, it illustrates some of the wrong reasons and expectations for going into business. Finally, it shows why the civil and public service, one of the fastest growing sectors by employment, may experience difficulties attracting and retaining competent, experienced, and hardworking professionals.

The dialogue and the research on motivation that has been done in Africa and reviewed by Blunt (1983) indicate that there are wide variations in sources of motivation across organizational levels and racial subgroups. The few managers and professionals at the top are motivated by material and higher-order needs *à la* Maslow (1954) and Hackman and Oldham (1980), whereas the majority of employees working in low-paying jobs are still driven by basic needs (such as food, clothing, housing, transportation, and drinking). For example, a study of motivation in Liberia showed that the African workers were motivated by lower-level needs (Howell, Strauss, and Sorensen 1975).

There are many countries in Africa where the workers do not earn a living wage. These places can be found in the urban areas of Uganda, the Sudan, Zaire, and parts of Nigeria. This is not limited to lower-level employees only because inflation rates make it almost impossible for employers to pay a decent living wage. Under these conditions, workers often engage in moonlighting practices, corruption, and abuse of organizational privileges for personal interests.

Organizational incentives are not only inadequate, but they often are inappropriate. In rural areas, farmers are not given enough incentives to boost production or to abandon traditional farming or pastoral practices in order to use modern methods. In the formal organizations, reward systems are not contingent on performance or any other desired behavior. In a recent study of six agricultural projects in six African countries, White (1986) found inadequate and inappropriate incentive practices in these countries. She also found that although incentives and monitoring are related, these countries did not have good performance-monitoring mechanisms.

Blunt (1982, 1983) has done an extensive review of the empirical studies of alienation and motivation in African organizations. He found that the urban African worker suffered from alienation, low self-esteem, isolation, normlessness, and powerlessness. Several reasons were given for these results. First, many workers found the discipline and structures of a modern working environment too imposing and restrictive. Second, there are problems of communication across organizational levels, especially in organizations where the workers and management belong to different racial or ethnic background. Blunt found, as for example, that

"Many of the subjects . . . indicated their displeasure at 'not being listened to' and not being allowed to explain their problems fully" (Blunt 1983: 49). In a society where age is a symbol of respect and status, it is not surprising that older men were most disturbed by the poor quality of their working lives.

Poor employment opportunities both in the rural and urban areas contributed to the alienation and poor morale. Within the urban employment sectors, lack of alternative employment opportunities forced workers to stay in dissatisfying jobs and not voice their dissatisfaction to management. This gave management the latitude to pay little or no attention to employee needs and, in some cases, to mistreat them. Between the rural and urban areas, studies have shown that given comparable alternatives, many African workers would rather work and live in their home villages or towns rather than in the big urban centers. They live in these big cities as the only way to meet their own and kinship financial obligations. They find these urban areas impersonal and take away their power, freedom, movement, and choice. Yet the rural areas offer no realistic employment opportunites. It is not surprising that tribal associations are active in most large African urban centers to provide the needed social and psychological support for the urban workers who are isolated from their natural social and family support systems.

Do U.S. theories of motivation apply in Africa? This question has been investigated by several researchers. For example, Blunt (1983) reviews the empirical evidence of several need theories of motivation (such as Maslow, McClellend, Herzberg, and Hackman and Oldham) and concludes that there are serious limitations in applying these theories either for theory development or organization interventions. He suggests that these theories should be used with caution. Kiggundu, Jorgensen, and Hafsi (1983) also concluded that both research and practice should emphasize *process* rather than *content* theories of motivation. However, a recent Zambian study of work motivation found support for both content and process theories of work motivation. Using the critical incidents method and questionnaires administered to 341 Zambian employees from different types of jobs, Machungwa and Schmitt (1983) found that work motivation in Zambia was determined by six factors: (1) the nature of work, (2) growth and advancement, (3) material and physical provisions, (4) relations with others, (5) fairness/unfairness in organizational practices, and (6) personal problems. All six factors were found to affect motivation both positively and negatively, but the powerful effects of inequity on employee behavior were evident in items relating to the degree of fairness of organizational practices. This study concludes that, with minor modifications, work motivation theories apply in the Zambian context.

Marketing

The prevailing marketing systems and practices reflect the physical, cultural, psychosocial, economic, and political infrastructure and realities of sub-Saharan Africa. For example, polyethnicity, multilingualism, and between- and within-country differences in economic performance, tastes, and purchasing power all make it difficult to develop an integrated marketing system. After reviewing several marketing studies and practices in West Africa, Simon-Miller (1984: 119-20) concluded that "the dual economy typical of sub-Saharan Africa leads to the dysfunctional coexistence of radically opposite distribution patterns unintegrated and poorly linked to the production system." The dual socioeconomic system leads to at least two distinctively different marketing systems: (1) the elite marketing that promotes conspicuous consumption and aims at consumer satisfaction in the context of Western marketing practices and (2) the basic-needs marketing based on functional marketing and ideally aimed at increasing the value of the goods and services only within the narrow context of satisfying the consumer's basic needs.

According to Simon-Miller (1984: 116), marketing conditions are "still the major obstacle to a private sector take-off" in sub-Saharan Africa. These conditions—which include declining agricultural yields and disposable incomes, and limited communication and transport infrastructure—are compounded by negative terms of trade, political risks, limited range of export and import commodities, and a rising international public debt. Even in large countries like Nigeria (about 100 million people), marketing is one of the most neglected managerial functions (Simon-Miller 1984).

The distribution systems are dominated by large foreign-owned rading houses, leaving the small retailing businesses to the small African traders. These big trading houses operate under the sole-agency rules, which makes it hard for indigenous firms to enter the wholesale or distribution market. Moreover, traditional trading and retail practices make it almost impossible to streamline marketing practices in these countries. For example, Simon-Miller (1984) found that in Nigeria, the Yoruba market women are strong not only because of their marketing functions as middlemen between the producers and consumers, but also because they occupy an important sociopolitical position. They are economically independent and receive a great deal of community social recognition. Women also play important marketing functions in Ghana and Kenya and help to bridge the gap between the rural and urban marketing practices, or between the subsistence and monetary economies.

Marketing science has not been applied to the problems of the agricultural sector. As a result, in addition to lower levels of production, agriculture suffers from problems of distribution, packaging and storage, pricing, competition with foreign tastes, and low adoption tastes. Marketing boards and cooperatives, in addition to their chronic management problems, have not effectively used marketing in linking producers with consumers. For example, in many cases, the buying and distribution systems for the outputs (such as crops) and inputs (such as fertilizers) are not streamlined but contain several middleman stages. Instead of working to stimulate markets and marketing, marketing boards and cooperatives have tended to serve as regulators of the marketing systems.

The African consumer has a very strong preference for foreign- (European-) made goods over locally made goods. Accordingly, all the marketing — distribution, advertising, brand naming, labeling, and so forth — reflect this dominant bias. For example, a study of Yoruba markets showed that of all the displays, only just over 2 percent carried locally (Yoruba-) made materials. Retailers' preference to stock and display imported goods is evidenced in retail stores in most African trading centers.

Consumer information and education is often inadequate either because of the advertising media and language used or because the foreign distributor did not take into account the psychocultural dynamics of the African consumer. Inadequate consumer information, especially for new product lines that are not traditionally used (such as infant formula, microwaves) by the consumers, can often lead to product misuse, abuse, or dangerous applications with long-term negative consequences. Low literacy rates as well as traditional cultural values and attitudes must be given due consideration in the development of an African marketing strategy.

Africa is a growing market, not only in terms of population but also in terms of disposable income and effective consumer, commercial, and industrial demand. The marketing system, however, operates under severe structural, physical, and attitudinal constraints that need to be changed. These constraints make it difficult to design and implement an efficient integrated marketing system in Africa. Policies and incentives are needed to ensure the development of local and national marketing systems consistent with national development goals and priorities. It is unlikely that an effective indigenous private sector will thrive unless such a marketing system exists. This in turn requires the development and effective management of modern organizations in all sectors of Africa.

Human Resource Management

It is often claimed that Africa has the three greatest assets: the land, the gods, and the people. The reference to land includes the continent's vast size, diversity, and natural resources. The reference to the gods relates to Africa's unique experiment in creating conditions whereby the higher and lower gods live side by side in apparent harmony. The reference to the people includes the total numbers, distribution, rapid rates of increase, and their determination to live, perseverance, and resilience. This section discusses the problems and prospects for one of Africa's greatest assets—its people.

In spite of the resilience of the African people, it is now generally recognized that the human condition and human resources constitute one of the most serious bottlenecks for development. As a recent World Bank report observed "the lack of human resources constitutes the major constraint on the development of the region. . . . The lack of skills and experience to man the modern public and private sectors has always been regarded as the major constraint on economic development in Africa, and hence, the most serious human resource problem" (Davies 1980: 55, 60).

The report goes on to suggest strategies for addressing the continent's human resource problems, including

1. Strengthening public administration at both the central and local government levels;
2. Putting more emphasis and making more investments in human resource development and management programs to improve the productive and absorptive capacity of the modern sector; and
3. Expanding and improving formal and nonformal education not only for academic and technical skills acquisition but, equally important, for changing attitudes and knowledge for the majority of the people in areas of health, sanitation, nutrition, family planning, and water supplies.

Implementation of these strategies, however, causes serious problems for most African countries. For example, although agriculture is by

Table 6-6. Sub-Saharan Africa: Basic Human Resource Management Statistics (percentage).

	Low-Income Countries		Middle-Income Countries	
	1965	1983	1965	1983
Labor force:				
Percentage of population of working age (15–65 years)	53	51	53	50
Percentage of labor force in:				
Agriculture	84	78	70	60
Industry	7	20	11	16
Services	9	13	19	24
Average annual growth of the labor force (%)	2.2	2.1	2.1	2.5
Average annual population growth (%)	2.6	2.8	2.6	2.9
Education:				
Enrollments in primary schools as a percentage of age group:				
Total	40	69	44	96
Male	52	79	54	99
Female	28	56	34	81
Enrollments in secondary schools (%)	4	14	5	17
Enrollments in higher institutions	LTO	1	LTO	3

Note: LTO = Less than one. Some of the figures do not exactly correspond to the years given in this table. Readers are encouraged to consult the original source.
Source: World Bank (1985b: Tables 21, 25).

far the most important sector by way of employment (see Table 6-6), the formal education systems are ill equipped to prepare students for employment in this sector. Instead, the system is heavily biased toward academic and urban education preparing student for a white-collar office type of employment that is almost unavailable. Second, again as Table 6-6 shows, opportunities for education are very limited indeed. Dropout rates are very high after elementary school because of the lack of adequate educational and learning facilities. Illiteracy is still a problem in most African countries. Although countries like Mali and Kenya are improving the quality and opportunities for effective human resource development in the rural areas by building and improving rural institutions, there is still a significant difference in the quality of education between the urban and rural areas.

In addition to the shortage of trained and experienced human resources in almost all sectors, recent studies show serious problems in effective utilization of available personnel. There is often a mismatch between the people's education, knowledge, and experience on the one hand, and the demands of the jobs they are asked to do on the other. Utilization problems can be caused by a wide range of factors, including inappropriate training and education, inadequate methods of recruitment, selection, placement, and staffing, poor supervision and management, lack of career paths, employee incompetency and obsolescence, and extraorganizational (such as political) interference.

It should also be pointed out that almost all of Africa's educational, training, socialization, and indoctrination in formal organizations is done drawing on Western scientific knowledge systems. Indigenous knowledge systems (IKS) are almost entirely neglected and are despised, especially by those who have made it through the formal educational system. Yet field research shows that IKS in Africa are important because they are holistic, provide a more complete analysis of the situation, and complement the alien and often misunderstood and scientific knowledge systems that tend to suffer from "disciplinary blinkers" (Bell 1979).

Studies show that African organizations may be experiencing serious employee motivation problems. The sources of these problems are varied and not well understood because of lack of adequate empirical research. For example, Kiggundu (1986b) seems to suggest that motivational problems are caused by organizational continued poor performance, which leads to employee frustration and alienation as the organization fails to provide the expected opportunity to satisfy the employee's salient needs. West African scholars tend to emphasize material rewards as the only source of employee motivation. For example, Kofi Ankomah (1985: 408), a Ghanaian management specialist with field experience in southern Africa, comes very close to Oshagbemi's position (see above section on motivation) when he writes, "Most people in postindependence African countries are not inspired to work because they lack desire to accomplish something. The African bureaucrat is often motivated to work by material things he can gain from work. He engages in those activities of work that will result either in immediate financial gains or possessing the potential for such."

In spite of all these human resource problems, the personnel function of a typical African organization is quite underdeveloped. Emphasis tends to be placed on maintenance personnel and industrial relations functions like payroll and salary administration, employee welfare benefits, and administration of the collective agreements where these may be in force. Personnel departments of organizations whose employees are facing severe economic hardship of deteriorating social services tend to spend most of their resources on employee social and welfare programs. For example, an increasing number of organizations in Africa are now involved in providing employees with transport to and from work, meals, housing, medical services, and recreation facilities. Big rural employers like mining companies are particularly active in community extraorganizational activities.

Development personnel and human resource development functions, like training and management development, organization development, career planning, job design, and personnel research, are largely neglected in most African organizations. The personnel departments tend to be poorly or inadequately staffed so that even if the personnel manager wanted to undertake some developmental work, staff shortages would make it extremely difficult. Although middle-income countries have active personnel professional associations, these are almost nonexistent in the low-income African countries. Moreover, the relative small size of the African organization by number of total employment means that the personnel function will remain relatively underdeveloped. Even in the United States, organizations with less than 250 employees do not have well-developed personnel functions. Because the average size of organizations in Africa is not likely to increase significantly in the near future, it would appear that one way of making sure that they have access to advanced personnel and human resource management systems and practices is to have these functions organized by sector or industry. For example, instead of each manufacturing plant's having its own personnel department, the national manufacturers' association could develop such a department and provide the developmental HRM services to individual member organizations. These and other new and innovative approaches to human resource management must be explored because it is very clear that Africa's development initiatives will continue to be frustrated as long as its human resources are not developed to their fullest potential.

SUMMARY AND CONCLUSION

In this chapter, we have discussed selected aspects of the context and process of organization and management in Africa. Under context, we have included various aspects of the sociopolitical context; the economic system; trade, money, banking, finance, and the public debt; transportation, communications, and information flows; and technology and technology transfer. It was concluded that these contextual factors significantly affect the internal management process of African organizations. The internal organization and management systems included organization structure, leadership and management, motivation and marketing. The discussion has emphasized the importance of organization and management for resolving Africa's current social, political, and economic crisis.

At the same time this chapter was written in the summer of 1986, the United Nations Special Session on the African Crisis was being conducted in New York City. This was an international forum where the African governments and the international community met to discuss the problems of and solutions to the crisis. In concluding this chapter, we analyze the final report of this forum and examine the extent to which it deals with issues similar to those discussed above. Three aspects of the report were of particular interest: the statement of the definition of the problem or crisis and its causes; the solutions suggested for the identified problem or problems and their causes; and the extent to which attention has been paid to the problems and potential solutions associated with organization and management, both context and process, of African organizations.

In the final report of the Ad Hoc Committee on the Critical Economic Situation in Africa adopted by the United Nations General Assembly (United Nations 1986), it was observed that the persistent economic crisis in Africa has been aggravated by a combination of exogenous and endogenous factors. The endogenous factors include deficiencies in institutional and physical infrastructure, ineffective economic policies, urban/rural disparities of income, wealth, and opportunities, insufficient managerial and administrative capacities, inadequate human resources development, lack of financial resources, demographic problems, and political instability leading to a growing refugee population.

The exogenous factors causing or aggravating the crisis included the recent international economic recession, decline in commodity prices, adverse terms of trade, decline in financial flows, increased protectionism, high interest rates, and heavy burden of debt and debt financing. Clearly, both the endogenous and exogenous factors discussed by this forum are similar to the issues discussed in this chapter. It is encouraging to note that there is a high degree of candor and consensus about the

African crisis and its causes. This is the first step toward searching for a long-term and permanent solution to the crisis.

The report's proposed solutions focus on increased production in all sectors. Specifically, it recommends priority developments in agriculture, sectors in support of agriculture, transport, and communication, defense against drought, desertification, human resource development, planning, and utilization, population control policies, policy reforms including management of the economy, exchange rate adjustments, salary and wage reductions, public employment freeze, improved efficiency for the parastatal organizations, and support for the private sector. It also emphasizes the need for broader participation of the people in development including women.

These priority development solutions are similar to some of the management context factors discussed in this chapter (such as agriculture, transportation, and communication, human resource development, and so forth). Although the final report reiterated the position of the Lagos Plan of Action, it is clear that the conservative pressures of the international financial institutions like the International Monetary Fund (IMF) and the World Bank, as well as the aid donor countries like the United States are strongly reflected in this document. The proposed public policy reforms and economic adjustments are very similar to the usual IMF conditions imposed on member countries in economic and financial difficulties (Mohiddin 1985).

On the surface, it does not appear as if the United Nation Session paid more attention to organization and management than it had on previous occasions. There are, however, some promising signs of increasing awareness of the need to increase organizational effectiveness through improved management practices. For example, the final report specifically states that the priority solutions indentified above would require "improvement of public management systems, institutions and practices, improvement of the performance of public enterprises; reforming the public services to make them more development-oriented services, greater mobilization of domestic savings, improvement of financial management, including debt and development aid, fiscal administration and control of public expenditure with a view to promoting the efficient use of resources and cutting on wastage and resource misallocation, reduction of foreign exchange leakages" (United Nations 1986: 12). The report also emphasizes the need to improve human resources development, planning, and utilization, to strengthen local institutions, and to improve coordination of foreign aid and technical assistance. All these imply direct improvements in the organization and management of African organizations both public and private.

The report, however, does not give specifics of *how* these improvements are to be brought about. These most critical but difficult details are left for each country to develop and implement on its own. Future research on organization and management should be directed toward improved understanding and informed policy options relating to these important questions. Whether or not Africa will pull out of its present doldrums may well depend on the quality of its organization and management practices ten to fifteen years from now and beyond.

REFERENCES

Adedeji, A. and T.M. Shaw, eds. 1985. *Economic Crisis in Africa*. Boulder, Colo.: Rienner.

Amoo, S. 1984. "Law and Development and the Expropriation Laws of Zambia." In *Law in Zambia*, edited by Muna Ndulo, pp. 245–69. Nairobi: East African.

Ananaba, W. 1979. *The Trade Union Movement in Africa*. London: Hurst.

Ankomah, K. 1985. "African Culture and Social Structures and Development of Effective Public Administration and Management Systems." *Indian Journal of Public Administration* 30(1, 2): 395–413.

Asiegbu, J.U.J. 1985. "Preliminary Thoughts on Indigenous African Technology and Development: An Exploratory Micro Study on the Umuabia-Igbo of South Eastern Nigeria." Seminar paper presented to the International Development Research Centre, Ottawa, Canada, Nov. 21.

Babatunde, T.D. 1986. "Technology and Industrial Development in Africa." In *Economic Crisis in Africa*, edited by A. Abebayo and T.M. Shaw, pp. 249–65. Boulder, Colo.: Rienner.

Bates, R.H. 1985. "The Analysis of Institutions." Paper presented to the Office of Rural and Institutional Development, Bureau of Science and Technology, U.S. Agency for International Development, Washington, D.C.

Bell, Martin. 1979. "The Exploitation of Indigenous Knowledge or the Indigenous Exploitation of Knowledge: Whose Use of What for What?" *IDS Bulletin* 10: 44–50.

Berg, E.J. 1981. *Accelerated Development in Sub-Saharan Africa: An Agenda for Action*. Washington, D.C.: World Bank.

———. 1984. "Accelerated Development Revisited." *CSIS African Notes* 31 (Aug. 5): 1–6.

———. 1985. "The Potentials of the Private Sector in Africa." *Washington Quarterly* (Fall): 73–83.

Blunt, P. 1982. "Work Alienation and Adaptation in Sub-Saharan Africa: Some evidence from Kenya." *Journal of Contemporary African Studies* 2(1): 59–79.

————. 1983. *Organization Theory and Behaviour: An African Perspective*. London: Longman.

————. 1984. "Conditions for Basic Needs Satisfaction in Africa through Decentralized Forms of Decision Making." *Journal of Applied Behavioral Science* 20(4): 403–21.

Browne, R.S., and R.J. Cummings. 1985. *The Lagos Plan of Action vs. The Berg Report*. Lawrenceville, Va.: Brunswick.

Canadian International Development Agency (CIDA). 1984. *Canadians and the Third World: CIDA's Year in Review, 1982–83*. Hull, Quebec: CIDA.

————. 1986. *Kenya: Country Program Review, 1985–90*. Hull, Quebec: CIDA.

Chambua, S.E. 1985. "Choice of Technique and Underdevelopment in Tanzania." Unpublished doctoral thesis, Department of Sociology and Anthropology, Carleton University, Ottawa, Canada.

Damachi, U.G., H.D. Seibel, and L.N. Trachtman, eds. 1979. *Industrial Relations in Africa*. London: MacMillan.

Dasah, B.Z. and M.N. Kiggundu. 1985. "Report on the Debriefing of the Canada–Kenya Business Forum." Canadian International Development Agency (CIDA), Briefing Centre, Hull, Quebec, CIDA.

Davies, David G. 1980. "Human Development in Sub-Saharan Africa." In *Poverty and the Development of Human Resources: Regional Perspectives*, edited by W. Bussink, pp. 53–95. Washington, D.C.; World Bank Staff Working Paper No. 406.

Elias, T.O., ed. 1972. *Law and Social Change in Nigeria*. Lagos: University of Lagos.

Emery, F.E., and E.L. Trist. 1965. "The Casual Texture of Organizational Environments. *Human Relations* 18: 21–32.

Escobar, J.K. 1982. "Comparing State Enterprises across International Boundaries: The Corporation Venezolana de Gueyana and the Compahia Vale de Rio Doce." In *Public Enterprise in Less-Developed Countries*, edited by L.P. Jones and R. Mullon, pp. 103–25. Cambridge: Cambridge University Press.

Faucheux, C., G. Amado, and A. Laurent. 1982. "Organizational Development and Change." *Annual Review of Psychology* 33: 343–70.

Frohlich, W. 1982. *The African Market System*. Vancouver: Tantalus Research.

Gallais, J., and A.H. Sidikou. 1978. "Traditional Strategies, Modern Decision-Making and Management of Natural Resources in the Sudan-Sahel." In *Management of Natural Resources in Africa: Traditional Strategies and Modern Decision Making*, pp. 11–32. Paris: UNESCO Technical Notes No. 9.

Ghai, Y. 1985. "The State and the Market in the Management of Public Enterprises in Africa: Ideology and False Comparisons." *Public Enterprise* 6(1): 15–26.

Gladwin, T.N., and V. Terpstra. 1978. "Introduction." In *The Cultural Environment of International Business*, edited by V. Terpstra, Cincinnati: Southwestern.

Goldstein, I.L. 1974. *Training: Program Development and Evaluation*. Monterey, Calif.: Brookes/Cole.

Hackman, J.R., and G.R. Oldham. 1980. *Work Redesign*, Reading, Mass.: Addison-Wesley.

Haddow, P.S. 1982. "The Post Graduate Training and Utilization of Professional Planners and Economists in the Government of Kenya: Recommendations to the Government and Donar Agencies." A report for the Ministry of Economic Planning and Development of the Government of Kenya and the Canadian International Development Agency, July.

Hafsi, T., M.N. Kiggundu, and J.J. Jorgensen. 1985. "Structural Configurations in the Strategic Apex of State-Owned Enterprises." Working Paper No. 85-07. Montreal: Ecole des heutes etudes Commerciales, (HEC), University du Montreal.

Henley, J.S. 1977. "The Personnel Professionals in Kenya." *Personnel Management* 9(2): 10–14.

Hofstede, G. 1980. *Culture's Consequences: International Differences in Work-Related Values.* Beverly Hills, Calif.: Sage.

Honadle, G. 1986. *Development Management in Africa: Context and Strategy — A Synthesis of Six Agricultural Projects.* AID Evaluation Special Study No. 43. Washington, D.C.: USAID.

Howell, P., J. Strauss, and P.F. Sorensen, Jr. 1975. "Research Note: Cultural and Situational Determinants of Job Satisfaction among Management in Liberia." *Journal of Management Studies* 12: 225–27.

Hull, R.W. 1980. *Modern Africa: Change and Continuity.* New Jersey: Prentice-Hall.

Ingle, M.D., and K.A. Smith. 1984. "Microcomputer Technology and International Development Management: An Assessment of Promises and Threats." Paper presented at the International Association of Schools and Institutes of Administration (IASIA) Conference, Bloomington, Ind., July 30–August 2.

Jorgensen, J.J. 1981. *Uganda: A Modern History.* London: Croom Helm.

———. 1985. "Managing after the Breakup of the East African Community." Paper presented at the Joint Meeting of the Canadian Association of Latin American and Caribbean Studies and Canadian Association of African Studies, Montreal, May 15–17.

Jorgensen, J.J., T. Hafsi, and M.N. Kiggundu. 1984. "Market Imperfections and Organizational Structure: The LDC Perspective." In *Marketing in Developing Countries*, edited by G.S. Kindra, pp. 172–82. London: Croom Helm.

———. 1986. "Towards a Market Imperfections Theory of Organizational Structure in Developing Countries." *Journal of Management Studies* 23(4) July: 417–42.

Kidwell, J., A. El Jack, and L. Ketchum. 1981. "Socio-Technical Study for Locomotive Maintenance Workshop at Sennar, Sudan." McLean, Va.: Parsons Brinckerhoff CENTEC International.

Kiereini, M. 1985. "Institutions in Rural Development: The Kenya Tea Development Authority." Unpublished research essay, Norman Paterson School of International Affairs, Carleton University, Ottawa.

Kiggundu, M.N. 1985. "Africa in Crisis: Can Organization Theory Help?" Paper presented at the National Meetings of the Academy of Management, San Diego, August 11–14.

———. 1986a. "Limitations of the Applications of Sociotechnical Systems in Developing Countries." *The Journal of Applied Behavioral Science* 22(4): 341–53.

———. 1986b. "Work Alienation and Institutional Decay in Developing Countries." Paper presented at the Eleventh World Congress of Sociology, International Sociological Association, New Delhi, India, August 17–22.

———. In press. *Managing Organizations in Developing Countries: An Integrative Approach.*

Kiggundu, M.N., J.J. Jorgensen, and T. Hafsi. 1983. "Administrative Theory and Practice in Developing Countries: A Synthesis." *Administrative Science Quarterly* 28(1): 66–84.

Killick, T. 1983. "The Role of the Public Sector in the Industrialization of African Developing Countries." In *Industry and Development*, pp. 57–88. New York: United Nations, No. 7.

Korten, D.C., and N.T. Uphoff. 1981. "Bureaucratic Reorientation for Participatory Rural Development." Unpublished manuscript, National Association of Schools of Public Affairs and Administration, Washington, D.C.

Machungwa, P.D., and N. Schmitt. 1983. "Work Motivation in a Developing Country." *Journal of Applied Psychology* 68(1): 31–42.

Maslow, A.H. 1954. *Motivation and Personality.* New York: Harper.

McHenry, D.E. 1985. "Political Bases for the Dissolution of a Public Corporation: A Nigerian Case." *Canadian Journal of African Studies* 19(1): 175–91.

Miles, R.H. 1980. *Macro Organizational Behavior.* Glenview, Ill.: Scott, Foresman.

Mintzberg, H. 1979. *The Structuring of Organizations.* Engelwood Cliffs, N.J.: Prentice-Hall.

Mohiddin, Ahmed. 1985. "Conditionality and the African State." Unpublished manuscript, Carleton University, Ottawa.

Moris, J.R. 1981. *Managing Induced Rural Development.* Bloomington, Ind.: International Development Institute.

Morrison, S. 1986. "Public Private Transitions." Personal communication, Jan. 30.

Mutukwa, K.S. 1979. "Politics of the Tanzania–Zambia Railway Project: A Study of Tanzania–China–Zambia Relations." Washington, D.C.: University Press of America.

National Association of Schools of Public Affairs and Administration (NASPAA). 1985. "Improving Management in Southern Africa." Final report to the Regional Training Council of the Southern African Development Co-ordination Conference (SADCC). Washington, D.C.

Nellis, J. 1985. "Public Enterprises in Sub-Saharan Africa." Washington, D.C.: World Bank. Public Sector Management Group.

Nicholson, N., E. Ostrom, D. Bowles, and R. Long. 1985. "Development Management in Africa: The Case of the Egerton College Expansion Project in Kenya." AID Evaluation Special Study, No. 35. Washington, D.C.: USAID.

Organization for Economic Cooperation and Development (OECD). 1978. "From Marshall Plan to Global Interdependence of the Industrialized Nations." Paris: OECD.

Oshagbemi, T.A. 1983. *Small Business Management in Nigeria.* London: Longman.

Page, Jr., J.M., and W.F. Steel. 1984. *Small Interprise Development: Economic Issues From African Experiences.* Technical Paper No. 26. Washington, D.C.: World Bank.

Paul, S. 1982. *Managing Development Programs: The Lessons of Success.* Boulder, Colo.: Westview Press.

Pelissier, P., and S. Diarra. 1978. "Traditional Strategies, Modern Decision-Making and Management of Natural Resources in the Sudan-Sahel." In *Man-*

agement of Natural Resources in Africa: Traditional Strategies and Modern Deci-sion-Making, pp. 33–56. Technical Notes No. 9. Paris: UNESCO.

Pfeffer, J. 1982. *Organizations and Organization Theory.* Boston: Pitman.

Ronen, S. 1986. *Comparative and Multinational Management.* New York: Wiley.

Shaw, T.M. 1986. "The African Crisis: Debates and Dialectics over Alternative Development Strategies for the Continent." in *Africa in Economic Crisis*, edited by J. Ravenhill, pp. 108–26. New York: Columbia University Press.

Shirley, M.M. 1983. *Managing State-Owned Enterprises.* World Bank Staff Working Paper No. 577, Management and Development Series No. 4. Washington, D.C.: World Bank.

Simon-Miller, F. 1984. "African Marketing: The Next Frontier." In *Marketing in Developing Countries*, edited by G.S. Kindra, pp. 115–29. London: Croom Helm.

Steeves, J.S. 1975. "The Politics and Administration of Agricultural Development in Kenya: The Kenya Tea Development Authority." Unpublished doctoral thesis, University of Toronto.

―――. 1978. "Class Analysis and Rural Africa: The Kenya Tea Development Authority." *Journal of Modern African Studies* 17(March): 123–32.

Tangri, R.K. 1985. *Politics in Sub-Saharan Africa.* London: Curry Heinemann.

Taylor, D.R.F., and R.A. Obudho, eds. 1977. *The Computer and Africa: Applications Problems and Potential.* New York: Praeger.

Ubeku, A.K. 1983. *Industrial Relations in Developing Countries: The Case of Nigeria.* London: MacMillan.

United Nations. 1986. "Report of the Ad Hoc Committee on the Thirteenth Special Session on the Critical Economic Situation in Africa." A/S-13/AC. 1/L.3. New York: United Nations.

Wallender, H.W. 1979. *Technology Transfer and Management in the Developing Countries.* Cambridge: Ballinger.

White, L.G. 1986. *Managing Development Programs: Managing Strategies and Project Interventions in Six African Agricultural Projects.* AID Evaluation Special Study No. 38. Washington, D.C.: USAID.

Williams, D. 1984. "Choice of Technology and Parastatal Firms." In *Technology Crossing Borders*, edited by R. Stobaugh and L.T. Wells, pp. 129–54. Boston: Harvard Business School Press.

World Bank. 1983. Kenya: "Agricultural Sector Memorandum." Report No. 4629-KE. Washington, D.C.: World Bank.

World Bank. 1981. Malawi: "The Development of the Agricultural Sector." Report No. 3459-MAI. Washington, D.C.: World Bank.

World Bank. 1985a. *World Debt Tables: External Debt of Developing Countries.* Washington, D.C.: World Bank.

―――. 1985b. *World Development Report 1985.* New York: Oxford University Press.

CHAPTER 7

Latin America

Fernando Quezada and James E. Boyce

In this chapter, commonly observed characteristics and trends of business management in Latin America are discussed within a broad description of the economy, the legal framework, and the sociopolitical context of this vast and diverse region. The authors identify as a pivotal determinant of strategy, style, and structure the propensity of managers in Latin America to concentrate both internal and external control mechanisms at the higher levels of the organizational hierarchies. It is further argued that although the observed managerial characteristics may be consistent with culturally based expectations, forces exogenous to the business management system per se present new challenges and opportunities that invite both strategic and structural adaptations that may lessen the concentration of control. Finally, the authors suggest areas where targeted empirical research can help to better understand the dynamics of managerial behavior in the Latin American context, particularly for the development of indigenous models of "professional" management. It is important to stress the limitations of attempting to offer generalizations on a multicountry, multiculture region with great differences in stage of development, political orientation, and other key factors.

SOME HISTORICAL CONSIDERATIONS

Both the early and more recent histories of the Latin American countries are as different and diverse as are their current cultures. Although many of the historical contrasts can be traced to the different colonial powers involved in each case, others are due to differences in the nature and level of sophistication of the indigenous populations at the time of the initial conquests. Similarly, the different resource endowments of the respective areas were key determinants of the patterns of exploitation. Perhaps the most notable of these patterns is the relatively advanced development of port cities in comparison to the hinderland areas.

Grunwald and Musgrove (1970: 7) divide Latin America economic history into three convenient intervals: the colonial era, from the early sixteenth century to the close of the wars of independence in the 1820s; the first century of independence, from the 1830s into the 1920s; and the years from the late 1920s to the present. These authors mention that in the colonial period permanent settlements were established only where precious metals or other valuable goods for export to Europe could be found. The territorial expansion and income growth of the colonial period economy were dependent on the development of the export sector. The colonial powers—Spain and Portugal—restricted manufacturing in the colonies, prohibited imports to the colonies from third countries, and restricted trade to certain favored ports in Spain and the New World. England was one of the countries that eventually gained access to the Brazilian market, and in subsequent years the laws were slowly relaxed.

During the first century of independence, the mercantilist system effectively disappeared. Power became concentrated in the hands of the primary producers—the landowners and the mining class. These groups controlled nearly all the region's exports and imports. This period also was one that occasioned large-scale European migration to the New World, bringing new talent and new capital resources.

"Modern times" in Latin America indirectly paralleled the changes in the industrialized economies in the sense that the global economy began playing a major role in the region. An important difference is that the manufacturing build-up in the advanced countries counted on a flow of raw materials from the less advanced countries in Latin America and elsewhere. During this period, many of the foundations were laid for current external dependence in Latin America. (This aspect will be discussed later in this chapter.) By the same token, governments began to intervene directly in the development of the manufacturing sector. Examples of this are the establishment of institutions like the Compania de Fomento de la Produccion en Chile and the Nacional Financiera in Mexico. In some basic industries, the public sector took over completely (Grunwald and Musgrove 1970: 14).

THE CULTURAL MILIEU

Many current cultural differences between and among Latin American countries stem from colonial origins, but they are also strongly related to the urban/rural distribution of the population and to the prevailing ethnic composition of the society. These latter factors have a direct bearing on societal groups' perspectives and beliefs about the extent to which they can or cannot influence the outcome of events in their lives.

The ethnic composition varies widely. Ninety-nine percent of the population in Argentina is of European descent, and only 1 percent is Indian. In contrast, approximately 5 percent of the population in Bolivia is of European extraction, 65 percent Indian, and 30 percent Mestizo.

Jean Franco (1970: 11) argues that although the business and commercial life of Latin America has been primarily influenced by the United States, the artistic and philosophical life of the region has been most profoundly affected by French thought. This may in part explain why artistic and philosophical pursuits are often valued over entrepreneurial ones in some Latin American sectors. This also explains why immigrants from societies that place relatively greater value on commerce (such as the Germans) do especially well in Latin American business.

Another author (Mander 1969: 207) makes the point that immigrants have been highly successful as entrepreneurs and top-level managers. He cites the Edwards family in Chile and Hans Neumann in Venezuela. One of the reasons is that newcomers are not burdened with ties to existing interest groups that may impede broad-based business development. Also, immigrants come looking for a better life and are willing to work hard to obtain it.

The comparative analysis by Geert Hofstede (1984) of approximately fifty countries suggests that Latin American societies, compared to the United States and Canada, are more likely to accept unequal distribution of power in institutions and organizations (large power distance). Similarly, persons in Latin America feel comparatively less comfortable in situations of uncertainty and ambiguity (strong uncertainty avoidance). The same societies may find a sense of security in perpetuating the status quo, even if it means a systematic reinforcement of sometimes imbalanced distribution of resources and power.

Referring to the third and fourth cultural dimensions dealt within Hofstede's analysis, Latin American societies tend to strongly prefer that a tightly knit social framework play a role in organizational and institutional

Table 7-1. Latin American Culture and Affected Business Functions.

Aspects of Latin American Culture	Examples of Business Functions Affected
Life follows a preordained course, and human action is determined by the will of God.	Planning, scheduling
People are intended to adjust to the physical environment rather than to alter it.	Work and motivation planning
Ideals are to be pursued regardless of what is reasonable.	Goal setting
Hard work is not the only prerequisite for success; wisdom, luck, and time are also required.	Motivation and reward system
A commitment may be superseded by a conflicting request, or an agreement may only signify intention and have little or no relationship to the capacity of performance.	Negotiating and bargaining
Schedules are important but only in relation to other priorities.	Long- and short-range planning
The individual employee has a primary obligation to his family and friends.	Loyalty, commitment and motivation
Employment is for a lifetime.	Motivation and commitment to the company
Family considerations, friendship, and other considerations partially determine employment practices.	Employment, promotions, recruiting, selection, reward
The removal of a person from a position involves a great loss of prestige.	Promotion
Education or family ties are the primary vehicles for mobility.	Employment practices and promotions
Decisions are expressions of wisdom by the person in authority, and any questioning would imply lack of confidence in his judgment.	Decision-making processes
Accurate data is not as highly valued.	Recordkeeping
Withholding information to gain or maintain power is acceptable.	Communications
Deference is to be given to persons in power or authority, and to offer judgments not in support of the ideas of one's superiors is unthinkable.	Communications

Table 7–1 continued.

Aspects of Latin American Culture	Examples of Business Functions Affected
Decisions may be made by those in authority and others need not be consulted.	Decisionmaking
Competition leads to unbalances and disharmony.	Promotion
Various kinds of work are accorded low or high status and some work may be below one's "dignity" or place in the organization.	Assignment of tasks, organization
Tradition is revered, and the power of the ruling group is founded on the continuation of a stable structure.	Planning
Symbols and the process are more important than the end point.	Communication, organization, planning
Persons are evaluated but in such a way that individuals not highly evaluated will not be embarrassed or caused to "lose face."	Rewards, promotion

Source: Adapted from Moran and Harris (1982: 299–300).

life (low individualism). Although somewhat variable, there is also a societal preference in Latin America for assertiveness and material success (high masculinity). The propensities displayed within these cultural dimensions are reinforced by the very symbols and rituals that they create in the sociopolitical realm.

The Osborns (1986: 7) compared managers from Latin American countries with U.S. managers using the Myers-Briggs Type Indicator (MBTI). They report that Latin American managers are significantly more extroverted and concerned with facts rather than concepts or in references. According to this study, Latin American managers also prefer orderly customs and procedures to being adaptable and flexible.

Moran and Harris (1982: 299–300) have described the relationships between the cultural orientations of Latin American managers and the business functions affected by these orientations (see Table 7–1).

THE SOCIOPOLITICAL CONTEXT

Latin American societies present a wide spectrum of political orientations that reflect greater or lesser governmental role in the economy;

greater or lesser role of the military in national policy; greater or lesser restrictiveness on free enterprise development and other factors. All of these aspects are often shown to be directly or indirectly related to the level of stability in the country. In Brazil, for example, the military took control over a highly unstable situation in 1964 and, after two decades of fairly strict oversight of developmental efforts, knew enough not to stand in the way of a society ready to return a civilian to the office of president (Dimenstein 1985).

Comparing Brazil to Mexico, Eliana Cardoso stresses that in the latter nation, political stability and economic growth have gone hand in hand. She illustrates the resiliency of the Mexican political system by mentioning that since its foundation in 1929 "the institutional Revolutionary party (PRI) has given the country not only all its presidents, but all of its senators and state governors as well. It has adjusted itself to the transformation of a rural society into an industrialized nation; it survived the anti-government movement in 1968; it outlived the political and economic crisis of 1976; and seems to be surviving the post-1982 economic slump, even if it is losing its popularity" (Cardoso 1986: 25). The same author presents Table 7–2, which summarizes the economic relationships and political spectrum in Mexico over the years.

Unlike the situations in countries such as Japan, where there is a close relationship between business and government, quite often these

Table 7–2. Political Spectrum, Growth, Inflation, and Real Wages in Mexico, 1947–85.

Period	President	Political Spectrum	GDP	Prices	Real Minimum Wage
			Percentage of Change during Period		
1947–52	M. Aleman	Right	5.8	11.2	3.8
1953–58	A. Ruiz-Cortines	Center	6.4	6.7	0.5
1959–64	A. Lopez Mateos	Left	6.7	2.2	11.1
1965–70	G. Diaz Ordaz	Right	6.8	3.6	4.0
1971–76	L. Echeverria	Left	6.2	14.1	2.3
1977–82	J. Lopez Portillo	Center	6.3	30.5	−3.3
1983–85	M. De la Madrid	Center-right	0.8	68.0	−8.9

Source: Cardoso (1986: 8).

sectors in Latin America have almost adversarial relationships. This is especially true in those countries where the state-dominated economy curtails the freedom of the private sector and where a lack of trust may prevail between the two.

Even the managerial and administrative training may vary from the public official to the private executive. It is common to find that the business elites are U.S. trained or trained in the U.S.-style executive programs. The governmental elites, particularly the political intellectuals, traditionally have been European trained.

THE ECONOMIC SYSTEM

Contrasts in the Latin American economies are illustrated by Table 7–3, which lists per capita gross domestic product for each country for 1983 (*Statistical Bulletin* 1984: 1–4).

Table 7–3. Latin American Per Capita Gross Domestic Product for 1983.

Country	U.S. $ (1982 prices)
Argentina	1,927.6
Bolivia	503.9
Brazil	1,698.8
Chile	1,603.2
Colombia	1,047.3
Costa Rica	1,465.0
Dominican Republic	1,214.0
Ecuador	1,077.8
El Salvador	635.6
Guatemala	1,172.5
Honduras	661.6
Mexico	2,080.7
Nicaragua	925.8
Panama	2,101.4
Paraguay	1,247.4
Peru	958.8
Uruguay	2,053.8
Venezuela	2,507.3

Source: Statistical Bulletin (1984: 30).

Table 7–4. Labor Force Structure, 1960–80 (percentage).

Country	% Population of Working Age (15–64 Years)		Agriculture		Industry		Services	
	1960	1982	1960	1980	1960	1980	1960	1980
Argentina	64	63	44	28	29	35	27	37
Bolivia	55	53	61	50	18	24	21	26
Brazil	54	55	52	30	16	24	33	46
Chile	57	62	31	18	20	19	50	61
Colombia	50	60	51	26	19	21	29	53
Costa Rica	50	59	51	29	19	23	30	48
Cuba	61	61	39	23	22	31	39	46
Dominican Republic	49	53	67	49	12	18	21	33
Ecuador	52	52	57	52	19	17	23	41
El Salvador	52	52	62	50	17	22	21	27
Guatemala	51	54	67	55	14	21	19	25
Haiti	55	53	80	74	6	7	14	19
Honduras	52	50	70	63	11	15	19	23
Mexico	51	52	55	36	20	26	25	39
Nicaragua	50	50	62	43	16	20	22	37
Panama	52	56	51	27	14	18	35	55
Paraguay	51	53	56	44	19	20	25	36
Peru	52	54	52	38	20	18	28	43
Uruguay	64	63	21	11	30	32	50	57
Venezuela	51	55	35	18	22	27	43	55
United States	60	66	7	2	36	32	57	66

Source: Statistical Abstract (1985: 212).

STRUCTURE OF THE LABOR FORCE

Although there have been notable shifts in labor force structure away from agriculture in recent years, a substantial proportion of the population still is engaged in this sector. Table 7–4 illustrates some of the similarities and contrasts in labor structure among the Latin American countries as well as the changes and shifts between 1960 and 1980. The most notable of these changes have occurred in Brazil, Venezuela, Mexico, and Uruguay. The rapid industrialization efforts, oil export dependency, altered agricultural development policies have even often jeopardized self-sufficiency in food production (Wilkie 1985). In considering socio-cultural as well as historical influences on Latin American management today, six features common to most Latin American countries can be highlighted.

Concentration of Wealth

All of the region's major productive assets are effectively owned or controlled by either the government, foreign investors, or by the national elites. Similarly, educational opportunities are often restricted to the more well-to-do sector of the society. One Argentinian author maintains that "at the very summit of Latin American society sit the old elites who jealousy guard their social, political and economic prerogatives" (Frame 1982: 49).

Public efforts to redistribute patterns of income and wealth generation in Latin America often result in a widening of the economic disparity. In Brazil, for example, during the 1960s, the real income of the richer half of the population grew by over 30 percent, whereas the income of the rest of the population is estimated to have grown less than 1 percent (Streeten and Burki 1978: 411). This is due in part to the fact that persons who are best able to take advantage of loan programs and other opportunities are those who already have resources and are better educated.

Regional Disparities

Latin American countries are generally characterized by a great contrast between the most developed urban areas and the impoverished and resource-poor rural areas. The lack of modernization of agriculture, health care, and education in the rural areas are compounded by problems of overpopulation. Outmigration from these areas exacerbate the problems in the burgeoning urban areas. In Mexico, the heavily populated industrial triangle of Mexico City, Monterrey, and Guadalajara reaped in large part the benefits of industrialization. Approximately two-thirds of manufacturing is located in this industrial triangle, which houses approximately one-fourth of the total population (Smith 1986: 2).

In 1976 Mexico City's population was 11.7 million. If the current trends continue, nearly doubling every ten years, the metropolitan area will house an estimated 30 million people by the year 2000 (Garza and Schteingart 1978). A 1986 Census Bureau report estimates that Mexico's overall population will increase by almost 42 percent, from 79.7 million in 1985 to 112.8 million in the year 2000. This population explosion has severe implications for the economic development of the entire country.

Economic Dualism

Beside the formal government regulated economy, an underground economy is at work primarily in the urban areas. The low availability of formal-sector jobs forces people to earn their living outside the regular market place (Mescher 1985: 1). In Peru, for example, 35 percent of the nation's urban population is engaged in business in the informal sector of the economy, which account for about 68 percent of its gross domestic product (see Table 7–5).

Two factors are sometimes mentioned as contributing to the economic dualism in Latin America: (1) an excessive population growth, especially in urban areas, that keeps the traditional sector growing at a higher rate than labor can be absorbed into the modern sector; and (2) an exogenous increase in the wage level (e.g., government-imposed wages), which may lead to labor-saving mechanizations in the modern sector and hence a reduction in labor absorption (Mescher 1985: 10). Other factors are certainly involved.

Table 7–5. Estimated Share of Informal Sector Employment in Total Urban Employment in Latin American Countries, 1980 (percentage).

Country	Percentage
Argentina	14
Bolivia	44
Brazil	17
Colombia	25
Costa Rica	11
Chile	19
Ecuador	32
El Salvador	23
Guatemala	31
Mexico	30
Panama	20
Peru	35
Uruguay	16
Venezuela	16

Source: PREALC (1983).

External Dependency

Partly stemming from its colonial heritage and dependence on the United States, and partly as continued by periods of heavy foreign investment in the exploitation of natural resources, major Latin American countries commonly find themselves in monoexport situations. This has led to heavy reliance on imports to meet the region's need for manufactured goods, with a resulting unfavorable trade balance. The decline of the markets for Latin American exports such as Mexican oil has occasioned serious debt payment problems for lack of hard currency. The international banking community has generally restructured the outstanding loans, but not without posing restrictions on government spending.

Celso Furtado (1970: 36) points out that the development of the modern sector in Latin America has been strongly influenced by U.S. and European multinational corporations. This has meant that many local entrepreneurs in order to be economically successful have often taken on auxiliary roles to these multinational firms—or have gone to work for the firms themselves.

One empirical study (Possas 1982) for Brazil, however, does describe a major multinational computer manufacturer as having a strategy that deliberately attempts to prevent the enterprise from becoming dependent on its suppliers and vice versa. It tries to diversify its suppliers in such a way that the items that it purchases never account for more than 17 percent of the supplier's sales. There are two motives for this diversification of the input sources: "The first is to prevent unforeseen events: if, for any reason, one of its suppliers ceases producing for a certain period, the enterprise can have recourse to other and its own production will not be curtailed (this is the reason for the geographical diversification, since often such stoppages affect a whole region). From the Brazilian subsidiary's standpoint it would be a tragedy to delay its output delivery, for this could mean losing the right to manufacture its products."

Even though both Brazil and Mexico have advanced considerably in the diversification of their production and exports, their economies remain vulnerable. A case study (Ramsaran 1985: 117) on investment policies in these countries points out that the present dynamic appears to rest heavily on the infusion of foreign investors. These "can easily overturn or cause to be modified nationalistic regulations which they may have been willing to tolerate in different circumstances. The greater the dependence on foreign capital, the more easily can domestic political behavior be affected. Even large countries like Brazil and Mexico which have been the significant progress in the industrial field have not been able to escape the implications of this relationship."

Dependency is also reflected in the way that certain segments of the labor force develop. In recent years, many multinational firms have started operations in the free trade zones of the Dominican Republic where the high population growth rate and comparatively young labor force is characteristic of other parts of Latin America (Stearns 1984: 4). Foreign investment in these zones has created low-skill factory jobs, primarily for young women. The demand for workers with higher skills and advanced education is limited to a few positions.

INFRASTRUCTURE

Transportation and Communications

The development of transportation and communications infrastructure in Latin American countries has steadily advanced with the help of external financing. Where traditionally the patterns of railway routes and waterway systems would primarily reflect the flow of natural resource and raw materials for export, national planners have recently sought to design transportation networks in a manner that effectively links major population settlements with secondary cities to encourage even demographic patterns. Similarly, large countries like Brazil seek to provide greater means of regional integration. That country's great Trans-Amazon Highway project was motivated by economic development considerations.

Because of the high-technology component of communications systems, foreign firms have played a key role in their development in Latin America. The heavy capital equipment investment required in the communications infrastructure results in extremely high costs for consumers of telephone services. On the whole this area is improving.

The wide variation in geographical sizes and level of wealth of countries in Latin America results in transportation networks that range from 56,000 kilometers of roads in Peru (6,000 of which are paved) to almost 2 million kilometers of roads in Brazil (of which less than 10 percent are paved).

Technology Development

If, as one political economist has stated (Montgomery 1979: 2), it is true that "technology almost certainly offers the best hope of improving the quality of life in the developing countries," the enhancement of Latin America's technological development capacity should be a first-order priority. As is typical in most less developed countries, however, the science and technology personnel in Latin America produce only an extremely small fraction of R&D worldwide. According to another author, Frame (1983: 42), one indicator of this is the average number of scientific papers produced by each country annually. He mentions that the average for Latin American countries is 119 papers per year compared to 9,500 papers per year produced in the average Western developed country. Although this author also stresses that data on R&D manpower and expenditures in less developed countries is highly unreliable, he offers evidence suggesting a strong link between the manpower and expenditures and the R&D performance illustrated by the papers generated and the technologies registered.

Many of the governments in Latin America have established science and technology agencies. Examples of these are the Consejo Nacional de Ciencia y Tecnologia (CONACYT) in Mexico; the Consejo Nacional de Ciencia and Tecnologia (CONCYTEC) in Peru; and the Consejo Nacional de Pesquisa (CNP) and the Instituto Nacional de Tecnologia (INT) in Brazil. The effectiveness of these agencies, however, ultimately rests on their ability to leverage private-sector investment in research and development efforts.

A representative of the Brazilian Secretariat for Industrial Technology mentions that R&D in that country has simply not kept up with Brazil's economic growth over the last two decades. A 1980 survey by Brazil's National Council for Scientific and Technology Development showed that only half of the medium and large companies in the country had R&D departments. Because periods of rapid growth pressure the local companies to obtain the greatest possible short-term investment return with a minimum of risk, the industrial strategies of these companies have favored the acquisition of foreign technology in the form of licenses, patents, and trademarks. The decreased availability of hard currency to make royalty payments should directly affect the continuation of this pattern.

SIGNIFICANT CHALLENGES FACING BUSINESS MANAGEMENT

Challenges that come from outside the organization can originate formidable pressures for organizational change. Three significant environmental factors challenging managers in Latin America are (1) inflation, (2) external debts of their respective countries combined with import restrictions, and (3) government regulations and preemptive actions.

Inflation

In recent years, nearly every Latin American country has experienced rampant inflation leading to heavy currency regulations, devaluation, and an active underground market for currency and certain capital goods. In 1983 alone the simple average rate of increase in consumer prices rose to 78 percent from 48 percent the previous year. The rate of increase weighted by population went from 86 percent to 131 percent in the same period. During 1983 prices increased more than five fold in Argentina and more than three and fourfold in Brazil and Bolivia, respectively (Economic Commission for Latin America and the Caribbean 1984).

Bolivia presents an extreme case of inflation that cannot be controlled by governmental measures alone. Today the underground economy accounts for 75 percent of Bolivia's economy. In terms of businesses operations, that means that Bolivia's businesses are almost restricted to a cash economy or even a barter economy. As a result, investments are minimal. Foreign businesses are withdrawing from the market, producing scarcity of imported goods. Labor unions are pressing for living wages at shorter time intervals. These factors contribute to the inflationary pressures and help to perpetuate the vicious circle with which the government has not been able to deal (Constable 1985: 8). In the case of runaway inflation in Argentina (where inflation at one point reached 1,000 percent), capital itself becomes virtually detached from the economy.

Local capital investment, however, has not grown at the pace one would expect. In part, this may be due to the flight of capital outside the country, but it also may be due to the fact that the needed production machinery can be acquired only with the hard currency, which is itself unavailable. The Organization of American States reports that overall consumption in the region fell by 4.3 percent in 1983, whereas overall investment, which grew at an average annual rate of 7 percent between 1978 and 1981, fell by 12.5 percent in 1982 and by almost 15 percent in 1983.

External Debt and Import Limitation

Table 7–6 illustrates the impressive growth of Latin American external debt over a ten-year period. The heavy debt burden carried by the major

Table 7-6. Latin America and the Caribbean: Some Indicators of External Indebtedness, 1983–84 (in billions of U.S. $).

	External Debt	External Debt Service	Debt Service Ratio	Per Capita External Debt
1973	33.3	4.4	13.8	119.9
1975	60.9	11.1	23.8	199.7
1977	94.1	18.4	29.6	294.1
1978	140.2	26.3	37.7	427.4
1979	172.8	35.6	38.0	514.0
1980	218.4	41.3	32.7	633.3
1981	266.9	51.5	37.1	755.1
1982	298.0	63.2	51.7	823.7
1983	319.2	66.8	64.6	861.9
1984	352.9	69.7	60.9	931.6

Source: Inter-American Development Bank (1984: Table A.1.01).

Latin American countries and the pressures from international banks to reduce public-sector spending have also led to more emphasis on private-sector investment and involvement. Carlos Salinas de Gortari, Secretary of Planning and Budget in Mexico, is quoted as saying the following about budget cutting (Lewis 1985: A25): "We've already done twice what Gramm-Rudman is trying to do in the U.S.; and we did in four years."

At the stated level, this is intended to be accomplished by a reduction in governmental regulation regarding business investments and the institution of specific programs involving resource allocation. Simultaneously, however, because currency restrictions continue in force or are often strengthened, the private-sector stimulation objectives are not always achieved.

A Council of the Americas (1983: 6) report points out that "To the extent subsidiaries are denied consistent, unpenalized access to scarce foreign exchange, it becomes increasingly desirable to curtail their activities." The report goes on to say that Latin America's debt/equity ratio could be put into better balance through greater investment flows. It mentions, however, that since the governments in debtor countries are too slow in changing investing and operating rules to encourage a shift in their debt/equity ratios, it is unlikely that U.S. multinational companies would be willing to substantially increase their investment there.

In principle, the devaluation of national currency, coupled with targeted import restrictions, should open the market for local manufacture of previously imported goods and services. One could expect an increase in opportunities for small- and medium-size firms with strengthened positions, at least in market terms.

However, the structural problems of Latin American economies (unbalanced growth, excessive dependency on few commodities, dependency on foreign markets) tend to limit the public advantages of entrepreneurship by rewarding short-term behavior more than long-term growth. Fortunes are often made in highly inflationary situations when speculators move their money around quickly and, at the appropriate time, get their money out of the country into hard currencies. This kind of entrepreneurial behavior may reward the individual but has negative consequences for the national economy. The type of entrepreneurs that are of special importance to Latin America therefore are those that have a long-term outlook and a willingness to ride through the ups and downs characteristics of the Latin American economies (Simonsen 1963).

Another key element of the debt reduction strategy is to encourage export-oriented production and, in some cases, tourism to stimulate a flow of hard currency to the country. Although Latin America's heaviest trading partner has been the United States, there is increasing interest in tapping the Japanese, European, and other markets ("Latin America's Bold New Partners" 1986). The local companies are thus also competing in markets traditionally dominated by industrialized countries. Although an important advantage of the local companies is their low cost for labor, they also have to conform to the production and quality standards set by the external market.

One key factor that will assuredly influence the economic structure of many Latin American countries is the eventual outcome of the continuous efforts relating to the regional integration of trade, particularly those of the Andean Common Market (ANCOM)—originally Bolivia, Chile, Colombia, Ecuador, and Peru (Carl 1986).

Government Regulations and Actions

The outside pressures to reduce government employment and services has also led to lessened governmental restriction on the private sector. The private sector has been asked to take over some selected government-owned enterprises and increase their use of the available human resources in the country. Additionally, governments in Latin America are playing an increasingly active role in encouraging entrepreneurship and risk-taking by making an effort to reduce some of the risks. Mexico's National Council for Science and Technology (CONACYT) initiated a program for joint investment for technological innovation with industry. Under the terms, CONACYT recovers its funds from successful projects but shares the risk with the industry in the event that project results do not work out.

Small-scale enterprises are not left out of the governmental promotional stream. Brazil has formally decreed a National Microenterprise Program where the cottage-type industry working in the informal sector of the economy is recognized for its potential in job creation. These microenterprises are exempted from a number of otherwise tedious licensing requirements in order to encourage the firms to come forth for minimal registry and economic census purposes.

Although the governments are seeking to promote entrepreneurial initiatives in the area of exports, a great deal of paperwork and delays are unfortunately characteristic of the ways in which the governments provide control over the related currency transactions. This action creates a disincentive for more activity of this type.

BUSINESS AND MANAGEMENT SYSTEMS

Industry Structure

Although the industrial structure in Latin America varies widely from country to country, Table 7-7 may help to illustrate the different levels and relative proportions of each sector. Mexico presents an example of a highly concentrated industrial sector. Over 50 percent of industrial output is produced by less than 2 percent of all industrial enterprises. This same 2 percent of industrial enterprises accounts for over 40 percent of employment. The government has provided tax incentives for smaller businesses, especially those willing to locate away from the major cities, but concentration of market demand and available infrastructure in those centers limited the success of these efforts. One of the obstacles to achieving a reversal of this situation has been an acute shortage of skilled workers (Cohen and Thirty 1983).

Bolivia, with a population base of just over 6 million, has close to half of its labor force dedicated to agriculture, 23 percent to services, 19 percent to industry and commerce, and 11 percent to government. Traditionally, mining has been the most important element of the Bolivian

Table 7–7. Structure of Urban Employment in a Developing Economy.

Subsector Designation				Percentage of Urban Labor Force
Senior government officials, military officers	Business leaders, corporate managers	University professors	Free professionals	3
Owner-entrepreneurs, middle-level officials, supervisors				2–5
Office workers, minor officials, teachers	Trade and service workers	Factory workers	Skilled construction workers	10–30
Trade and service workers, domestic servants		Workmen		35–45
Handicraft workers	Street traders, service workers	Casual construction workers	"Underground" occupations	20–25
		Unemployed workers		5–15

Source: Adapted from Friedmann and Sullivan (1974).

economy. Although tin has constituted almost 60 percent of exports, recent declines in the world prices for this commodity have forced the government to reduce its own participation in tin exploitation (Graham 1986).

Management Philosophy and Organizational Processes

Managerial settings in each Latin American country not only differ markedly in cultural and environmental context but also in the respective industrial and organizational factors in each situation. Although no generalizations are entirely defensible, it is not uncommon to read or hear the following descriptions and characterizations of business management in Latin America.

The Philosophy and Practices of Latin American Managers Tend to Be Authoritarian. Managerial orientation in Latin America is based on a concern common to managers in any part of the world; that is, the concern for maintaining or maximizing *control* over the variance in conditions affecting the firm or organization. A premium is placed on increasing the certainty of outcomes to protect the business from unforeseen and potentially threatening situations.

Decisionmaking is therefore highly centralized. Teamwork is often sacrificed in favor of individuals and individual areas of responsibility. In surveys to diagnose organizational problems and needs of various firms in Colombia, for example, it was commonly reported that managers often suffered from a focus limited to their area of responsibility. It was also reported that they did not necessarily work well with peers in addressing overall organizational goals and objectives.

A separate angle of this same problem is that there exists a lack of trust between individuals at different organizational levels. Information is not freely shared between people of different or even similar rank. This often interferes with improvement of decisionmaking and job performance. The lack of information sharing, coupled with the strict role definition, practically eliminates any form of collective decisionmaking or coordination. The inability to be more open with the information, both vertically and horizontally, inhibits adaptive change in organizations and works to stifle initiative and innovation. It is interesting to note that Argyris and Schon (1978) used a Latin American case study to illustrate limited learning situations in organizations.

A Strong Legacy of Family-Style Management Exists in Latin America. Typically, many business organizations in Latin America have evolved from small family enterprises with paternalistic management structures. Responsible positions tend to be staffed with relatives and friends. Understandably, this practice can and does interfere with the uniform quality of managerial performance and internal communications. Under these circumstances, there are fewer formal incentives to keep current professionally. In time this also takes its toll on both managerial and technical performance.

In countries such as Colombia and Ecuador, where small family enterprises are growing to medium-size firms, there is a shortage of qualified middle-level managers. This restricts the growth and productivity of these firms and the professionalization of their management teams.

In this context, workers strive to please and conform. Nonsupervisory employees can be characterized as having a strong desire to do what is expected and to take pride in their work. However, they usually do only what they are told—no more, no less. They have little formal incentive to contribute to the overall improvement of the operations. Often, persons in authority are more to be feared than to be trusted according to line workers in one assembly plant in northern Mexico visited by the authors.

A Strong Concern for Social (Interpersonal) Relationships Is Reflected in the Latin American Business Management Systems. Because good relationships among colleagues have a high priority, perceived organizational problems do not always get addressed forthrightly. Both managers and workers can find it difficult to say no to a request. A superior's judgment is rarely questioned, despite the fact that input could improve the quality of the decision.

The personalization of management extends to the interorganizational realm. Although some business leaders may hold a certain mistrust toward government, they are likely to participate in the political process through interpersonal means, using friends as the basis for working relationships. Similarly, interactions with labor unions, churches, business associations, and consumers are preferably handled on a personal level. In Latin American countries run by military governments with special conditions such as censure policies and security limitations, personal contacts become even more important.

The paternalism reflected in the management structures in Latin America is also characteristic of the manner in which government often deals with businesses. The fiscal incentives for the private sector are accompanied by many governmental regulations and bureaucratic processes that are difficult to deal with in a manner other than through interpersonal relationships. There is a tendency to deal only with persons at the top rather than at lower functional levels to make sure that one's interests are dealt with "properly."

Societal Status Differences Carry over to the Business Place. Family, education, and social class are important factors in Latin American societies in general. Definite class distinctions exist in organizational life as well. Aside from their effect on promotional opportunities, they can raise communication barriers as well.

Status consciousness, the marked definition of roles, and the perceived need to maintain greater control are factors that make for situations that do not allow much flexibility in task assignments. For example, the authors have observed manufacturing plants in Mexico where an engineer will not "lower himself" to carry out a shop floor task that is normally done by a worker.

"Sellers' Market" Conditions in Latin America Can Have the Effect of Lessening Managerial Concerns for Product Quality. Because many manufacturers in Latin America are in a virtually monopolistic position within their respective countries, they can sell almost everything they produce. Under these conditions, business organizations can become relatively static. There is less reason to change when competition is not seen as an immediate problem. When confidence in the future business climate is also lacking, a short-term perspective results. It is perhaps indicative that industrial research and development budgets are characteristically low in Latin America.

Organization Structure

There is no reason to expect that the determinants of organization structure in Latin America are any less or any more dominated by cultural factors than they would be in other societies. To be sure, culture and other overall situational influences particular to Latin America affect structural configurations and adaptation in organizations. It is also a fact that efforts on the part of the larger Latin American firms to adopt matrix type structures have met with certain obstacles in the area of cross-functional coordination and team building. Depending on the size and nature of the firm, functional structures with strict division of areas are common.

Human Resources/Personnel

The descriptions of managerial characteristics in Latin America suggest that the human resources in organizations or business establishments there comprise as much of an unknown factor as would the outside environment in which the organization is operating. The differentiation of social status between management and workers is reinforced by a concentration of organizational power at the higher levels.

The personnel and human resource policies of business firms in Latin America vary in direct relation both to the level of unionization of the labor force and to the level of sophistication in the firm. For example, one management scholar (Derr 1981: 2) who studied career development in Mexico notes that there is a strong distinction between firms in the northern and southern regions of the country. This is in part due to the decreased role of the labor unions in northern Mexico and in part due to the advanced level of management training in the northern industrial cities such as Monterrey, where there is a marked U.S. orientation in management circles.

Even then, this author points out specific peculiarities in managerial career advancement. In addition to needing the right family background and recurring a protective senior sponsor, he mentions three factors needed to enable promotion (Derr 1981: 6): "First, one must get good 'report cards' or performance appraisal ratings by his superior. Second, it is critical to understand the subtleties of the organizational culture—its myths, rituals, symbols and norms—and to abide the essential mores which are rites of passage. For example, in one corporation it is useful for executives to be seen on occasion with subordinates carrying their briefcases. Third, one needs good job assignments or experiences which will make him visible to others and give him the experiences that will qualify him to be considered for an upper-level position. Fourth, and most important, one has to be perceived as a good subordinate, one who has the ability to make the boss appear competent and successful and who relieves him of much of his work load."

Management education in Latin America has done well in the past two decades. Business degrees are offered at both public and private universities at both the graduate and undergraduate level. Additionally, executive training programs have been developed in all the major Latin American countries. The Association of Latin American Business Schools (CLADEA) was formed to help members schools address problems of common interest. Additionally, this group has served as a vehicle for members to interact with other similar associations such as the American Association of Collegiate Schools of Business (AACSB) in the United States and the European Foundation for Management Development (EFMD).

THE EVOLVING MANAGERIAL RESPONSE

What has been or is likely to be the managerial response to the environmental trends of inflation, debt crisis, and governmental reactions described in this chapter? Can we expect a business and management system to alter the assumptions and beliefs on which it is based? Is it likely that the management and business systems would be able to manipulate or influence the sociopolitical institutions in which they are embedded?

Will the structural patterns of managerial control be tightened, loosened, or perhaps shifted to reflect a greater concern for the nature and rate of the environmental change itself?

The changing attributes in a Latin American manager's task environment can be related to particular consequences in that manager's strategy and style. The pressing effects of the highly inflationary economies in Latin America, for example, increase the amount of uncertainty that the manager faces, along with an increased level of risk for the business. Under these circumstances, given what was described earlier as the culturally based uncertainty avoidance propensity in Latin America, we can expect the manager to want to increase his or her control over the business and its perceived environment. This in turn leads to an even more centralized decisionmaking process and is again consistent with our comments on power distance.

The increased risk under inflationary conditions may also reduce the incentive for production innovation on the part of both managers and workers. Comparatively speaking, it is likely that given similar conditions in the United States or Canada, one would see more capital spending because in that credit market, inflation tends to decrease the cost of long-term investments. In certain Latin American countries, however, the rate is so high that credit is not easily obtainable, especially in light of the external pressures on government to reduce its debt burden.

If the import restrictions occasioned by Latin America's debt crisis are opening opportunities for local businesses to provide goods and services to replace items that are no longer being imported, we can also expect that this phenomena would translate into greater turbulence (that is, marked and frequent changed) in the business environment, as well as increased risks on the part of industries that would need to depend on the local suppliers. The uncertainty avoidance discussed earlier would suggest that the managerial strategy would favor greater vertical integration measures such as acquiring equity investment in supplier firms or outright purchase of the same.

The increasing government restrictions vis-à-vis currency transactions would require that the managers in Latin America orient their strategy to increased long-term planning and optimization of efforts and resources. Although many governments are producing long-range economic development plans with input from various sectors of the economy, these plans often contain difficult compromises among various sectors and therefore are sometimes viewed with skepticism or at least caution by potential business investors (Peroni 1985: 21).

Opportunities for Management Research in Latin America

Little empirical management research has been carried out in Latin America to examine objectively and systemically the management tools that are most effective for varying situations in those cultures. Although inheriting somewhat authoritarian traditions from centuries of colonial dominance, managers in Latin America now study in business schools and in executive seminars about management as it is taught in the United States and other industrialized countries. The difficult task is left to the manager to discern what is applicable and useful in the respective Latin American cultural context from these externally generated models, theories, and cases.

The use of various forms of participative management that is increasing in industrialized countries can permit employees at all levels to contribute their thinking and judgment to productive and creative organizational performance. The right adaptation of participative management schemes might allow Latin American firms to make better use of their human resources and increase their competitiveness. We need to know how to render this a viable tool for Latin American management systems without destroying the cultural integrity from which their energies are derived.

REFERENCES

Argyris, C., and D.A. Schon. 1978. *Organizational Learning: A Theory of Action Perspective.* Reading, Mass.: Addison-Wesley.

Cardoso, Eliana A. 1986. "What Policymakers Can Learn from Brazil and Mexico." *Challenge* 29: 25.

Carl, B.M. 1986. *Economic Integration among Developing Nations.* New York: Praeger.

Cohen, R. and K. Thirty. 1983. "Mexico: Crisis of Confidence." Case 0-383-148. Cambridge, Mass.: Harvard Business School.

Constable, P. 1985. "Bolivian Black Market." *The Boston Globe,* Aug. 16, p. 8.

Council of the Americas. 1983. "The Impact of the Economic Crisis in Argentina, Brazil, Mexico and Venezuela on the United States Companies Operating There." Technical Report.

Derr, B. 1981. "Career Development in the Industrial 'Grupos' of Northern Mexico." Unpublished paper, University of Utah, Salt Lake City.

Dimenstein, Gilberto, et al. 1985. *O Complo que eleque Tancredo.* Rio de Janeiro: JB.

Economic Commission for Latin America and the Caribbean. 1984. *Economic Survey of Latin America and the Caribbean.* New York: ECLAC.

Frame, J.D. 1982. *International Business and Global Technology.* Lexington, Mass.: Lexington Books.

Franco, J. 1970. *The Modern Culture of Latin America*. New York: Penguin.

Friedmann, John, and Flora Sullivan. 1974. "The Absorption of Labor in the Urban Economy: The Case of Developing Countries." *Economic Development and Cultural Change* 22(3) (April).

Furtado, C. 1970. *Obstacles to Development in Latin America*. New York: Doubleday.

Garza, G., and M. Schteingart. 1978. "Mexico City: the Emerging Megalopolis." *Latin American Urban Research* 6: 51–86.

Graham, B. 1986. "Bolivia: The Paz Government Turns away from Tin." *The Boston Globe*, Dec. 7, p. A10.

Grunwald, J., and Philip Musgrove. 1970. *Natural Resources in Latin American Development*. Baltimore: Johns Hopkins University Press.

Hofstede, G. 1984. "Cultural Dimensions in Management and Planning." *Asia Pacific Journal of Management* (January): 81–99.

Inter-American Development Bank. 1984. *External Debt and Economic Development in Latin America*. Washington, D.C.: Inter-American Development Bank.

"Latin America's Bold New Partners." 1986. *New York Times*, Aug. 12.

Lewis, F. 1986. "Choices for Mexico." *New York Times*, Aug. 12, p. A25.

Mander, J. 1969. *The Unrevolutionary Society*. New York: Harper.

Mescher, M. 1985. "The Informal Economy in Latin America: Theories, Methods and Measures." Unpublished paper, Mescher Associates, Washington, D.C.

Montgomery, J. 1974. *Technology and Civic Life*. Cambridge, Mass.: MIT Press.

Moran, R.T., and Philip Harris. 1982. *Managing Cultural Synergy*. Houston: Gulf.

Osborn, T.N., and D.B. Osborn. 1986. "Leadership Training in a Latin American Context." *Issues and Observations* 6(2): 7–10.

Peroni, G.F., and M. Burt. 1985. *Paraguay: Laws and Economy*. Asuncion: Edidora. Litocolor.

Possas, M.L. 1982. "Multinational Enterprises, Technology and Employment in Brazil: Three Case Studies." Working Paper. Geneva: International Labor Office.

Ramsaran, R. 1985. *U.S. Investment in Latin America and the Caribbean*. New York: St. Martin's Press.

Silveira, M.P. 1985. *Research and Development Linkages to Production in Developing Countries*. Boulder: Westview Press.

Simonsen, M.H. 1963. "The Role of Government and Free Enterprise." In *Latin America: Evolution or Explosion?*, edited by Mildred Adams, pp. 123–42. New York: Dodd, Mead.

Smith, P.J. 1986. "Growth and Debt: The Mexican Crisis of 1982." Unpublished paper, Tufts University, Medford, Mass.

Statistical Bulletin of the Organization of American States. 1984. 6: 1–4, 30.

Stearns, K. 1984. "Dominican Students and the International Economy." Unpublished monograph, Cornell University, Ithaca, N.Y.

Streeten, P. and S.J. Burki. 1978. "Basic Needs: Some Issues." *World Development* 6: 411–421.

PRELAC (Programa Regional del Empleo para América Latina y el Caribe). 1983. "El Sector Informal Urbano: Definición de Políticas y Requerimientos Estadísticos." Santiago, Chile: Oficina Internacional del Trabajo.

U.S. Census Bureau. 1986. "World Population Profile 1985." Washington, D.C.: U.S. Government Printing Office.

Wilkie, J. 1985. *Statistical Abstract of Latin America*, Vol. 24. Los Angeles: University of California Press.

CHAPTER 8

Comparative Analysis, Conclusions, and Future Directions

Raghu Nath and Kunal K. Sadhu

Chapter 1 of this book proposed an open systems framework for comparative management in which the business and management system continuously interacts with the environment and each is influenced by the other. Using that framework as a broad guideline, various authors developed the subsequent six chapters each focussed on one region or country. The purpose of this final chapter is threefold: to develop a comparative analysis highlighting similarities as well as differences among the six regions and countries discussed in the book; to present some conclusions and their implications for managerial action and research; and to outline some future directions for the comparative management field.

COMPARATIVE ANALYSIS

We read each chapter independently and developed lists of the major themes occurring in each chapter, which were then merged into a single list. Common themes were grouped together, as were themes that applied to more than one region or country. Themes that represented unique aspects of a given country or region were labeled as "other." Final results of this comparative analysis are summarized in seven tables that address the following dimensions:

1. The cultural milieu,
2. The sociopolitical context,
3. The economic system,

4. The infrastructure,
5. The industry structure,
6. Management philosophy and orientation,
7. Organization structure, processes, practices, and other stakeholders.

The first five tables are about various aspects of the environment, and the last two are about different aspects of the business and management system.

ENVIRONMENT

This section presents the results of the comparative analysis of various aspects of the environment—that is, the cultural milieu, the sociopolitical context, the economic system, the infrastructure (legal system, technology, transportation, and communication), and the industry structure.

The Cultural Milieu

Table 8-1 summarizes the cultural milieu in terms of the four dimensions of Hofstede (1980) as well as other unique factors. As the table indicates, there are some striking similarities among regions and countries.

First, similarities exist betweenNorth America and the Anglo group of countries from Europe, a fact established by Hofstede (1980). North America and the Anglo countries of Europe share a strong individualistic culture, their orientation is masculine, with low to medium power distance and low to medium uncertainty avoidance.

Second, people from the Near Eastern and the Balkanic clusters from Europe and Latin America believe in collectivism, a high power distance, a high uncertainty avoidance, and masculinity. It is interesting to note that Quezada and Boyce (Chapter 7) speculate that, philosophically, Latin America looks to Latin Europe. Although Latin Europe and Latin America share the high power distance and the high uncertainty avoidance, Latin Europe tends to be more individualistic and more feminine than Latin America.

It is also interesting to contrast Japan with some of the other regions and countries. Japan appears to have similar beliefs as Latin America and the Near Eastern and Balkanic states. However, the Japanese culture exhibits both a high and low power distance and masculine and feminine orientation. This paradoxical existence of opposing tendencies within Japan is unique and is rarely reported elsewhere. Also, Japan's

Table 8-1. The Cultural Milieu.

Region/Country	Hofstede's Dimensions				Other Dimensions
	Individualism-Collectivism IC	Power Distance PD	Uncertainty Avoidance UA	Masculinity-Femininity MF	
North America (USA)	Individualism	Low	Medium	Masculine	
Japan	Collectivism	High and low	High	Masculine and feminine	Amae (mutual dependence); authority is respected but superior must be a warm leader
Europe:					
Anglo	Individualism	Low/medium	Low/medium	Masculine	
Germanic	Medium individualism	Low	Medium/high	Medium/high masculine	
West Slavic					
West Urgic					
Near Eastern Balcanic	Collectivism	High	High	Medium masculine	
Nordic	Medium/high individualism	Low	Low/medium	Feminine	
Latin Europe	Medium/high individualism	High	High	Medium masculine	
East Slavic	Collectivism	Low	Medium	Masculine	
China	Collectivism	Low	Low	Masculine and feminine	Emphasis on tradition, Marxism, Leninism, and Mao Zedong Thought
Africa	Collectivism	High	High	Feminine	Colonial traditions; tribal customs
Latin America	Collectivism	High	High	Masculine	Extroverted; prefer orderly customs and procedures

cultural milieu appears to be the antithesis of the prevailing norms in North America.

Finally, Africa and Latin America exhibit similar cultural norms except on the masculinity/femininity dimension. This is somewhat puzzling because these two regions are not normally perceived as similar.

It is to be noted that only some of the data in Table 8–1 come from empirical research (Hofstede 1980). For example, in the case of Europe, data for the European cluster of democratic countries are empirically based; however, cultural norms prevailing in socialist states of Europe have been hypothesized by Banai and Levicki. Research needs to be conducted to confirm or refute these hypotheses.

Finally, there are some important elements of culture that have not been captured by the Hofstede dimensions. Some of these are highlighted in the "other" column of the Table 8–1. For example, in China there is a great emphasis on tradition, Marxism, Leninism, and Mao Zedong Thought. In many ways, these cultural elements have a greater influence on Chinese society than the four cultural dimensions of Hofstede. From the comparative management perspective, there is a great advantage in imposing a common framework such as that of Hofstede. The disadvantage is that important elements outside of the framework are ignored.

The Sociopolitical Context

Table 8–2 provides a summary of the salient aspects of the sociopolitical context of the six regions and countries. Although similarities exist among the cultural dimensions, in the sociopolitical domain the similarities are few. The number of political parties, the relationship between government and business, and the nature of the public and private sectors vary by country or region. Ideology, interest groups, political parties, or social needs dominate to make each country or region unique.

In the United States there are two dominant political parties, whereas in Japan one party has dominated the postwar era. In Europe, the democratic states have multiple political parties of various ideologies, whereas in the socialist countries a single party prevails. The same is true in China. However, as Tung points out, the socialist doctrine in China is a judicious blend of Lenin-Marxism and Confucianism. In Africa tribal affiliations and their relative power base is important in the political arena, whereas the military plays a major role in Latin America.

Of the six nations and regions studied, five carry out some degree of centralized planning. The United States is an exception. Japan, on the

Table 8-2. The Sociopolitical Context.

| Dimension | Region/Country | | | | | |
	North America (USA)	Japan	Europe	China	Africa	Latin America
Political parties	Two political parties	One dominant political party	Multiple parties dominated by ideology	Single political party	Multiple political parties dominated by ideology and tribal affiliations	Military is influential in politics; one-party (PRI) rule in Mexico
Private/ public sector	Separate and distinct	Close relationship	Separate and distinct in democratic states; state capitalism dominates in socialist states	State capitalism dominates	State capitalism and indigenous ownership coexist	MNCs influential; both state and private ownership exist simultaneously
Business/ government relationship	Distant; business influence government by PACs (lobbying); government intervenes by regulation	Government and business closely intertwined; business openly involved in the political process	In democratic states, government involved in limited areas; in socialist states, government involved in all spheres	Each factory has a party committee and a working committee; ideology tends to dominate over innovation	Business entities consist of commissors and engineers; external environment is to be managed politically	Government intervenes in terms of export, promotion, foreign remittance controls, etc.

Table 8–2 continued.

				Region/Country			
Dimension	North America (USA)	Japan	Europe	China	Africa	Latin America
Centralized planning	None	Government provides administrative guidance (MITI)	Centralized in socialist states; free enterprise in democratic states	Centralized and dominated by party ideology	Centralized	Centralized but influenced by MNCs
Others	Foreign and defense policy used to influence business	Keiretsu/Zaibatsu; civil service and business leaders exchange positions (Amakudar); trading company acts as the integrator (Sogo So-sha); social needs of paramount importance	Strong monarchical tradition; strong religious beliefs; strong preindustrial value system	Proletariat dictatorship; democratic centralism; socialist democracy; socialist spiritual civilization; incentives for innovation	Tribal democracy; stakeholders include tribal chiefs, the military, students, women, and political parties	European philosophy influential; U.S. business tradition important; political economic relations

other hand, has a unique system; the Japanese government through its Ministry of International Trade and Industry (MITI) provides administrative guidance toward the development of a national consensus.

Relationships between private and public sectors also vary from region to region. In the European socialist countries, China, and parts of Africa, state capitalism dominates. In Japan prominent businesspeople play a major role, whereas in Latin America, MNCs from the developed world exercise a great deal of influence. In the United States private and public sectors are separate and distinct; in Japan there is a very close relationship between private and public sectors. By the practice of *amukdar* (heavenly descent) in Japan, retired civil servants join business and thus provide a critical link between private and public sectors.

In some countries or regions (Africa, China, and socialist Europe) the distinction between commissors and engineers remains pronounced; the former devise policy and take care of the boundary spanning activities, and the latter execute the policy. Normally, the commissors are an arm of the dominant political party, and their job is to ensure that the enterprise actions are pure in terms of the party ideology. Thus, enterprises in socialist Europe, China, and Africa have a dual authority structure.

In addition to the above, some unique characteristics emerge. Democratic states in Europe have a strong preindustrial value system, strong Christian beliefs, and a strong monarchical tradition. They are also the home of many of the world's revolutionary and radical political parties. Thus, democratic Europe has a strong tradition of ideological tolerance unlike any of the other countries or regions. On the other hand, the socialist countries (socialist Europe, China, and some countries of Africa) have a dominant ideology and a single party to implement the ideology.

Finally, Japan has a unique sociopolitical context. Like the United States, it has a democratic political system and a free enterprise ideology. But unlike the United States, Japan has a well-integrated institutional framework that is characterized by close relationships between business and government. This institutional framework (such as Keiretsu and Zaibatsu) enables Japan to develop a true national consensus.

The Economic System

Various aspects of the economic system are highlighted in Table 8–3. First, all six countries and regions owe allegiance to some form of capitalism as the guiding business philosophy, and this ranges from free enterprise to state capitalism with various shades in between. For example,

Table 8-3. The Economic System.

Dimension	Region/Country					
	North America (USA)	*Japan*	*Europe*	*China*	*Africa*	*Latin America*
Guiding business philosophy	Free enterprise; capitalistic	Capitalistic but under the influence of government	State capitalism in socialist states; free enterprise in democratic states	State capitalism or collectives	State capitalism and indigenous entrepreneurship	State capitalism; indigenous entrepreneurs; large organizations under MNC influence
Nature of economy	Mixed	Mixed	Mixed in democratic states; state dominated in socialist states	State domination	Mixed	Mixed
Nature of markets	Large domestic market; service sector large and expanding	Large export; service sector small	Self-contained in economic blocs and political blocs	Potentially large	Potentially large	Potentially large
Parallel economy	Small, confined to arms and drugs		Small		Large	Significant portion
Banking system	Highly developed	Highly developed	Highly developed in democratic states; state controlled in socialist states	Less developed	Primitive	Less developed

Agriculture/industry proportion	Low	Low	Low in some countries, high in others	High	High	High
Employee productivity	Medium	High			Low	Low
Balance of payment	Unfavorable	Highly favorable	Varies from country to country		Unfavorable	Highly unfavorable
Others	Large stable middle class	Large middle class; export-oriented industry	Codetermination; major trading centers	Debate on law of value, law of market; export activity valued; production orientation; four modernizations efforts	Currencies tied to colonial masters; small tax base; malnutrition; agriculture and mineral production important; low productivity	Wide variation in per capita GDP; export oriented; inflationary; high external debt; agriculture and mineral production important; external dependency

we have free enterprise in the United States, whereas state capitalism dominates China. Europe, Africa, and Latin America have aspects of both. Japan has free enterprise system, but the government through MITI provides administrative guidance.

Second, economies are mixed in all regions and countries. Whereas the private sector dominates in the United States, Japan, democratic Europe, and some countries of Latin America, the public sector plays a dominant role in others, such as socialist Europe, China, and some countries of Africa.

Third, the market potential for all six regions and countries is immense. The United States has a large and stable middle class; Japan is aided by its competitiveness in international markets; Europe by its economic and political blocks—the EEC and COMECON; and China, Latin America, and Africa by their large populations.

The dichotomy of developing versus developed dictates other aspects of the economic environment. For example, parallel economies flourish in the developing nations of Africa and Latin America and constitute a significant portion of the nation's GNP. In contrast, the informal sector is rather small in the developed countries of North America and democratic Europe. The banking system and capital markets are either primitive or less developed, the ratio of agricultural workers to industrial workers is high, and employee productivity is low in the developing countries of Africa, Latin America, and China. The reverse is true for the developed countries of Europe, United States, and Japan. Also, the balance of payment has generally been unfavorable for the developing countries. Lately, the United States and some developed countries of Europe have also experienced unfavorable balance of payments. In recent years, only Japan and Germany have registered favorable balance of payments.

Some unique features also characterize the economic system of some of these countries and regions. Latin America suffers from chronic high inflation and a very high level of external debt. Many African currencies are tied to their previous colonial masters, and China has recently instituted the four modernizations efforts. Employee codetermination is a major feature in many countries of Europe. Finally, there is a great emphasis on exports in Japan, China, and many countries of Europe.

The Infrastructure

Table 8–4 highlights various aspects of the infrastructure—that is, the legal system, technology, transportation, and communication.

Table 8–4. The Infrastructure.

Dimension	Region/Country					
	North America (USA)	Japan	Europe	China	Africa	Latin America
The Legal System						
Nature of society	Litigious	Consensus	Not litigious	Mediation and reconciliation	Dualistic	
Antitrust laws	Strong	Weak implementation	Varies by country			
Patent laws	Strong		Strong			
Other		MITI prevails over FTC; weak environmental protection	Romano-Germanic laws; natural law; private property; customary law; tolerance for cartels	Distaste for laws; revolutionary humanitarianism; new laws for foreign companies	Customary and European law; multiplistic legal structure	
Technology						
Type of research/technology	Both basic and applied research	Mostly applied research	Both applied and basic research	Technically backward; progress in few selected areas	Old technology	New technology in mineral extrusion; otherwise old technology
Level of technological expertise	High	High	High	Low	Very low	Low

Table 8-4 continued.

Dimension	Region/Country					
	North America (USA)	Japan	Europe	China	Africa	Latin America
Technical man-power skills	Good	Good	Good	Good in certain areas, poor in others	Primitive	Good in certain areas
R&D expenditures	High; supported by government	High; supported by government	High		Low; copy technology from advanced nations	Low
Other	Leader in high technology	Better on production process than product innovation; moving from applied to basic		Incentives for innovation	Poor copier of technology	
Transportation and communication						
Telecommunication	Good	Good	Good/fair	Poor	Primitive	Poor
Road system	Good	Good	Good/fair	Poor	Primitive	Poor
Air system	Good	Good	Good	Poor	Primitive	Poor
Postal system	Good	Good	Good/fair	Poor	Primitive	Poor
Record keeping	Good	Good	Good/fair	Poor	Primitive	Poor
Other	Major expressways			Press extremely powerful	Plans for trans-African highway	

The Legal System. The legal system of the United States is unique. Unlike other regions and countries, U.S. society is litigious and strongly enforces antitrust and patent laws. Although some other countries (such as Japan and Germany) have antitrust laws on the books, they implement them rarely. In fact, in these countries there is a great tolerance for cartels. Some European countries also have strong patent laws.

The legal system in China and Africa, particularly as it relates to the industrial sector, is in its infancy. In the case of China, commercial laws are now being developed to enable foreign companies to operate in China. Although some attempts are being made in some African countries to develop a unified legal structure, the present legal system in Africa is dualistic, based on both customary and European law. Unlike in the United States, there is a great emphasis on consensus in Japan and mediation and reconciliation in China.

Technology. Technology tends to clearly separate developed from developing nations. For example, the level of technological expertise is high in the developed nations of North America, Europe, and Japan, but it is low in the developing nations of Latin American, Africa, and China. Similarily, R&D expenditures are high in the developed nations and low in the developing countries. Although it has made considerable progress in few selected areas of technology, China is technically backward compared to the developed nations. Africa is characterized by old technology, a very low level of technological expertise, and primitive technical manpower skills.

The United States continues to be the leader in high technology, and this lead is particularly significant in the areas of basic research. Japan, on the other hand, excels in applied research, particularly in the development of better production technologies. MNCs in Latin America use the state-of-art technology in the extraction of minerals, but old technology is the norm in other industries. Africa not only uses old technology but has been a poor copier of technology. Finally, in recent years, China has provided incentives for innovation.

Transportation and Communication. The contrast between developed and developing nations is most obvious in the case of transportation and communication systems. As can be seen from the Table 8–4, developed countries of North America, Europe, and Japan have good to fair transportation and communication systems, and the developing countries of China and Latin America have poor transportation and communication systems. Like the technology area, this part of the infrastructure is primitive in the case of Africa. Unique aspects of the transportation and communication systems are the major expressways in North America and the powerful press in China.

The Industry Structure

Various aspects of industry structure in the six regions and countries are outlined in Table 8–5. As can be seen from the table, industry is migrating from rural to urban areas in Europe, Africa, and Latin America. On the other hand, the shift in the United States is from urban to rural areas. Some have argued that the shift toward rural areas is symptomatic of the postindustrial era.

Large and small companies coexist in all regions and countries, although there are differences in the proportion of large versus small companies among regions and countries. Privately owned larger firms control 25 percent of sales in the United States. On the other hand, larger firms are owned by the state in China and Africa and by MNCs in Latin America. Japan is unique in that many smaller firms serve as subcontractors to larger firms. China has tried to encourage the formation of smaller firms that are owned by private entrepreneurs.

There are significant differences in terms of sectoral distribution among developed and developing nations. For example, only 3 percent of the U.S. economy but 80 percent of the Chinese depend on agriculture.

In terms of markets, developed nations of North America, democratic Europe, and Japan have competitive markets. On the other hand, developing nations of Africa, Latin America, and China as well as socialist states of Europe have seller's markets.

Finally, the developing nations of Africa, Latin America, and China are characterized by concern for production, whereas developed nations of North America and Japan have concern for price and quality. Japan, of course, excels in terms of concern for quality.

BUSINESS AND MANAGEMENT SYSTEM

Management Philosophy and Orientation

Management philosophy and orientation is summarized in Table 8–6. In most regions and countries (except Japan), management philosophy can be best characterized by theory X (McGregor 1960), under which author-

Table 8-5. The Industry Structure.

Dimension	Region/Country					
	North America (USA)	Japan	Europe	China	Africa	Latin America
Rural/urban	Shift towards rural		Shift towards urban		Shift towards urban	Shift towards urban
Mix of large/small companies	Coexist; larger firms control 25% of sales	Coexist; larger firms pay higher wages; smaller firms as subcontractors to larger firms	Coexist; in democratic countries, larger firms control large proportion of sales; in socialist countries, small firms are privately owned	Large firms state owned or collectives; smaller firms entrepreneurally owned	Coexist; large firms state owned and centralized	Coexist (smaller firms in informal sector); many large firms controlled by MNCs; large companies are centralized
Sectoral distribution	Agriculture 3%; manufacturing 12%; service 9%; information 65%			Agriculture 80%	Mostly agriculture	Bolivia mostly agriculture; Mexico high concentration of industry in urban areas
Nature of markets	Competitive	Competitive globally	Competitive in democratic states and seller's market in socialist states	Seller's market	Seller's market	Seller's market
Other	Concern for price and quality	Concern for price and quality; each industrial group has a bank		Concern for production	Concern for production	Concern for production

Table 8–6. Management Philosophy and Orientation.

Dimension	Region/Country					
	North America (USA)	Japan	Europe	China	Africa	Latin America
Theory (X or Y)	Mostly theory X	Theory Y	Mostly theory X		Theory X	Theory X
Management style	Tending toward participative style	Participative	Authoritative in socialist and participative in democratic societies	Participative (mandated)	Authoritative	Authoritative (lack of trust); paternal
Decision authority	Manager have decisionmaking prerogatives	Managers *alone* do not have decisionmaking prerogatives; consensus decisions	Codetermination in several democratic states; workers participate in socialist states	Workers participate	Managers decide	Societal status differences carry on at work place; managers have the elite status
Emphasis on	Rational	Social	Rational	Social	Manager's benefit	Control maximization
Management production distinction	Clear distinction	No clear distinction	Varies from country to country		Clear distinction	Clear distinction
Managerial orientation	Owners' interest	Managers look after subordinates	Owners interest in democratic and party interest in socialist states	Party and workers interest	Managers like status quo	Managers oriented to social relation

	Short-term	Long-term	Short-term	Short-term	Short-term	Short-term
Short- versus long-term horizon						
Other	Adaptive to recent trends in management theory		Human nature is mixed; mastery of man over nature	Managers need to be politically sound and technically competent; peaceful cooperation	Low loyalty; innovation risk-taking not rewarded; narrowly defined job tasks	Family-style management; workers strive to please and conform

ity is used in managing employees. In theory X–dominated business systems, decision authority usually rests with the manager, who has an elite status. Management style tends to be authoritative with emphasis on rationality and control maximization. The distinction between management and production cadres is clear, and the decision time horizon tends to be short term.

As can be seen from Table 8–6, Africa and Latin America have a theory X orientation, authoritative management style, clear distinction between management and production staff, and a short-term decision horizon. Decision authority is vested in the managers, who have elite status, and emphasis is on the manager's benefit and control maximization. Therefore, workers in Latin America try to please and conform, whereas workers in Africa have low loyalty and an aversion to innovation and risk taking.

In the United States and democratic countries of Europe, the prevailing management philosophy is theory X, although these countries are trying to move toward a participative style (theory Y). In the United States, managers have decisionmaking prerogatives, but in many countries of democratic Europe there is a mandated codetermination policy. Emphasis is on rational decisionmaking, and a clear distinction exists between management and production cadres. Managerial orientation is to protect owners' interests; therefore, the time horizon is short term.

In China and the socialist countries of Europe, worker participation is mandated. Although managers are asked to look after both the party's as well as workers' interests, in practice, party interests dominate. Also, the time horizon is short term.

Finally, Japan has a unique management philosophy and orientation characterized by theory Y and participative management style. There is no clear distinction between management and production cadres, and managers look after subordinates' interests. Emphasis is on social interaction and consensus decisions. The time orientation tends to be long term.

Organization Structure, Processes, Practices, and Stakeholders

Table 8–7 highlights various aspects of organizations in the six regions and countries.

Organization Structure. In most of the countries and regions (except Japan) a formal organization structure is considered important. In the developing countries of Africa and Latin America, organization structure is functional, hierarchical, authoritarian, and centralized. In the developed economies of North America and democratic Europe, various types of organization structures exist. China and socialist Europe have a two-tier structure—that is, political and technical. In Japan alone, formal structure is of secondary importance and close working relationships exist within groups.

Decisionmaking Processes. The decisionmaking (except in Japan) is mainly top down and follows the rational school, which necessitates a short time horizon. In contrast, the Japanese make decisions by consensus. This is probably a result of the cultural ethos (described by Namiki and Sethi in Chapter 3).

Communication Process. In Japan the communication process is ritualistic, such that "all" opinions are considered—a result of the requirements of the Japanese society. In other countries and regions (North America, China, Africa, and Latin America) the communication process is vertical (top down) and is not considered important. In China, there is a dual chain of command. And fear tends to characterize the communication process in Africa.

Group Process. In the area of group process, task orientation prevails in North America and Latin America, but Japan has a strong maintenance orientation. Structure tends to be more important in the United States, whereas process is more important in Japan and China. Africa is characterized by poor motivation and alienation.

Human Resource Management. There are large differences among the six regions and countries in terms of human resource management practices. Africa is characterized by the underdeveloped state of human resource management—low wages and poor performance monitoring. In Latin America, human resource management varies depending on the state of unionization. Promotion is usually based on family connections rather than merit. Human resource management tends to be poor except in MNC-dominated industries. In China the state is very active in the recruitment process because of the large number of job applicants. Promotion decisions are based on both political and technical criteria. In recent years there has been emphasis on skill training.

In Europe class distinctions are still important, and managerial skills

Table 8-7. Organization Structure, Processes, Practices, and Stakeholders.

Dimension	Region/Country					
	North America (USA)	Japan	Europe	China	Africa	Latin America
Organization structure	Formal structure important; various types are functional, product, geographic; matrix and network	Formal structure of secondary importance; departmental; strong middle management; close working relationship within group	Formal structure important; power dependent on education, social class, party affiliation; two tiers in socialist states	Two tier, i.e., political and technological; political determines policy	Highly centralized; hierarchical; authoritarian; shortage of quality leadership	Authoritarian; centralized; functional; matrix has experienced difficulty
Decisionmaking process	Rational; short-term; top down	Consensus; long-term	Rational; short-term	Rational; control by state; top down	Rational; short-term; top down	Rational; short-term; top down
Communication process	One-way vertical; process may be important	Ritualistic; process important		Vertical, dual; process not important	Vertical, fear; process not important	Vertical; process not important; social consideration important
Group process	Goal/task orientation; poor maintenance; structure *more* important than process	Informal within group, formal across groups; strong maintenance; structure *less* important than process		Clearly laid down tasks; process *more* important than structure	Poor motivation; alienation	Task oriented; continue existing social differences; difficulty with team building

Human resource management	Faddish; emphasis on recruitment and placement	Job rotation to develop generalists; life-time employment; seniority-based wage system	Managers develop general management skills by either job rotation or rising to the top of specialization; class distinction important	Few jobs for large numbers of applicants; recruitment by state (political-technical criteria); promotion emphasis on skill training	Underdeveloped; low wages; poor performance monitoring	Poor except in MNC-dominated industries; depends on unionization; need right family connection
Union management relations	Adversarial, suspicious, mistrusting; recent givebacks	Societal pressure towards consensus	Confrontational in some countries, not in others	Mandated cooperation	Low membership; corruption; severely restrictive laws regarding union activity; unions have little say	
Unions	National (industrial); local (craft)	Company based	Affiliated with major political parties	Geographic units; affiliated with the communist party	Few ties with the international labor movement; low membership; corruption; severely restrictive laws regarding union activity; unions have little say	
Other stake holders	Consumer unions, environmental agencies, etc.	Banks	The party, banks or consumer groups based on social ideology	Communist party	Foreign interests	Foreign MNCs

are developed through experience including job rotation. The United States is characterized by fads, and the emphasis tends to be on recruitment and placement.

Japan has a seniority-based wage system. There is an emphasis on lifetime employment, and job rotation is used to develop generalists. Unlike the United States, human resources are highly valued in the Japanese system.

Union/Management Relations and Unions. The union/management relations tend to vary from confrontational to consensus building. This is governed by the history of the union/management relations in the specific country or region. In the United States, the relationship between the unions and management traditionally has been confrontational. In Japan, on the other hand, the unions tend toward consensus and compromise because of societal pressures. Europe has a traditional alliance of unions with a political party, and union/management relations vary depending on which party is in power. In Africa antilabor legislation by the ruling elite severely restricts union activity. China's mandated cooperation requires the union to work through the work council.

Unions tend to be organized along different lines in various regions and countries. For example, in the United States industrial unions are nationally organized, and craft unions are local. In Japan industrial unions are company based. In Europe and China unions have affiliations with major political parties.

Other Stakeholders. These appear to vary across countries and regions. In North America consumer unions, environmental advocates, and agencies seem to be important. In Japan the banks and the trading companies are the major stakeholders of big business. In socialist countries, the party is the major stakeholder. Finally, in the developing countries of Africa and Latin America, foreign interests or MNCs appear to be the major stakeholders of large enterprises.

CONCLUSIONS

This section draws three major conclusions about the findings of this book. First, chapters in this volume yield a picture of great diversity among the six regions and countries. This diversity exists along environmental as well as management system dimensions. We therefore believe that developing a unified global strategy may not be possible except in a very limited competitive strategy arena, as was suggested by Porter (1986). International business strategy must be responsive to the wide diversity reported in this volume. Also, organization design and management practices must be tailored to the specific situation prevailing in a particular region or country. We hope therefore that this volume provides valuable input to the development of a situationally responsive international business strategy by providing specific knowledge about how these six countries and regions differ from each other and how each region or country is unique.

Second, in spite of the wide diversity, comparative analysis has highlighted some similarities among these regions and countries. Some of these similarities encompass all or most of the six regions and countries; other similarities are confined to two or three regions and countries. It therefore may be possible to cluster countries based on some of these similarities. To the extent that management know-how can be easily transferred within these clusters, this may facilitate implementation of international business strategy. Clustering of countries along common dimensions also has significant implications for future comparative management research.

Third, many of the authors included a section on how history affected environment as well as the business and management system. Several chapters as well as the comparative analysis section in this chapter contain references to outcome factors such as effectiveness, survival, growth, development, and so forth. We therefore conclude that the framework outlined in Chapter 1 needs to be expanded to include these two additional sets of factors—that is, historical antecedents and outcomes. Figure 8-1 presents an outline of this expanded model or modified framework for comparative management.

This model has implications for research, theory building, and managerial action. Most important, it is an interactive, dynamic model. Historical antecedents affect the environment as well as the business and management system, and these in turn interact with each other to influence the outcomes. Feedback about the outcomes modifies the perception of historical antecedents as well as influences the environment, business, and management systems. In such a dynamic interacting framework, the traditional dichotomy between independent and dependent variables does not matter. For example, any environmental factor (such as the cultural milieu) can be treated as an independent variable if we consider its effect on the business and management system or outcomes. It can also be considered as a dependent variable because historical antecedents

Figure 8–1. Modified Framework for Comparative Management.

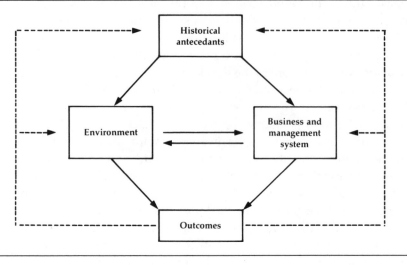

------ Feedback loops

affect the cultural milieu. As Banai and Levicki (Chapter 4) point out, the cultural milieu has been treated by scholars as an independent as well as a dependent variable. In terms of the model, both ways of treating this variable are equally legitimate.

Major research as well as theory building implications of the above model arises from the fact that outcomes are a result of the historical antecedents, the environment, the business and management system, as well as interactions among these three sets of variables. However, most of the research in comparative management has been focused at a rather simplistic level. For example, the frequently cited work by Hofstede (1980) has focused on only four dimensions of culture. But this volume clearly demonstrates that this four-dimension culture theory omits many significant aspects of the cultural milieu. Also, in addition to the cultural milieu, other aspects of history, environment, and the business and management system need to be considered in order to develop an adequate understanding of a given region or country. Thus, the major implication of the model is that, although studies like those by Hofstede are useful, there is a need for comparative studies based on comprehensive frameworks like the one employed in this volume.

Finally, the implications of the model for managerial action are clear. In order to operate effectively in a given country, international business strategy must take into account all of the variables outlined in the model. There is reason to believe that effective MNCs already do this. For example, the director of worldwide strategic planning of IBM, Abraham Katz, reported at the annual meeting of the Academy of Management in New York (held in August 1979) that IBM employs a comprehensive framework in developing its worldwide strategy.

FUTURE DIRECTIONS

Although this volume has made a beginning, a number of steps need to follow. As was indicated in Chapter 1, this is the first attempt, after the work of Harbison and Myers (1959), to develop an in-depth profile of different regions and countries from a comparative management perspective. This volume has focused on the regional level, and yet authors of the regional chapters (Europe, Africa, and Latin America) have clearly demonstrated that large differences exist among countries within each of these regions. In order to understand and appreciate these differences, it is essential that research should focus on the next lower level. This level could be a cluster of countries along cultural, political, and economic dimensions. Ronen and Shanker (1985) have demonstrated how countries can be clustered according to similarities on certain cultural dimensions.

Second, various authors had to extrapolate, conjecture, or hypothesize when empirical data were not available. For example, regarding the cultural milieu in China, Tung had to extrapolate from the available empirical data about Taiwan. Similarly, Banai and Levicki hypothesized about the cultural milieu in socialist countries of Europe because empirical data were available only for the democratic states of Europe. Field research needs to be conducted to either confirm or refute these extrapolations and hypotheses. For Africa and Latin America there was a lack of empirical data about several aspects of environment as well as the business and management systems. This gap needs to be closed.

Third, we need to use the expanded open-systems framework, as reported earlier, for future work in the comparative management field. Careful consideration needs to be given to what specific factors ought to be included as historical antecedents and outcomes. Although some chapters in this volume describe some of these specific factors, a delphi process involving comparative management experts from various nations may be a way to address this problem.

In conclusion, we hope that this book has made a valuable contribution to the comparative management field. Much remains to be done before the comparative management field realizes its full potential.

REFERENCES

Harbison, F., and C.A. Myers. 1959. *Management in the Industrial World.* New York: McGraw-Hill.

Hofstede, G. 1980. *Cultures Consequences: National Differences in Work Related Values.* Beverly Hills, Calif.: Sage.

McGregor, D. 1960. *The Human Side of Enterprise.* New York: McGraw-Hill.

Porter, M.E., ed. 1986. *Competition in Global Industries.* Boston: Harvard Business School Press.

Ronen, S., and O. Shankar. 1985. "Clustering Countries on Attitudinal Dimensions: A Review and Synthesis." *Academy of Management Review,* 10(3): 435–54.

Name Index

Subject Index

About the Editor

Raghu Nath is on the faculty of the Joseph M. Katz Graduate School of Business, University of Pittsburgh, where he has been coordinator of the International Interest Group and director of the Management Training Laboratory. Dr. Nath is the president of INSOHP, which specializes in organizational system and international business development. He is also program chairman of the Partnerships for Development Dialogue Conference, which brings together leaders of industry, labor, government, media, universities, and international organizations from developed and developing countries to discuss issues of mutual interest.

Raghu Nath is the author of over fifty articles, book chapters, and books. In addition, his work has been cited in many leading newspapers and business periodicals. He has served on the editorial boards of several professional journals and has been chairman of the International Division of the Academy of Management.

Dr. Nath has consulted with international organizations, government departments, and multinational corporations, among them the United Nations, the World Bank, the Departments of State and Navy, NASA, IBM, GE, Westinghouse, and ALCOA. His research interests and areas of consultation include comparative and cross-cultural management, international corporate strategy, technology transfer from developed to developing countries, strategic issues in institution building, organization development and design, crisis management, design of knowledge network, management of strategic change, and development of human resources.

About the Contributors

Douglas B. Allen is pursuing a doctorate in organization behavior and industrial relations at The University of Michigan School of Business Administration. He received an M.B.A. from Harvard and a B.S. in sociology from the University of Zimbabwe. He has worked at Chrysler Corporation World Headquarters in Highland Park, Michigan, developing and implementing management improvement and employee participation programs and at the Baha'i National Center in Wilmette, Illinois, providing advisory support for professionals preparing for overseas relocation.

Moshe Banai is assistant professor of management at Baruch College, City University of New York. He received his Ph.D. from the London Business School. Dr. Banai has many publications in the field of human resource management in multinational corporations. He is a consultant to major international companies in Israel, Europe, and the United States.

James E. Boyce is professor of management emeritus at Michigan Technological University in Houghton, Michigan, where he has also served as area coordinator for management in the School of Business and Engineering Administration. After earning a Ph.D. in industrial psychology at Purdue University, he spent several years doing research and training in management in Colombia, Ecuador, and Mexico. His professional career also includes several production and planning posts at General Motors. His current research relates to the quality of work life programs at the General Motors assembly plants along the Mexican border.

Moses N. Kiggundu is an associate professor of management, School of Business, Carleton University, Ottawa, Canada. He has worked as an employee, teacher, consultant, and researcher to various organizations in Africa. His active research interests include international management with a special focus on administrative theory and practice in developing countries. Dr. Kiggundu's articles have appeared in many leading journals, including *Administrative Science Quarterly, Journal of Management Studies,* and the *Journal of Applied Behavioral Sciences.* He is currently writing a book on the management of organizations in developing countries.

Cyril J. Levicki is assistant professor of management at Baruch College, City University of New York. He received his Ph.D. from the London Business School and is the editor of a book on small businesses in Europe. Dr. Levicki is a leading consultant on strategic planning to major British domestic and international companies.

Edwin L. Miller is professor of industrial relations at The University of Michigan School of Business Administration. He received his Ph.D. from the University of California, Berkeley and joined Michigan's faculty in 1964. Professor Miller is a fellow of the Academy of Management, and he currently serves on the academy's Board of Governors. He has published over forty articles and several commissioned papers for books of readings and has edited two books. His research interests focus on the relationships between human resource management and the global strategic planning process and on the comparison between human resource management subsystems of U.S. multinational corporations and foreign multinational corporations.

Nobuaki Namiki is associate professor at the California State University, Sacramento, where he teaches business policy and international business courses. He coauthored *The False Promise of the Japanese Miracle* with S. Prakash Sethi and Carl Swanson and has published in such journals as *California Management Review* and *Journal of Business Strategy.* His primary research interests lie in the areas of global strategy, comparative management, competitive strategy in export markets, and the Japanese management system. Professor Namiki is also a consultant on trade between Japanese and American companies.

Fernando Quezada has taught management and economics at the Monterrey Institute of Technology in Mexico and the University of São Paulo, Brazil, and has served as consultant to both business and government in those countries. He is currently project director of the Biotechnology center of Excellence in the Executive Office of Economic Affairs of the Commonwealth of Massachusetts and adjunct professor of cross-cultural technology transfer at the Lesley College Graduate School in Cambridge, Massachusetts. He received his graduate training in public administration and planning at the University of California, Los Angeles and the Massachusetts Institute of Technology.

Kunal K. Sadhu is a doctoral candidate at the Joseph M. Katz Graduate School of Business at the University of Pittsburgh. After obtaining a Postgraduate Diploma in business administration (M.B.A.) from the Indian Institute of Management, Ahmedabad, he worked as a management executive in the areas of planning, control, and marketing for nine years before joining the Graduate School of Business at the University of Pittsburgh in 1983. His research interests include strategic planning, management control systems, and planning for international business.

S. Prakash Sethi is professor at Baruch College and associate director of its Center for Management. He was founder and director of the Center for Research in Business and Social Policy at the University of Texas at Dallas. Dr. Sethi is the author of numerous books and articles on public policy issues and international business practices. He serves as consultant to some of the leading American corporations.

Rosalie L. Tung is professor of business administration and director of the International Business Center at the University of Wisconsin, Milwaukee. She earned a Ph.D. from the University of British Columbia and is the author of seven books. Dr. Tung has published widely on the subjects of international management and organizational theory in leading journals. She was invited as the first foreign expert to teach management at the Foreign Investment Commission (now known as the Ministry of Foreign Economic Relations and Trade), the highest agency under the Chinese State Council, which approves all joint ventures and other major forms of foreign investment. Dr. Tung is actively involved in management development and consulting activities around the world.